MATHS ON TARGET

Year 4

Stephen Pearce

Elmwood Press

First published 2008 by
Elmwood Press
80 Attimore Road
Welwyn Garden City
Herts. AL8 6LP
Tel. 01707 333232

Reprinted in 2009

ISBN 9781 902 214 924

Numerical answers are published in a separate book.

Typeset and illustrated by Tech-Set Ltd., Gateshead, Tyne and Wear.
Printed and bound in Spain on behalf of JFDi Print Services Ltd.

PREFACE

Maths on Target has been written for pupils in Year 4 and their teachers.

The intention of the book is to provide teachers with material to teach all the objectives as set out in the yearly programme in the renewed Primary Framework for Mathematics.

The structure of **Maths on Target** matches that of the renewed framework. It is arranged in five blocks, A–E, each of which consists of three units. To ensure progression throughout the year the units are best taught in the order in which they appear in both this book and the exemplar planning structure for Year 4 in the renewed framework.

	Block A	Block B	Block C	Block D	Block E
Term 1	Unit 1	Unit 1	Unit 1	Unit 1	Unit 1
Term 2	Unit 2	Unit 2	Unit 2	Unit 2	Unit 2
Term 3	Unit 3	Unit 3	Unit 3	Unit 3	Unit 3

Each unit in **Maths on Target** consists of lessons based upon the learning overview for that unit in the renewed framework. Each lesson is divided into four sections:

Introduction: the learning intention expressed as an 'I can' statement and, where necessary, clearly worked examples.

Section A: activities based upon work previously covered. This generally matches the objectives for Year 3 pupils. This section can be used to remind children of work previously covered, as well as providing material for the less confident child.

Section B: activities based upon the objectives for Year 4 pupils. Most children should be able to work successfully at this level.

Section C: activities providing extension material for the faster workers and for those who need to be moved quickly onto more challenging tasks. The work in this section generally matches the objectives for Year 5 pupils. Problems in Section C can also provide useful material for discussion in the plenary session.

The correspondence of the three sections A–C to the objectives for different year groups provides a simple, manageable structure for planning differentiated activities and for both the formal and informal assessment of children's progress. The commonality of the content pitched at different levels also allows for progression within the lesson. Children acquiring confidence at one level find they can successfully complete activities at the next level.

The author is indebted to many colleagues who have assisted him in this work. He is particularly grateful to Sharon Granville and Debra Turner for their invaluable advice and assistance.

Stephen Pearce

CONTENTS

	Page
BLOCK A UNIT 1	
Numbers	2
Place Value and Partitioning	4
Ordering Numbers	5
Negative Numbers	6
Multiplying and Dividing by 10/100	8
Multiplication Facts	9
Mental Strategies (+/−)	10
Money Problems	11
Number Puzzles	12
Darts	13
BLOCK B UNIT 1	
Addition and Subtraction Facts	14
Magic Squares	15
Rounding	16
Multiplication Facts	17
Word Problems	18
Three-Dimensional Shapes	19
Two-Dimensional Shapes	20
BLOCK C UNIT 1	
Collecting Data	22
Interpreting Data	24
BLOCK D UNIT 1	
Metric Units	26
Reading Scales	27
Mental Addition/Subtraction	28
Horizontal and Vertical Lines	29
Position	30
Units of Time	31
Reading the Time	32
Time Problems	34
Timetables	35
BLOCK E UNIT 1	
Multiplication Facts	36
Word Problems	37
Number Patterns and Relationships	38
Multiples Problems	39
Recognising Fractions	40
Fractions of Amounts	41
Fraction Pairs Making One	42
Equivalent Fractions	43
Decimal Fractions	44
BLOCK A UNIT 2	
Mental Strategies (+/−)	45
Decimal Fractions	46
Written Method for Addition	48
Written Method for Subtraction	49
Multiplication Facts	50
×/÷ by 10/100 and by Multiples of 10/100	51
Written Method for Multiplication	52
Written Method for Division	53
Number Puzzles	54
BLOCK B UNIT 2	
Multiplication Facts	55
Word Problems	56
Multiplication Facts for 8	57
Doubling and Halving	58
Two-Dimensional Shapes	59
Visualising 3-D Shapes	60
Three-Dimensional Shapes	61
BLOCK C UNIT 2	
Metric Units	62
Reading Scales	63
Presenting Data	64
Interpreting Data	66
BLOCK D UNIT 2	
Measuring Length	68
Perimeter	70
Metric Units of Length	72
Written Method (+/−)	73
Written Method (×/÷)	74
Word Problems	75
Angles	76
Compass Directions	78
BLOCK E UNIT 2	
Multiplication Facts for 7	79
Multiples Problems	80
Mixed Numbers	81
Fractions that Total 1	82
Equivalent Fractions	83
Fractions of Quantities	84
Fractions and Decimals	85

BLOCK A UNIT 3
Number Sequences 86
Mental Strategies (+/−) 87
Written Method for Addition 88
Written Method for Subtraction 89
Written Method for Multiplication 90
Written Method for Division 91
Rounding Remainders Up or Down 92
Number Problems 93
Word Problems 94

BLOCK B UNIT 3
Multiplication Facts for 9 95
Multiplication and Arrays 96
Doubling and Halving 97
Using Addition and Subtraction Facts 98
Mental Strategies (+/−) 99
Word Problems 100
Drawing 2-D Shapes 101
Making 3-D Shapes 102

BLOCK C UNIT 3
Reading Scales 103
Presenting Data 104
Interpreting Data 106
Metric Units 108

BLOCK D UNIT 3
Capacity 109
Measuring Lengths 110
Time Problems 111
Timetables 112
Measurement Problems 113
Angles 114
Area and Perimeter 116

BLOCK E UNIT 3
Ordering Fractions 118
Equivalent Fractions 119
Fractions and Decimals 120
Fractions of Quantities 121
Written Method for Multiplication 122
Written Method for Division 123
Ratio and Proportion 124
Multiplication Facts 126

REVIEW PAGES
Crossnumber Puzzles 127
Counting and Number 128
Fractions and Decimals 129
Calculations 130
Measures 131
Shape 132
Handling Data 133
Mental Arithmetic 134
Times Tables 136

A1 NUMBERS

I can read and write whole numbers.

Numbers are made up from digits.

There are ten digits: 0, 1, 2, 3, 4, 5, 6, 7, 8 and 9.
3 is a single digit number, 32 is a two-digit number, and so on.

The way we read a digit depends upon its place in the number.
274 is read as two hundred and seventy-four.
2748 is read as two thousand seven hundred and forty-eight.

TAKE CARE when a number has zeros in it.
3600 is read as three thousand six hundred.
3060 is read as three thousand and sixty.
3006 is read as three thousand and six

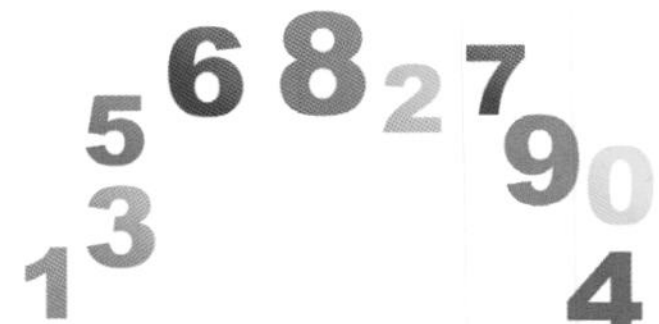

Copy the table, writing each distance in figures.

	Place	Road distance to London (kilometres)
1	Lincoln	two hundred and eleven
2	Bristol	one hundred and ninety-six
3	Leeds	three hundred and four
4	Aberdeen	eight hundred and thirty-two
5	Land's End	four hundred and seventy-eight
6	Manchester	two hundred and ninety-eight
7	Edinburgh	six hundred and twenty-eight
8	Cardiff	two hundred and fifty-three
9	Penzance	five hundred and fifteen
10	Nottingham	two hundred and nine

These figures also show the distance between London and other places by road.
Write each distance in words.

11. Birmingham 188 km
12. Exeter 291 km
13. Liverpool 325 km
14. Newcastle 460 km
15. York 333 km
16. Cambridge 87 km
17. Inverness 885 km
18. Gloucester 139 km
19. Blackpool 364 km
20. Dundee 721 km

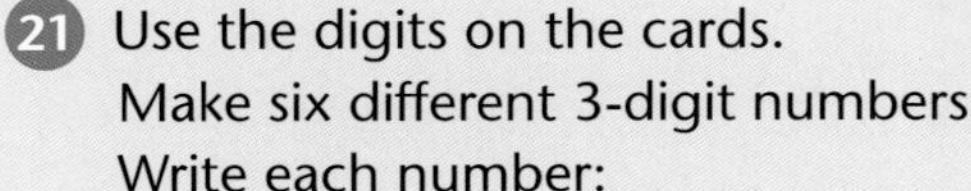

21. Use the digits on the cards.
    Make six different 3-digit numbers.
    Write each number:
    a) in figures **b)** in words.

4	5	9

B

Copy the table, writing each distance in figures.

1

River	Length (kilometres)
Amazon	six thousand seven hundred and fifty
Nile	six thousand six hundred and seventy
Yangtze	six thousand three hundred
Mississippi	six thousand and twenty
Yenisey	five thousand five hundred and forty
Hwang He	five thousand four hundred and sixty-four
Ob	five thousand four hundred and nine
Parana	four thousand eight hundred and eighty
Congo	four thousand seven hundred
Lena	four thousand four hundred

The figures below give the lengths of the same rivers in miles. Write each distance in words.

2. Amazon 4194 miles
3. Nile 4145 miles
4. Yangtze 3915 miles
5. Mississippi 3741 miles
6. Yenisey 3442 miles
7. Hwang He 3395 miles
8. Ob 3361 miles
9. Parana 3032 miles
10. Congo 2920 miles
11. Lena 2734 miles

C

One thousand thousands is one million (1 000 000).

Copy these sentences writing the number in figures.

1. The Moon is about a quarter of a million miles from the Earth.
2. The population of Sheffield is about half a million.
3. One tenth of a million people watched the football match.
4. Kieran won three quarters of a million pounds on the Lottery.
5. A billion is one thousand million.
6. Every year one and a half million people use the airport.

7. Use the digits on the cards.
Make as many five-digit numbers as you can with a value of between 25 000 and 28 000.
Write each number:
a) in figures **b)** in words.

I can partition numbers into 1000s, 100s, 10s and 1s.

Example

Th	H	T	U
3	6	9	8

The 3 has a value of 3000.
The 6 has a value of 600.
The 9 has a value of 90.
The 8 has a value of 8 units.

Knowing the value of the digits means that you are able to partition numbers.

Example 3698 = 3000 + 600 + 90 + 8

A

Copy and complete.

1. 128 = 100 + 20 + □
2. 369 = 300 + □ + 9
3. 427 = □ + 20 + 7
4. 584 = 500 + □ + 4
5. 392 = □ + 90 + 2
6. 655 = 600 + 50 + □
7. 716 = 700 + □ + 6
8. 925 = □ + 20 + 5

Write down the value of the digit underlined.

9. $3\underline{2}8$
10. $17\underline{9}$
11. $\underline{8}46$
12. $5\underline{8}5$
13. $\underline{4}51$
14. $3\underline{6}2$
15. $71\underline{4}$
16. $\underline{3}07$

Add 100 to:

17. 290
18. 428
19. 781
20. 19

Take 10 from:

21. 171
22. 596
23. 224
24. 162

B

What is the value of the digit underlined?

1. $2\underline{3}6$
2. $\underline{5}47$
3. $\underline{2}184$
4. $439\underline{5}$
5. $1\underline{6}38$
6. $54\underline{4}0$
7. $\underline{7}063$
8. $492\underline{2}$

Partition these numbers as in the example.

9. 1637
10. 2452
11. 3985
12. 2174
13. 4538
14. 5843
15. 7296
16. 8310

What needs to be added or subtracted to change:

17. 382 to 352
18. 2794 to 2294
19. 1068 to 7068
20. 4856 to 4456
21. 7321 to 9321
22. 1627 to 1697
23. 5340 to 5840
24. 8915 to 3915
25. 6218 to 6298
26. 2831 to 2231

C

Take 50 from:

1. 6187
2. 523
3. 1258
4. 4740
5. 25 901

Add 600 to:

6. 2317
7. 769
8. 55 834
9. 4627
10. 8

Take 400 from:

11. 814
12. 23 636
13. 5380
14. 92 742
15. 2075

Add 5000 to:

16. 2317
17. 815
18. 36
19. 95 423
20. 47 840

What needs to be added or subtracted to change:

21. 48 915 to 35 915
22. 6238 to 6198
23. 32 281 to 33 381
24. 1010 to 100 010

Copy and complete.

25. 12 594 = □ + 94
26. 16 350 = □ + 50
27. 7936 = 7006 + □
28. 28 517 = 20 017 + □

A1 ORDERING NUMBERS

I can put numbers to 10 000 in order.

Example
Put these numbers in order with the smallest first. 6513 5613 6315
Look at the thousands first. 6513 5613 6315
If the thousands are the same look at the hundreds. 6513 6315
The correct order is 5613, 6315, 6513.

A

Which number is smaller?

1. 68 or 86
2. 93 or 39
3. 351 or 315
4. 428 or 482

Which number is larger?

5. 932 or 923
6. 548 or 584
7. 126 or 162
8. 654 or 645

Place these sets of numbers in order starting with the smallest.

9. 382 283 823 238
10. 714 417 174 471
11. 325 532 523 352
12. 649 469 496 694

Answer True or False.

13. $62 > 26$
14. $308 < 380$
15. $10 \times 8 > 3 \times 30$
16. $100 \div 2 < 50$

B

Copy and put < or > in the box.

1. 2471 ☐ 2741
2. 3856 ☐ 3568
3. 9706 ☐ 9670
4. 2843 ☐ 3248
5. 9999 ☐ 10 000
6. 4756 ☐ 4675
7. 7030 ☐ 6859
8. 1859 ☐ 1958

Put these numbers in order, starting with the smallest.

9. 2635 3256 2536 3526
10. 1984 1849 1498 4189
11. 6472 7462 6724 7246
12. 3748 3874 3784 3478

What needs to be added or subtracted to change:

13. 3128 to 3168
14. 4890 to 4590
15. 2761 to 8761
16. 8903 to 8203
17. 6452 to 6472
18. 7139 to 3139

C

Work out the number that is halfway between these numbers.

1. 3460 ←☐→ 3660
2. 2000 ←☐→ 2500
3. 4530 ←☐→ 4610
4. 19 500 ←☐→ 21 500
5. 950 ←☐→ 1050
6. 2095 ←☐→ 2125
7. 1440 ←☐→ 1500
8. 17 280 ←☐→ 17 290

What needs to be added or subtracted to change:

9. 7368 to 7200
10. 2495 to 2365
11. 1830 to 1900
12. 5634 to 4034?

13. Use these digits once each. Make two 3-digit numbers which give:

a) the largest possible total
b) the smallest possible total
c) the largest possible difference
d) the smallest possible difference.

I can recognise and order negative numbers.

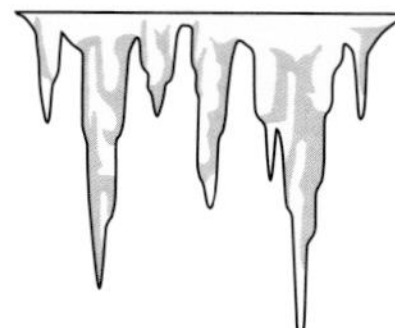

Negative numbers
Below zero
Have a minus sign

Positive numbers
Above zero

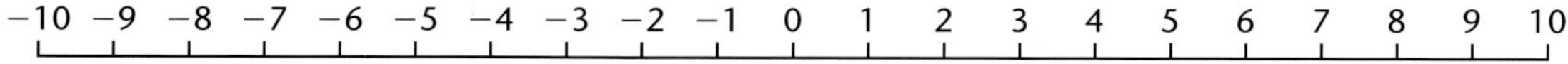

We often use negative numbers in the context of temperature.

Example

The temperature is 4°C. It falls 5°. What is the new temperature?
Answer −1°C

A

Use the number line above.

1. Count on 4 from −10
2. Count on 3 from −5
3. Count on 7 from −2
4. Count on 5 from −5
5. Count on 2 from −1
6. Count on 4 from −3
7. Count on 6 from −4
8. Count on 8 from −2

Copy and complete by filling in the boxes.

9. □ □ −3 −2 □ 0 1 2 □ 4 5
10. −10 −8 □ −4 −2 □ 2 □ □ 8 10
11. 5 4 □ □ 1 0 □ □ −3 −4 −5
12. 10 8 6 4 2 0 −2 □ □ □ □

Look at the scale.

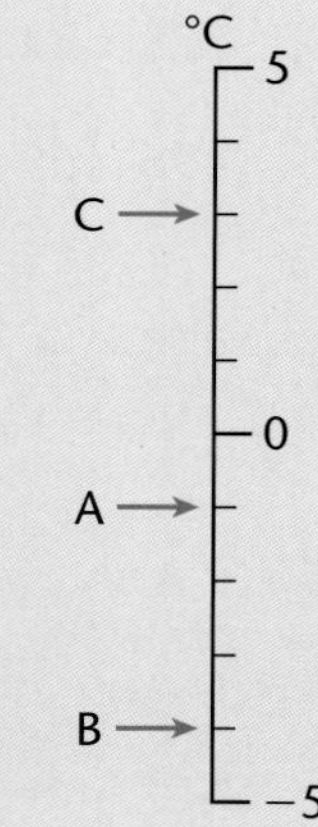

13. What temperatures are shown by the letters?
14. Which letter shows the coldest temperature?
15. Give the difference in temperature between:
    a) A and B
    b) B and C
    c) A and C.
16. What would the temperature be if it was:
    a) at B and rose 3°C
    b) at B and rose 5°C
    c) at A and rose 2°C
    d) at A and fell 2°C?

B

Use the number line on page 6.

1. Count on 6 from −5
2. Count on 8 from −10
3. Count on 10 from −6
4. Count on 6 from −4
5. Count back 8 from 5
6. Count back 7 from 0
7. Count back 15 from 8
8. Count back 13 from 4

17. What temperatures are shown by the letters?
18. Which letter shows the coldest temperature?
19. Give the difference in between
    a) A and B
    b) A and C
    c) B and C.
20. What would the temperature be if it was:
    a) at A and fell 7°?
    b) at B and rose 9°?

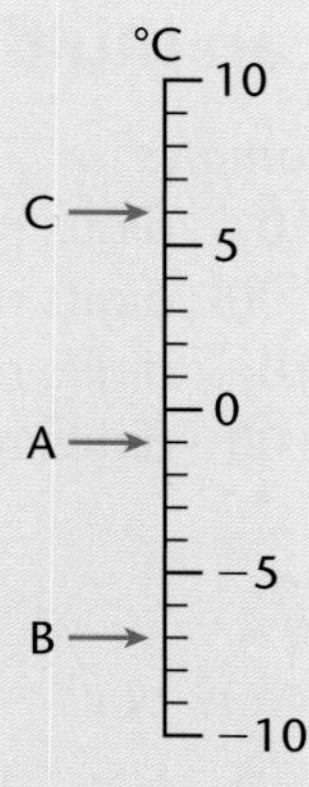

Copy and complete the sequences.

9. 3 2 □ □ □ −2 −3
10. □ □ □ 1 2 3 4
11. □ □ −4 −6 −8 −10 □
12. −10 □ −8 □ −6 □ −4
13. −10 −8 □ −4 □ □ 2
14. −7 □ □ −1 1 3 5
15. 6 4 2 □ □ □ −6
16. 5 □ 1 □ −3 □ −7

Put > or < in each box.

21. 4 □ − 4
22. −3 □ 2
23. 0 □ − 3
24. −2 □ − 4
25. −1 □ 6
26. −4 □ 0
27. −3 □ − 5
28. −8 □ 2

C

Find the difference between:

1. −6 and −4
2. −2 and 2
3. −3 and 5
4. −1 and 3
5. −4 and 2
6. −1 and −7
7. 0 and −4
8. 2 and −3

Put these numbers in order, smallest first.

9. 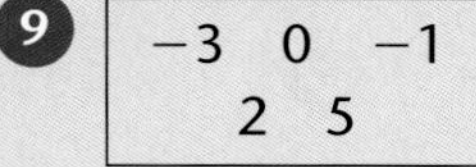
   −3 0 −1
   2 5
10. 4 −3
    −1 −5 1
11. 3 0 −4
    −2 1
12. 2 −4
    4 −1 0

Copy and complete these tables showing changes in temperature.

13.

Monday	Change	Tuesday
3°C	−4°C	−1°C
−1°C	+3°C	
0°C	−5°C	
4°C	−7°C	
−6°C	+2°C	
−2°C	+4°C	

14.

Monday	Change	Tuesday
7°C	−4°C	3°C
−2°C		3°C
−4°C		−1°C
1°C		−3°C
0°C		−6°C
−3°C		4°C

A1 MULTIPLYING AND DIVIDING BY 10/100

I can multiply and divide numbers up to 1000 by 10 and 100.

Examples

$\times 10$	digits move one place to the left	$62 \times 10 = 620$	$624 \times 10 = 6240$
$\times 100$	digits move two places to the left	$7 \times 100 = 700$	$73 \times 100 = 7300$
$\div 10$	digits move one place to the right	$350 \div 10 = 35$	$3590 \div 10 = 359$
$\div 100$	digits move two places to the right	$500 \div 100 = 5$	$5400 \div 100 = 54$

A

Work out

1. 16×10
2. 20×10
3. 58×10
4. 100×10
5. $50 \div 10$
6. $910 \div 10$
7. $600 \div 10$
8. $730 \div 10$
9. 4×100
10. 7×100
11. 2×100
12. 6×10
13. $300 \div 100$
14. $800 \div 100$
15. $500 \div 100$
16. $1000 \div 100$

How many 10ps make:

17. £1
18. £30
19. £6
20. £12
21. £42
22. £50?

How many 1ps make:

23. £1
24. £5
25. £10
26. £12
27. £3
28. £20?

29. A model of a house is ten times smaller than the house. How tall is the house if the model is 2 m tall?

B

Multiply by:

(10) (100)

1. 176
2. 49
3. 300
4. 220
5. 9
6. 17
7. 60
8. 48

Divide by:

(10) (100)

9. 7550
10. 5000
11. 6440
12. 4090
13. 3200
14. 700
15. 9000
16. 8300

Copy and complete.

17. $\square \times 10 = 630$
18. $\square \times 100 = 2800$
19. $\square \div 10 = 400$
20. $\square \div 100 = 51$
21. On a map 1 cm shows 100 m.
    a) How long is a road which is 20 cm long on the map?
    b) How wide is a lake on the map if the actual lake is 1500 m wide?

C

Copy and complete.

1. $\square \times 10 = 3860$
2. $\square \div 10 = 632$
3. $\square \times 100 = 7000$
4. $\square \div 100 = 6$
5. $\square \times 1000 = 4000$
6. $\square \div 1000 = 21$
7. $\square \times 10 = 95\,000$
8. $\square \div 10 = 350$
9. $\square \times 100 = 28\,000$
10. $\square \div 100 = 194$
11. $\square \times 1000 = 60\,000$
12. $\square \div 1000 = 11$

How many grams make:

13. 1 kg
14. 3 kg
15. 10 kg
16. $\frac{1}{2}$ kg
17. $2\frac{1}{2}$ kg
18. 14 kg?

19. A model bridge is 100 times smaller than the bridge.
    a) How tall is the bridge if the model is 12 cm tall?
    b) How wide is the model if the bridge is 750 metres wide?

A1 MULTIPLICATION FACTS

I know my 2, 3, 4, 5, 6 and 10 times tables.

A

What is

1. 7×2
2. 8×4
3. 3×10
4. 6×3

5. 4×6
6. 9×5
7. 8×3
8. 6×4

9. 7×5
10. 4×10
11. 9×2
12. 5×6

13. $40 \div 5$
14. $50 \div 10$
15. $36 \div 4$
16. $18 \div 6$

17. $21 \div 3$
18. $12 \div 2$
19. $30 \div 5$
20. $28 \div 4$

21. $16 \div 2$
22. $27 \div 3$
23. $36 \div 6$
24. $100 \div 10$

B

Copy and complete.

1. $\square \times 3 = 15$
2. $\square \times 5 = 20$
3. $\square \times 2 = 12$
4. $\square \times 10 = 80$

5. $\square \times 4 = 20$
6. $\square \times 6 = 42$
7. $\square \div 5 = 2$
8. $\square \div 3 = 8$

9. $\square \div 10 = 7$
10. $\square \div 2 = 8$
11. $\square \div 4 = 7$
12. $\square \div 6 = 4$

Write the answer only.

13. 6×30
14. 8×50
15. 5×20
16. 9×60

17. 3×40
18. 2×100
19. 8×20
20. 9×30

21. 3×50
22. 8×60
23. 10×100
24. 6×40

25. $300 \div 6$
26. $210 \div 3$
27. $80 \div 2$
28. $450 \div 5$

29. $160 \div 4$
30. $600 \div 10$
31. $250 \div 5$
32. $180 \div 2$

33. $320 \div 4$
34. $150 \div 3$
35. $300 \div 10$
36. $360 \div 6$

C

Copy and complete.

1. $\square \times 40 = 280$
2. $\square \times 50 = 300$
3. $\square \times 30 = 120$
4. $\square \times 5 = 500$

5. $\square \times 7 = 140$
6. $\square \times 3 = 180$
7. $\square \div 50 = 7$
8. $\square \div 40 = 9$

9. $\square \div 20 = 6$
10. $\square \div 7 = 60$
11. $\square \div 8 = 30$
12. $\square \div 4 = 100$

Write the answer only.

13. 2×7
14. 9×7
15. 5×7
16. 7×7

17. 3×8
18. 8×8
19. 4×8
20. 6×8

21. 5×9
22. 2×9
23. 7×9
24. 9×9

25. $21 \div 7$
26. $42 \div 7$
27. $56 \div 7$
28. $28 \div 7$

29. $16 \div 8$
30. $72 \div 8$
31. $40 \div 8$
32. $56 \div 8$

33. $36 \div 9$
34. $54 \div 9$
35. $27 \div 9$
36. $72 \div 9$

I can add or subtract to the nearest multiple of 10 and adjust.

Examples

$46 + 29 = 46 + 30 - 1$
$= 76 - 1$
$= 75$

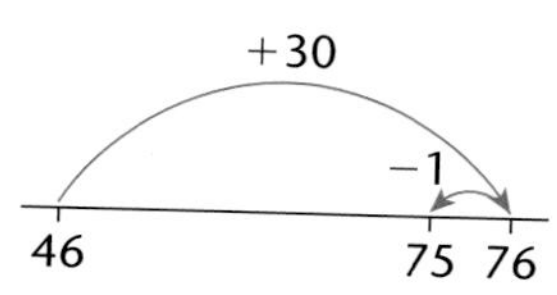

$85 - 31 = 85 - 30 - 1$
$= 55 - 1$
$= 54$

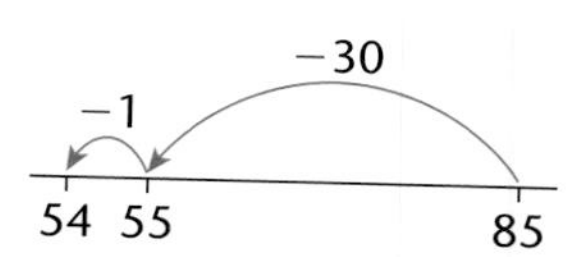

A

Work out

1. 62 + 9
2. 48 − 19
3. 36 + 21
4. 69 − 31
5. 54 + 19
6. 65 − 19
7. 63 + 31
8. 84 − 21
9. 48 + 19
10. 56 − 19

B

Work out

1. 73 + 29
2. 67 − 19
3. 97 + 48
4. 85 − 29
5. 48 + 31
6. 93 − 51
7. 74 + 62
8. 176 − 61
9. 68 + 39
10. 154 − 49

C

Copy and complete

1. ☐ + 68 = 324
2. ☐ − 39 = 193
3. ☐ + 52 = 817
4. ☐ + 59 = 238
5. ☐ − 99 = 369
6. ☐ + 61 = 547
7. ☐ + 72 = 263
8. ☐ − 48 = 267
9. ☐ + 96 = 514
10. ☐ + 78 = 147

I can add or subtract by partitioning.

Examples

$45 + 37 = 40 + 30 + 5 + 7$
$= 70 + 12$
$= 82$

$63 - 47 = 63 - 40 - 7$
$= 23 - 7$
$= 16$

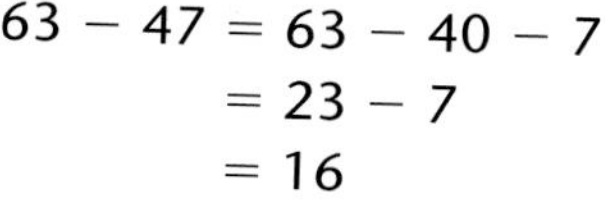

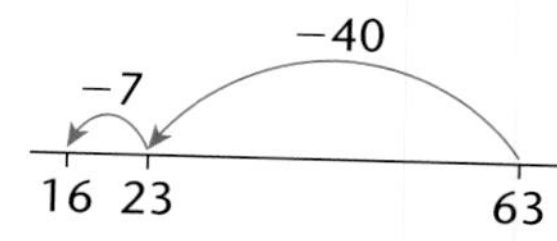

A

Work out

1. 26 + 52
2. 42 + 25
3. 68 − 35
4. 97 − 53
5. 43 + 45
6. 33 + 46
7. 79 − 26
8. 88 − 24
9. 54 + 35
10. 96 − 51

B

Work out

1. 26 + 57
2. 44 + 39
3. 86 − 42
4. 96 − 68
5. 36 + 59
6. 67 + 28
7. 78 − 36
8. 65 − 27
9. 38 + 46
10. 83 − 54

C

Copy and complete

1. 326 + ☐ = 578
2. 438 + ☐ = 694
3. 428 + ☐ = 536
4. 174 − ☐ = 26
5. 283 − ☐ = 64
6. 857 − ☐ = 352
7. 649 − ☐ = 66
8. 736 − ☐ = 514
9. 462 − ☐ = 141
10. 525 − ☐ = 218

A1 MONEY PROBLEMS

I can solve problems involving money using a calculator if needed.

Examples

What is the cost of 4 books at £2.95 each?

£2.95 × 4 Press C [2] [.] [9] [5] [×] [4] [=] → 11.8 Answer = £11.80

John spends 82p. He pays with a £2 coin. How much change should he have?

£2.00 − £0.82 Press C [2] [.] [0] [0] [−] [0] [.] [8] [2] [=] → 1.18 Answer = £1.18

A

Work out mentally.

1. 25p + 16p
2. 35p + 27p
3. 42p + 19p
4. 54p + 29p
5. 68p − 15p
6. 47p − 23p
7. 72p − 31p
8. 56p − 19p
9. Nick has 85p. Karen has 31p less. How much does Karen have?
10. Rona has 42p. Joss has half as much. How much do they have altogether?
11. Kumar earns 50p a day doing the washing up. How much does he earn in three weeks?
12. Four lollies cost £2·40. What does one lolly cost?
13. Stamps cost 30p each. There are 10 stamps in a book. What do two books cost?

B

Use a calculator.

1. £3·40 + 68p
2. £2·70 + 45p
3. £6·30 − 77p
4. £5·00 + 83p
5. £2·37 × 10
6. £4·16 × 5
7. £18·50 ÷ 5
8. £14·40 ÷ 4
9. Find the total cost of four pens at £1·30 each and three pencils at 27p each.
10. Calvin buys a shirt and a tie for £17·40. The tie costs £5·65. How much does the shirt cost?
11. Four friends share the cost of a meal. The bill is £37·60. How much should they each pay?
12. Ava buys four sandwiches and pays with a £10 note. She gets £2·80 change. How much does one sandwich cost?

C

Use a calculator.

1. £3·18 + 84p + 29p
2. £2·27 + 65p + 48p
3. £10·00 − 79p − 34p
4. £14·38 − £2·50 − 67p
5. £23·75 × 6
6. £19·95 × 8
7. £13·20 ÷ 12
8. £38·40 ÷ 16
9. Theatre tickets cost £17·50 for adults and half price for children. What will be the cost of tickets for two adults and three children?
10. Vernon spends £145·60 on newspapers in one year. How much does he spend in one week?
11. Anna earns £16·20 every hour. She works seven hours each day. How much will she earn in five days?

A1 NUMBER PUZZLES

I can solve puzzles involving addition and subtraction.

A

Match each shape to one of the numbers in the ring.

1

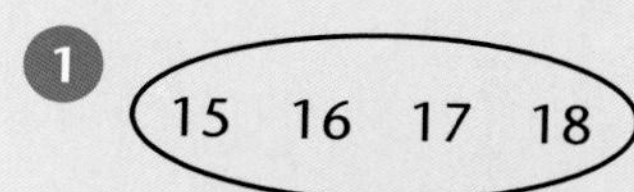

○ + △ = 35
◇ − □ = 1

2 25 35 45 55

■ + ◆ = 70
● − △ = 20

Copy and complete by writing the missing digit in the box.

3 23 + □4 = 37
4 □1 + 25 = 56
5 □6 + 19 = 35
6 □8 + 33 = 61
7 46 − □3 = 13
8 □2 − 35 = 7
9 75 − 5□ = 18
10 3□ − 14 = 16

Check the answers by doing the inverse operation.

11 I choose a number.
I add 14.
I take away 23.
My answer is 8.
What number did I choose?

B

Match each shape to one of the numbers in the ring.

1 34 48 68 78

□ − ○ = 44
◇ + △ = 116

2 26 27 28 29

■ + ● = 55
◆ − △ = 1

Copy and complete by writing the missing digits in the boxes.

3 4□ + □2 = 54
4 4□ + □8 = 73
5 □6 + 1□ = 41
6 □8 − 1□ = 21
7 5□ − □1 = 16
8 6□ − □4 = 34
9 3□ − □1 = 9
10 □1 − 3□ = 25

Check the answers by doing the inverse operation.

11 I choose a number.
I subtract 27.
I add 44.
My answer is 91.
What number did I choose?

C

What number is shown by each shape?

1 △ + ○ = □
□ + 14 = ◇
◇ − ○ = 53
The square is 66.

2 ● + ◆ = △
● − ■ = ◆
◆ − ■ = 7
The square is 28.

Copy and complete by writing the missing digit in the boxes.

3 $$\begin{array}{r} \square\ 2 \\ +\ 2\ \square \\ \hline 5\ 9 \\ \hline \end{array}$$

4 $$\begin{array}{r} \square\ 5 \\ +\ 3\ \square \\ \hline 7\ 9 \\ \hline \end{array}$$

5 $$\begin{array}{r} 5\ \square \\ +\ 1\ 2 \\ \hline 7\ 0 \\ \hline \end{array}$$

6 $$\begin{array}{r} \square\ 8 \\ +\ 3\ 8 \\ \hline 9\ 6 \\ \hline \end{array}$$

7 $$\begin{array}{r} \square\ 8 \\ -\ 2\ \square \\ \hline 2\ 5 \\ \hline \end{array}$$

8 $$\begin{array}{r} 6\ \square \\ -\ \square\ 6 \\ \hline 5\ 1 \\ \hline \end{array}$$

9 $$\begin{array}{r} \square\ 5 \\ -\ 3\ 9 \\ \hline 4\ 6 \\ \hline \end{array}$$

10 $$\begin{array}{r} 5\ \square \\ -\ 2\ 8 \\ \hline 2\ 5 \\ \hline \end{array}$$

Check the answers by doing the inverse operation.

11 Find a pair of numbers:
a) with a sum of 45 and a difference of 7
b) with a sum of 100 and a difference of 18.

A1 DARTS

I can solve puzzles involving addition and subtraction.

On a dartboard the outer ring doubles the score and the inner ring trebles the score. (Trebles means times by 3.)

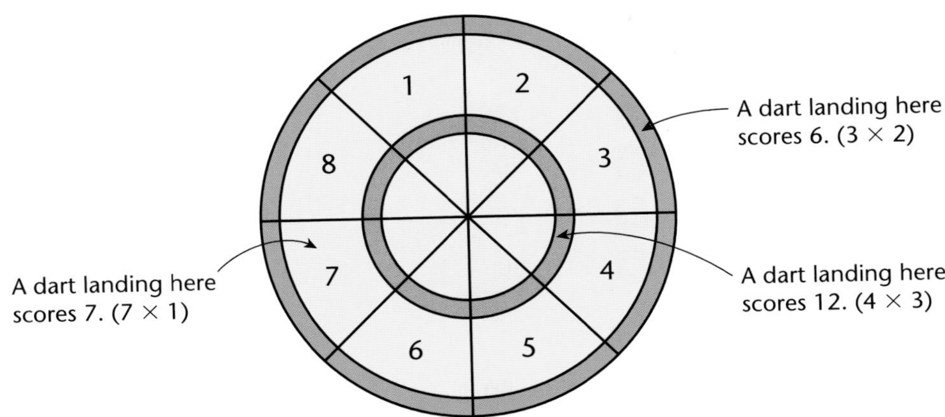

A

Use one dart only in all the questions in this section.

1. What is the highest possible score?
2. Find two ways of scoring:
   a) 8 **b)** 2 **c)** 4 **d)** 12
3. Which number can be scored in three different ways?
4. Write down one way of scoring:
   a) 9 **b)** 14 **c)** 21 **d)** 10 **e)** 15 **f)** 16
5. There are four numbers lower than 20 that you cannot score. What are they?

B

In this section use two darts only. Both darts must score.

1. What is the highest possible score with two darts?
2. Find two ways of scoring:
   a) 34 **b)** 39
3. Find four ways of scoring:
   a) 36 **b)** 33 **c)** 32 **d)** 29
4. How can you score:
   a) 35 **b)** 37 **c)** 38 **d)** 40?
5. Explore different ways of scoring these numbers.
   a) 17
   b) 26
   c) 31

C

In this section use three darts only. All three darts must score.

1. What is the highest possible score using three darts?
2. How can you score 59?
3. There are three ways of scoring 58. What are they?
4. Which numbers in the 60s cannot be scored?
5. Explore different ways of scoring these numbers:
   a) 47 **b)** 51 **c)** 55
6. Design a dartboard of your own. Investigate the scores that can be made on it, and the scores that cannot be made.

B1 ADDITION AND SUBTRACTION FACTS

I can use addition and subtraction facts for all numbers up to 20 and state the addition fact corresponding to any subtraction fact and vice versa.

A

Work out.

1. 8 + 6
2. 7+ 7
3. 5 + 8
4. 7 + 9
5. 9 + 8
6. 6 + 7
7. 9 + 6
8. 9 + 9
9. 6 + 8
10. 8 + 7
11. 8 + 8
12. 8 + 9
13. 7 + 6
14. 9 + 7
15. 7 + 8
16. 15 − 7
17. 17 − 8
18. 14 − 6
19. 13 − 7
20. 16 − 9
21. 15 − 8
22. 18 − 9
23. 13 − 5
24. 16 − 8
25. 16 − 7
26. 17 − 9
27. 14 − 7
28. 13 − 6
29. 15 − 9
30. 15 − 6

Copy and complete.
Use the three given numbers only.

31. 23 + 16 = 39
    □ + □ = □
    39 − □ = □
    □ − □ = □
32. 46 + 17 = 63
    □ + □ = □
    □ − □ = 17
    63 − □ = □

B

Work out.

1. 60 + 110
2. 50 + 90
3. 70 + 70
4. 60 + 80
5. 70 + 90
6. 160 − 80
7. 150 − 70
8. 170 − 90
9. 150 − 60
10. 180 − 90
11. 700 + 600
12. 800 + 700
13. 900 + 800
14. 600 + 600
15. 500 + 800
16. 1400 − 700
17. 1300 − 400
18. 1600 − 900
19. 1700 − 800
20. 1100 − 700

For each fact below write three related facts.

21. 48 + 16 = 64
22. 67 − 29 = 38
23. 45 + 38 = 83
24. 58 − 26 = 32

C

Copy and complete.

1. 60 + □ = 140
2. 90 + □ = 160
3. 70 + □ = 150
4. 50 + □ = 140
5. 90 + □ = 150
6. 140 − □ = 70
7. 170 − □ = 80
8. 150 − □ = 90
9. 180 − □ = 90
10. 160 − □ = 70
11. 900 + □ = 1300
12. 6000 + □ = 15 000
13. 800 + □ = 1600
14. 3000 + □ = 12 000
15. 600 + □ = 1300
16. 15 000 − □ = 8000
17. 1400 − □ = 800
18. 16 000 − □ = 9000
19. 1300 − □ = 500
20. 17 000 − □ = 9000

For each set of numbers write four related + and − facts .

21. 123, 214, 337
22. 72, 37, 109
23. 600, 170, 430
24. 340, 700, 360

B1 MAGIC SQUARES

I can use addition and subtraction facts to solve puzzles.

Example
In a magic square the sum of each row, column and diagonal is the same.

13	4	7
2	8	14
9	12	3

(↔) Rows (↔)
$13 + 4 + 7 = 24$
$2 + 8 + 14 = 24$
$9 + 12 + 3 = 24$

(↕) Columns (↕)
$13 + 2 + 9 = 24$
$4 + 8 + 12 = 24$
$7 + 14 + 3 = 24$

(↗) Diagonals (↖)
$13 + 8 + 3 = 24$
$7 + 8 + 9 = 24$

Copy and complete the following magic squares.

A

1

10	6	2
		7

2

		8
5		9
		4

3

2		6
	5	
		8

4

9	10	5
		7

B

1

	7	
6	11	10

2

	2	
	10	
4	18	

3

9		
	12	
	8	15

4

		8
		15
14		10

C

1

		7	14
13		12	
16	5	9	4
	10		

2

5	16		2
	7		13
	11	12	
17	4		

3

3		10	
	9		4
17	8	12	
6			18

4 Now try to make some magic squares of your own. Start with a 3×3 square.

B1 ROUNDING

I can round numbers to the nearest 10 and 100 and money to the nearest pound and I can use rounding to estimate an answer.

Examples

To NEAREST 10
Look at the units.
5 or more, round up.
Below 5, round down.
138 rounds to 140
134 rounds to 130

To NEAREST 100
Look at 10s and units.
50 or more, round up.
Below 50, round down.
374 rounds to 400
1620 rounds to 1600

APPROXIMATING
125 + 43 → 130 + 40 → 170
29 × 3 → 30 × 3 → 90
893 − 216 → 900 − 200 → 700
£3·74 × 5 → £4 × 5 → £20

A

Round to the nearest 10.

1. 21
2. 35
3. 47
4. 83
5. 69
6. 51
7. 78
8. 42
9. 26
10. 97

Round to the nearest 100.

11. 230
12. 370
13. 450
14. 620
15. 910
16. 880
17. 790
18. 540
19. 360
20. 650

Round to the nearest pound.

21. £2·70
22. £8·50
23. £5·20
24. £1·80
25. £9·30
26. £6·40
27. £3·60
28. £2·10
29. £7·90
30. £4·80

B

Approximate by rounding to the nearest 10.

1. 62 + 57
2. 49 + 78
3. 128 − 31
4. 92 − 49
5. 153 − 64
6. 39 × 2
7. 32 × 3
8. 18 × 5
9. 21 × 4
10. 47 × 6

Approximate by rounding to the nearest 100.

11. 360 + 440
12. 420 + 290
13. 850 − 270
14. 490 − 160
15. 1130 − 580

Approximate by rounding to the nearest pound.

16. £4·60 × 3
17. £9·20 × 5
18. £2·84 × 7
19. £5·17 × 2
20. £7·50 × 6

C

Copy the sentences, writing the numbers to the nearest 1000, with the word 'about'.

1. 2813 patients were treated at the hospital.
2. The supermarket sold 1479 bottles of wine.
3. 135 268 people live in the town.
4. There are 29 500 books in the library.

Approximate by rounding to the nearest 10.

5. 129 + 133
6. 608 + 199
7. 552 − 347
8. 743 − 126

Approximate by rounding to the nearest pound.

9. £14·92 × 6
10. £23·27 × 8
11. £13·56 × 4
12. £38·83 × 5

B1 MULTIPLICATION FACTS

I can recall the multiplication and division facts for the 2, 3, 4, 5, 6 and 10 times tables.

A

Copy and complete.

1. $7 \times 2 = \square$
2. $10 \times 4 = \square$
3. $6 \times 3 = \square$
4. $9 \times 5 = \square$
5. $8 \times 10 = \square$
6. $6 \times \square = 30$
7. $7 \times \square = 28$
8. $9 \times \square = 18$
9. $4 \times \square = 40$
10. $8 \times \square = 24$
11. $\square \times 3 = 21$
12. $\square \times 5 = 40$
13. $\square \times 10 = 100$
14. $\square \times 2 = 12$
15. $\square \times 4 = 36$
16. $24 \div 4 = \square$
17. $16 \div 2 = \square$
18. $50 \div 5 = \square$
19. $15 \div 3 = \square$
20. $70 \div 10 = \square$

These are harder.

21. $\square \div 5 = 35$
22. $\square \div 10 = 90$
23. $\square \div 3 = 27$
24. $\square \div 4 = 32$
25. $\square \div 2 = 4$

B

Write the answers only.

1. 3×6
2. 10×6
3. 7×6
4. 9×6
5. 6×6
6. 2×6
7. 5×6
8. 0×6
9. 8×6
10. $36 \div 6$
11. $6 \div 6$
12. $60 \div 6$
13. $24 \div 6$
14. $48 \div 6$
15. $30 \div 6$
16. $54 \div 6$
17. $18 \div 6$
18. $42 \div 6$

Copy and complete.

19. $\square \times 6 = 18$
20. $\square \times 6 = 42$
21. $\square \times 6 = 24$
22. $\square \times 6 = 36$
23. $\square \times 6 = 0$
24. $\square \times 6 = 48$
25. $\square \times 6 = 30$
26. $\square \times 6 = 54$
27. $\square \div 6 = 5$
28. $\square \div 6 = 8$
29. $\square \div 6 = 10$
30. $\square \div 6 = 4$
31. $\square \div 6 = 7$
32. $\square \div 6 = 1$
33. $\square \div 6 = 9$
34. $\square \div 6 = 6$

C

Write the answers only.

1. 40×6
2. 200×6
3. 500×6
4. 70×6
5. 30×6
6. 800×6
7. 400×6
8. 700×6
9. 90×6
10. 600×6
11. $120 \div 6$
12. $600 \div 6$
13. $240 \div 6$
14. $6000 \div 6$
15. $3600 \div 6$
16. $300 \div 6$
17. $4800 \div 6$
18. $1800 \div 6$
19. $420 \div 6$
20. $5400 \div 6$

Work out by multiplying by 6 and doubling.

21. 3×12
22. 10×12
23. 5×12
24. 2×12
25. 8×12
26. 6×12
27. 4×12
28. 9×12
29. 7×12
30. 20×12
31. There are six chairs in every stack. There are 24 stacks. How many chairs are there?
32. Eggs are packed into boxes of 6. How many boxes are needed for 96 eggs?

I can solve word problems.

Example

An ice cream costs 50p for one scoop and 30p for each extra scoop.
How much will an ice cream with four scoops cost?

$30p \times 3 = 90p$
$90p + 50p = 140p$
Answer
The ice cream costs £1·40.

A

1. Callum has 83 stamps. 48 are British. How many are foreign?
2. How many 5 cm lengths of string can be cut from 40 cm?
3. A coin weighs 20 g. How much do eight coins weigh?
4. There were eight teams at a 5-a-side football tournament. How many players were there?
5. During the football season Joe's team scored 64 goals. Harry's team only scored half as many. How many goals were scored by the two teams altogether?

B

1. A motorist needs to drive 231 miles. He stops for petrol after 86 miles. How much further does he have to go?
2. A mug of tea holds one quarter of a litre. How many mugs can be filled from a 5 litre urn?
3. Three shelves each had 25 books and there were nine books on another shelf. How many books were there altogether?
4. Sixty children entered a fancy dress competition. One quarter of them came as witches. How many children wore a different costume?
5. Ross is 87 cm tall. Dee is 57 cm taller. How tall is Dee in metres and centimetres?
6. T-shirts cost £2·50 each. Ned buys a pack of 3 for £5·75. How much has he saved?

C

1. A factory produces 655 cars. 168 are painted white. How many cars are painted other colours?
2. A serving of breakfast cereal weighs 30 g. How many servings are there in a three quarter kilogram box?
3. How many hours are there in 4 weeks?
4. There are 19 more boys than there are girls in a school. There are 138 girls. How many children are there in the school?
5. The top shelf is one and a half metres long. The bottom shelf is 64 cm shorter. What is the combined length of the shelves?
6. Cherri buys 3 ice creams and a lolly for £3·45. The lolly costs 75p. How much does each ice cream cost?

B1 THREE-DIMENSIONAL SHAPES

I can describe the faces and count the faces, edges and vertices of 3-D shapes.

A

Match each of the shapes A to L with one of the names of 3-D shapes.

cone
cube
cuboid
cylinder
hemi-sphere
hexagonal based prism
octagonal based prism
pentagonal based prism
sphere
square based pyramid
triangular based prism
triangular based pyramid

A

D

G

J

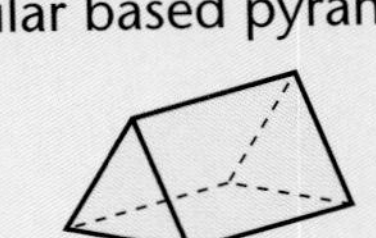

B

E

H

K

C

F

I

L

B

Describe the faces of:

1. a square based pyramid
2. a triangular based prism
3. a cuboid
4. an octagonal based prism.

Which 3-D shape has:

5. 2 circular faces
6. 10 vertices
7. no edges
8. 12 identical length edges?
9. This net of an open cube has one square too many. Copy it, cut off one square and fold to make an open cube.

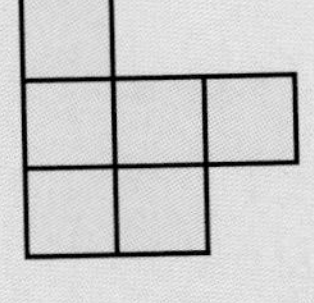

10. Copy the net again. Cut off a different square to make an open cube.

C

1. Copy and complete this table showing the features of 3-D shapes.

Name	Faces	Edges	Vertices
cuboid			
	8		
		8	
			6
	6		
		24	
			4
	7		

2. This net of a closed cube has one square too many. Copy it, cut off one square and fold to make a closed cube.
3. Copy the net again. Cut off a different square to make a closed cube.

I can name 2-D shapes and describe their properties.

2-D shapes with straight lines are called polygons.
(Equal lines are shown with dashes and equal angles are marked.)

A three sided polygon is a triangle.

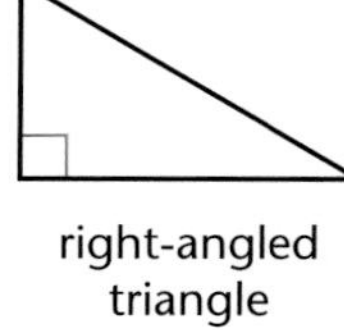
right-angled triangle

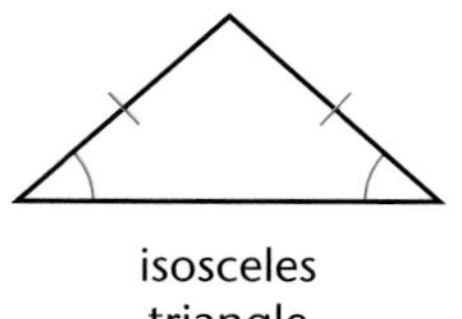
isosceles triangle

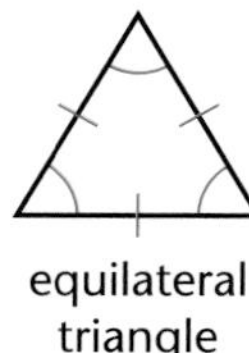
equilateral triangle

A four sided polygon is a quadrilateral.

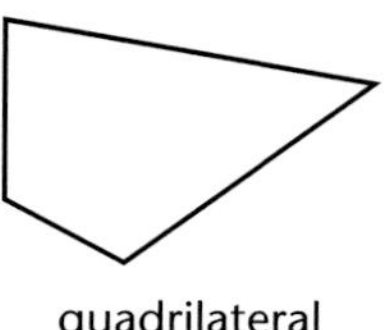
quadrilateral

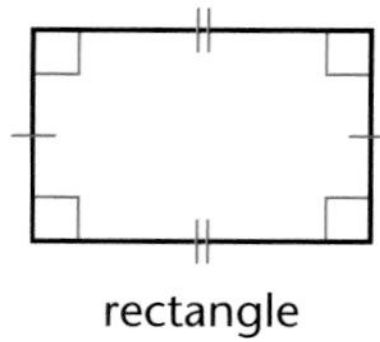
rectangle

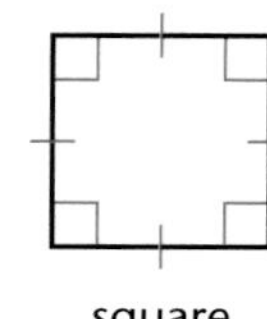
square

Other polygons are:

5 sides – pentagon 6 sides – hexagon 7 sides – heptagon 8 sides – octagon

A regular polygon has all sides equal and all angles equal.

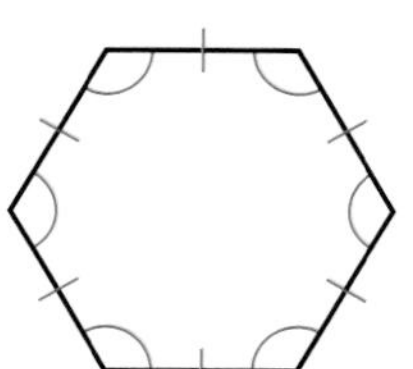

An irregular polygon has sides and angles which are not all equal.

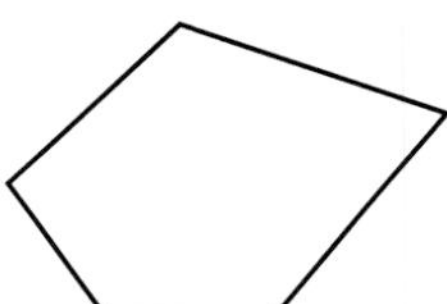

1 Copy the Carroll diagram and write the letters in the correct places.

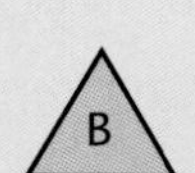
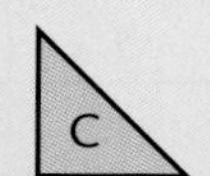

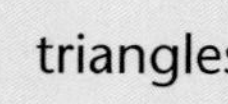

	symmetrical	not symmetrical
triangles		
not triangles		

2 Write the names of all the shapes in question **1**.

3 Draw a quadrilateral with equal angles but not equal sides.

4 Draw a quadrilateral with equal sides but not equal angles.

5 Which of the above shapes A–H:

a) have all sides equal
b) have 2 or more equal angles
c) is an isosceles triangle
d) is a regular pentagon?

B

1. Copy the Carroll diagram and use it to sort the shapes I–Q.

	has a right angle	no right angle
regular		
not regular		

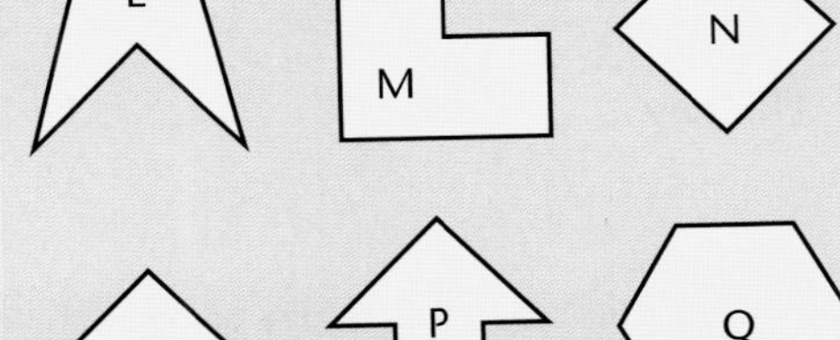

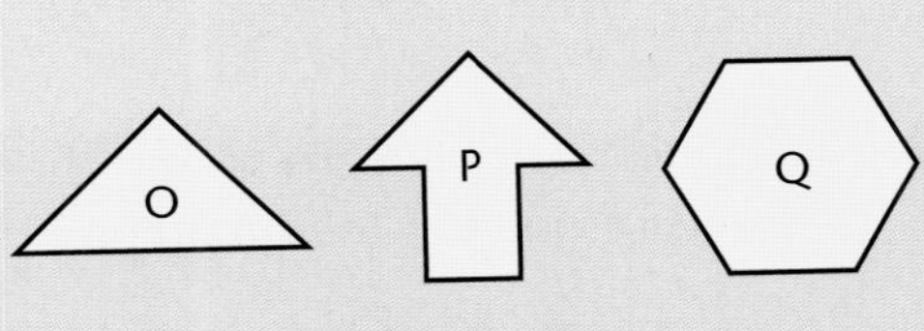

2. Write the names of the above shapes.
3. Which of the shapes have:
   a) 2 or more equal sides
   b) 2 or more right angles?
4. Draw a hexagon with equal sides but not equal angles.
5. Draw a hexagon with equal angles but not equal sides. (You may find it helpful to use triangular paper.)
6. What is the largest number of right angles possible in a quadrilateral which is not a square or a rectangle?
   Draw diagrams to illustrate your answer.

C

1. Copy the Carroll diagram.
   Look at the shapes in Sections A and B.
   Write the letters A to Q in the right places in your diagram.

	has 2 or more equal angles	does not have 2 or more equal angles
has 5 or more sides		
does not have 5 or more sides		

2. What is the common name for a regular quadrilateral?
3. What is the common name for a regular triangle?
4. Draw an isosceles triangle with one angle:
   a) greater than 90°
   b) less than 90°.
5. Draw a quadrilateral with three angles greater than 90°.
6. An equilateral triangle cannot have a right angle.
   Explain why.
7. What is the largest number of right angles possible in:
   a) a pentagon
   b) a hexagon?
   Draw diagrams to illustrate your answer.
8. Investigate the maximum number of right angles in other polygons.

I can collect, organise and present data.

Example

The ages of children in a Junior Football Club.

9	10	7	8	8	11	9	10
9	10	10	9	8	10	9	9
7	8	10	9	9	10	9	8
11	9	8	10	7	8	10	8
8	9	11	8	9	11	10	9

A tally chart showing the ages:

Age		Tally	Total
7	–	|||	3
8	–	~~||||~~ ~~||||~~	10
9	–	~~||||~~ ~~||||~~ |||	13
10	–	~~||||~~ ~~||||~~	10
11	–	||||	4

The ages in the tally chart can be presented in a horizontal or vertical bar chart.

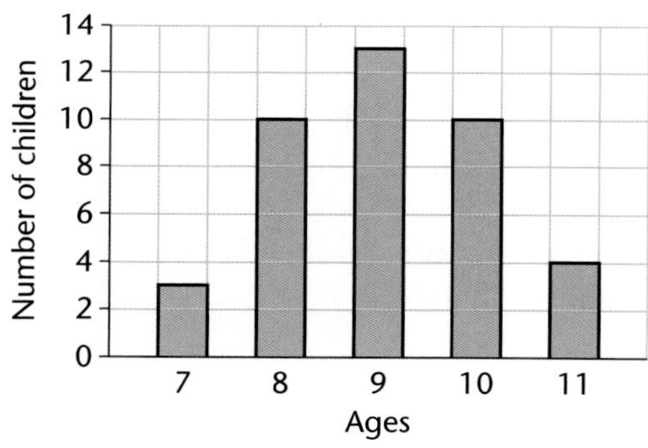

A

1. In their games lessons a class had played netball, football, rounders and hockey. At the end of the year they were asked to choose their favourite sport. These are the results.

N	F	R	H	R	F
H	N	F	R	F	N
H	F	H	N	F	H
F	F	R	F	H	N

Copy and complete the tally chart.

Games	Tally	Total
Netball	~~||||~~	5
Football		
Rounders		
Hockey		

2. The school football team scored these numbers of goals in their matches.

2	0	1	3	2	0	1	2
3	1	2	2	0	2	3	0
2	4	2	0	3	2	3	4

Copy and complete the tally chart.

Goals	Tally	Total (Matches)
0	~~||||~~	5
1		
2		
3		
4		

3. Present your results in a bar chart or a pictogram.

B

Class 4 made parachutes using squares of cotton cloth. They then investigated the rate at which the parachutes fell.
They identified these variables.

a) the size of the cotton square
b) the length of the string
c) the weight attached
d) the drop height
e) the drop time

1. Write the units of measurement used for each of the above variables (**a–e**).

2. One group decided to investigate how the weight attached affected drop time. Which of the above variables **a–e** did they:
   a) change each time
   b) measure for their results
   c) make sure they kept the same?

3. They presented their results in a table. What were their headings?

4. Complete their predicted conclusion.
   The greater the weight ….

5. The children in 4Z were asked how many children were there in their family. These are the results:

2	3	1	2	4	3	1	2
3	4	2	3	1	5	3	2
2	1	2	5	3	2	2	3
2	3	4	1	2	3	2	1

   a) How many children are in 4Z?
   b) Make a tally chart to organise the results.
   c) Make sure that your tally total matches the number of children in the class.
   d) Present the results in a horizontal bar chart.

C

Using the variables **a–e** listed in Section B, plan a different investigation.

1. Identify:
   a) the variable you would change
   b) the variable you would measure for your results
   c) the variable you would make sure did not change,

2. If your results were presented in a bar chart what would you label each axis.

3. Write a predicted conclusion for your investigation.

4. John wanted to know how long the words were in his reading book. He found that in one passage the words had these numbers of letters:

3	3	4	4	4	3	7	4	2	2
2	7	2	6	2	8	2	2	4	5
2	7	5	2	3	4	6	3	5	2
3	5	7	2	2	7	4	3	5	6
5	3	2	8	2	4	6	7	3	4

   Make a tally chart and then draw a vertical bar chart to show the results.

5. Make a tally chart of the lengths of the words in Section C on this page. Draw a bar chart to show the results.

6. Investigate the lengths of the words in your reading book.

I can use tables and bar charts to find information.

Example

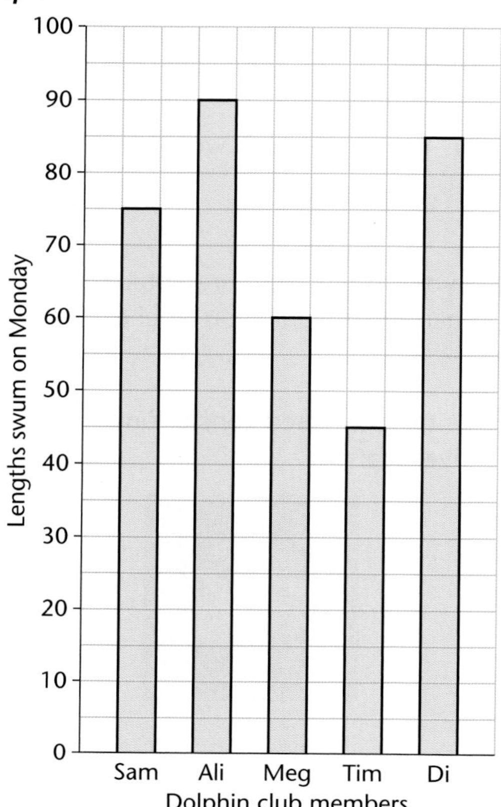

Look at the bar chart.

1. What information is shown?
   The axis labels show that it is the number of lengths swum by Dolphin members on Monday.
2. What is the value of one numbered division? *10 lengths*
3. What is the value of one unnumbered division? *5 lengths*
4. How many lengths did Meg swim? *60*
5. Who swam most lengths? *Ali*
6. Who swam 85 lengths? *Di*

The School Breakfast Club kept a record of the bowls of cereal and slices of toast eaten in one week.

Day	Cereal	Toast
Monday	9	23
Tuesday	12	28
Wednesday	16	12
Thursday	11	18
Friday	14	30

1. On which day were the fewest bowls of cereal eaten?
2. On which day were the most slices of toast eaten?
3. How many slices of toast were eaten on Tuesday?
4. How many more bowls of cereal were eaten on Wednesday than on Thursday?
5. How many bowls of cereal were eaten altogether?

The children in Class 4 chose their favourite colours.

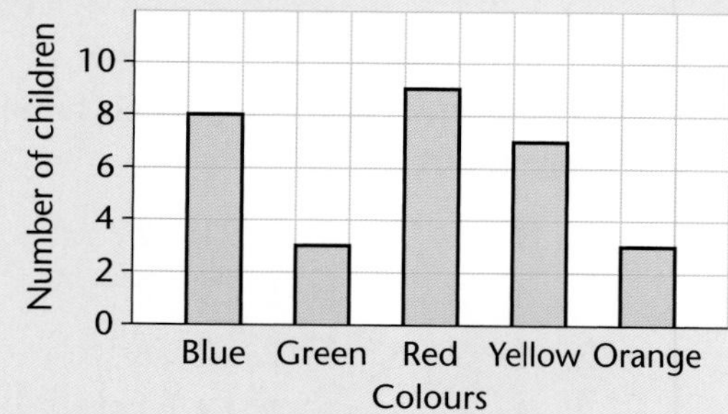

6. Which colour was chosen most often?
7. How many more children chose blue than chose green?
8. How many fewer children chose orange than chose yellow?
9. How many children are there in this class?
10. Kevin says that over half the class chose red or yellow. Is he right? Explain why.

Four football teams played each other twice in a tournament. These were the results.

Team	Won	Drawn	Lost
City	3	0	3
Rovers	1	1	4
Town	3	1	2
United	2	4	0

1. How many games:
   - **a)** did Town draw
   - **b)** did City lose
   - **c)** did Rovers win?
2. Which team:
   - **a)** lost 4 games
   - **b)** drew 4 games
   - **c)** lost 0 games?
3. Two points were awarded for a win and one for a draw. Work out the total points for each team. Draw a table with the teams in points order.

This bar chart shows the numbers of vowels in the first page of a book.

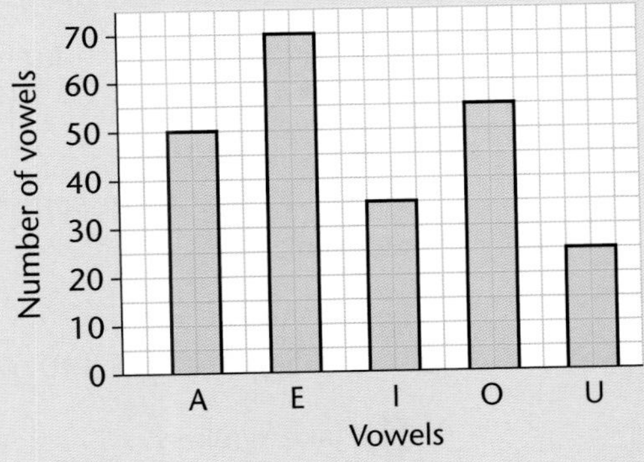

4. Which was the most common vowel?
5. Which was the least common?
6. Which letter appeared:
   - **a)** twice as often as U
   - **b)** half as often as E?
7. How many vowels were there altogether?

Class 4 studied parachutes. This table shows the results of one group's investigation.

Drop height ( )	Drop Time ( )
2	1
4	2
6	3
8	4

1. What are the two missing units of measurement in the table headings?
2. Which variable did the children change each time?
3. What did they measure to find their results?
4. What question were they investigating?
5. Complete the conclusion. *The greater the drop height ….*

This bar chart shows the numbers of jumps by members of a parachute club.

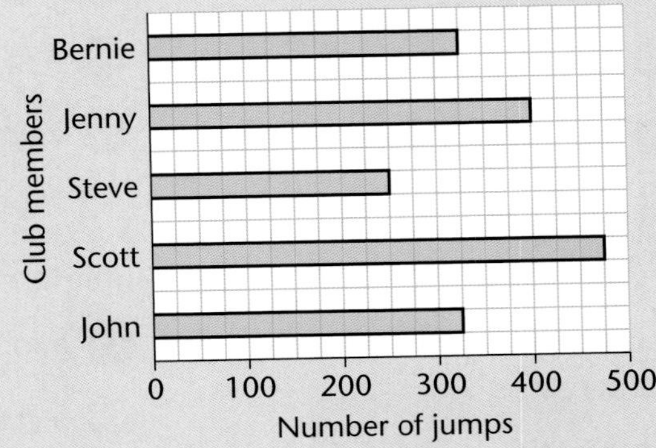

6. How many jumps has Steve made?
7. How many more jumps has Scott made than John?
8. How many fewer jumps has Bernie made than Jenny?
9. How many jumps have the five members made altogether?

D1 METRIC UNITS

I can choose and use metric units to measure lengths, weights or capacities.

LENGTH
100 cm = 1 m
1000 m = 1 km

WEIGHT
1000 g = 1 kg

CAPACITY
1000 ml = 1 litre

Remember Kilo = 1000
1 kilogram = 1000 g
1 kilometre = 1000 m

A

Copy and complete.

1. 1 km = ☐ m
2. 2 m = ☐ cm
3. 3 kg = ☐ g
4. 2 litres = ☐ ml
5. 3 km = ☐ m
6. 3 m = ☐ cm
7. 1 kg = ☐ g
8. 3 litres = ☐ ml
9. 2 km = ☐ m
10. 1 m = ☐ cm
11. 2 kg = ☐ g
12. 1 litre = ☐ ml

Choose the more sensible estimate.

13. a feather
    1 g or 100 g
14. a wine glass
    10 ml or 100 ml
15. a bottle's height
    25 cm or 50 cm
16. a bag of potatoes
    200 g or 2 kg

B

Copy and complete.

1. $\frac{1}{2}$ kg = ☐ g
2. 5 litres = ☐ ml
3. 200 cm = ☐ m
4. $\frac{1}{2}$ km = ☐ m
5. 6 kg = ☐ g
6. 3000 ml = ☐ litres
7. $\frac{1}{2}$ m = ☐ cm
8. 2000 m = ☐ km
9. 4000 g = ☐ kg
10. $\frac{1}{2}$ litre = ☐ ml
11. 4 m = ☐ cm
12. 7 km = ☐ m

Suggest a suitable metric unit to measure:

13. a lorry's height
14. a cushion's weight
15. a bath's width
16. a bath's weight
17. a bath's capacity
18. a newspaper's weight
19. the length of Africa
20. a baby's weight

C

Copy and complete.

1. 250 ml + ☐ = 1 litre
2. 94 cm + ☐ = 1 m
3. 580 m + ☐ = 1 km
4. 390 g + ☐ = 1 kg
5. 110 ml + ☐ = 1 litre
6. 76 cm + ☐ = 1 m
7. 90 m + ☐ = 1 km
8. 820 g + ☐ = 1 kg
9. 670 ml + ☐ = 1 litre
10. 46 cm + ☐ = 1 m
11. 530 m + ☐ = 1 km
12. 210 g + ☐ = 1 kg

Copy the sentence choosing the most sensible estimate.

13. An apple weighs (15 g, 150 g, 1500 g).
14. Jake walked (40 m, 400 m, 4000 m) in one hour.
15. A bottle of perfume holds (20 ml, 200 ml, 2 litres).
16. A box of cornflakes weighs (34 g, $\frac{3}{4}$ kg, 3 kg).

I can read a scale by counting on from the last numbered interval.

Work out the measurement shown by each arrow.

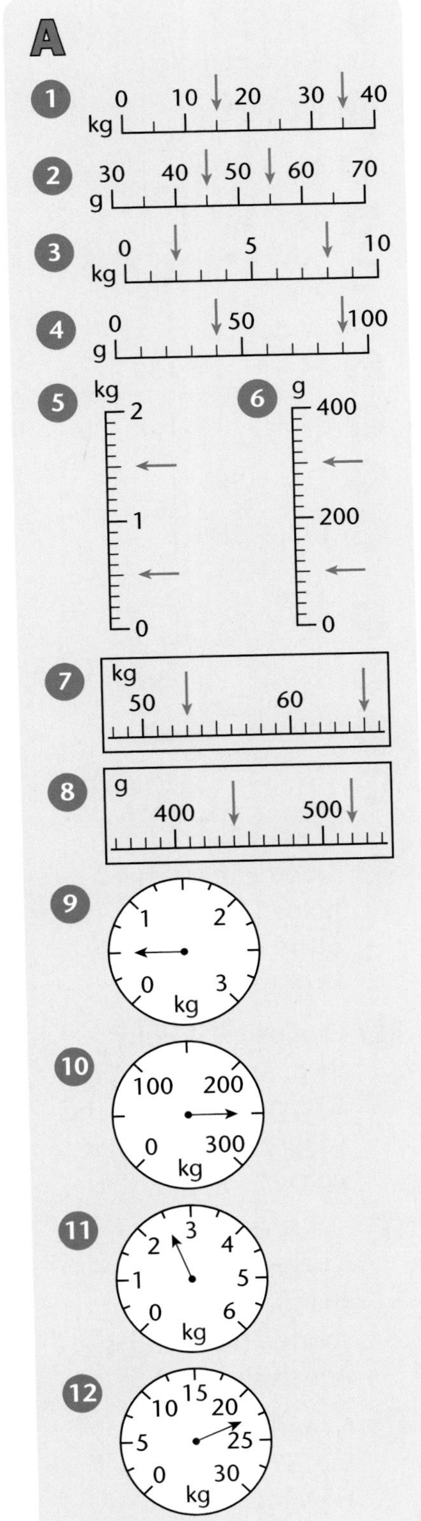

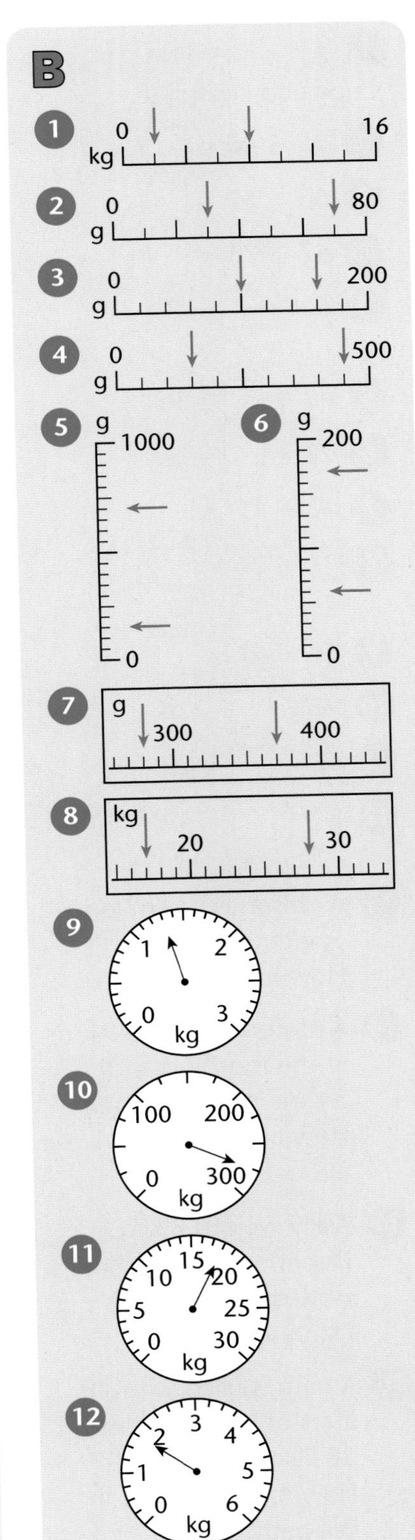

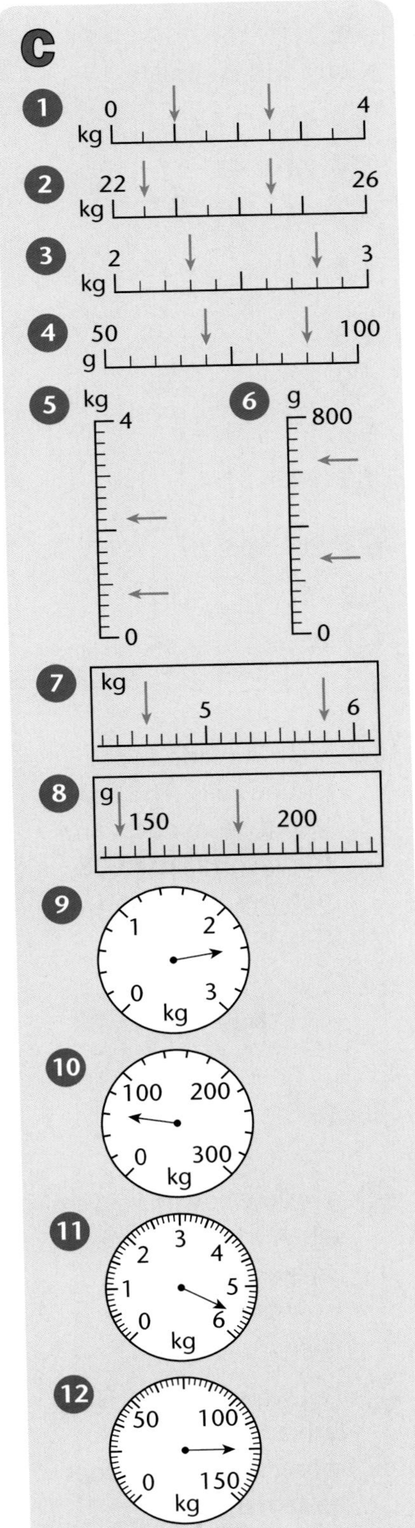

D1 MENTAL ADDITION/SUBTRACTION

I can add and subtract mentally pairs of two-digit numbers and use this to solve problems.

A

Copy and complete

1. 41 + 17 = ☐
2. 26 + 43 = ☐
3. 32 + 35 = ☐
4. 43 + ☐ = 75
5. 54 + ☐ = 78
6. 32 + ☐ = 96
7. 64 − 21 = ☐
8. 56 − 32 = ☐
9. 98 − 63 = ☐
10. 79 − ☐ = 52
11. 85 − ☐ = 44
12. 67 − ☐ = 33
13. Sharon made two phone calls. The first lasted 34 minutes and the second lasted 28 minutes. How long was she on the phone?

14. A yellow flower is 76 cm tall. A white flower is 34 cm shorter. How tall is the white flower?
15. Tim weighs 32 kg. His father weighs 25 kg more. How much does his father weigh?

B

Copy and complete.

1. 35 + 46 = ☐
2. 56 + 37 = ☐
3. 47 + 28 = ☐
4. 62 + ☐ = 81
5. 48 + ☐ = 93
6. 28 + ☐ = 59
7. 43 − 17 = ☐
8. 71 − 26 = ☐
9. 64 − 41 = ☐
10. 92 − ☐ = 36
11. 56 − ☐ = 27
12. 84 − ☐ = 49
13. A ribbon is 95 cm long. Sue cuts off 36 cm. How much is left?
14. A motorist drives 49 km in the morning and 34 km in the afternoon. How far does she drive altogether?
15. Wally weighs 83 kg. Daphne weighs 56 kg. How much lighter is Daphne?
16. A bath is filled with 48 litres of hot water and 28 litres of cold water. How much water is in the bath?

C

Copy and complete.

1. 89 + 32 = ☐
2. 65 + 58 = ☐
3. 96 + 46 = ☐
4. 77 + ☐ = 161
5. 54 + ☐ = 130
6. 83 + ☐ = 162
7. 110 − 42 = ☐
8. 133 − 56 = ☐
9. 124 − 95 = ☐
10. 154 − ☐ = 86
11. 152 − ☐ = 68
12. 191 − ☐ = 92
13. A bottle of vinegar holds 150 ml. 68 ml is used. How much is left?
14. One parcel weighs 96 g. Another weighs 67 g more. What is the weight of the heavier parcel?
15. Sally's shadow is 117 cm long. Anne's shadow is 48 cm shorter. How long is Anne's shadow?
16. A candle is 125 mm tall. 39 mm is used. How much is left?

D1 HORIZONTAL AND VERTICAL LINES

I can recognise horizontal and vertical lines.

Examples

Horizontal lines —— top and bottom of the flag
Vertical lines —— sides of the flag
Diagonal lines —— the cross on the flag

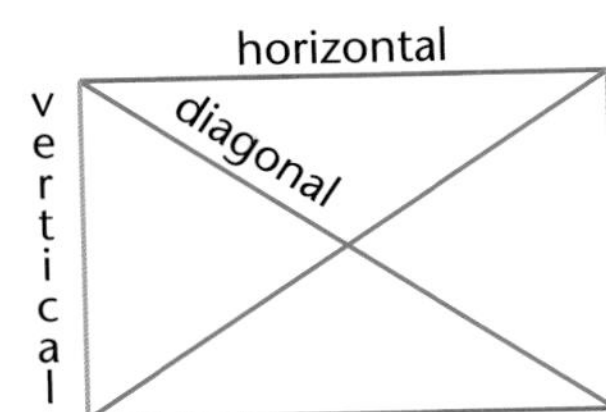

A

Use squared paper.
Copy each flag in a 6 × 4 grid. Use one colour pen to show all the horizontal lines.
Use a different colour pen for all the vertical lines.

1. 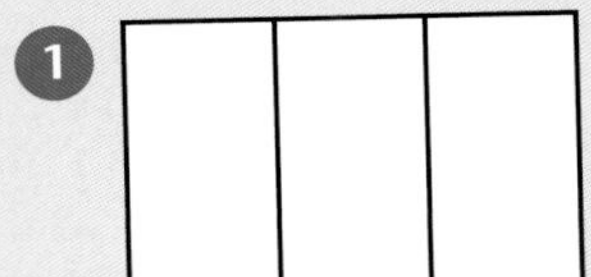
2. 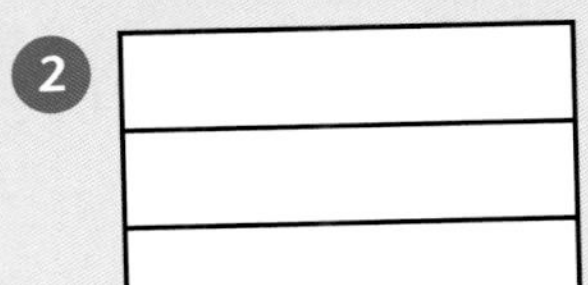
3. 
4. 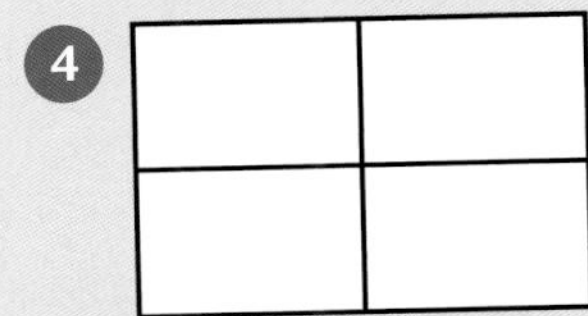

B

Use squared paper.
Copy each flag in a 6 × 4 grid. Use different colour pens to show:

a) all the horizontal lines
b) all the vertical lines
c) all the diagonal lines.

1. 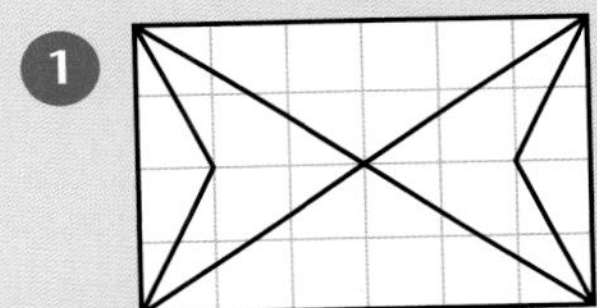
2. 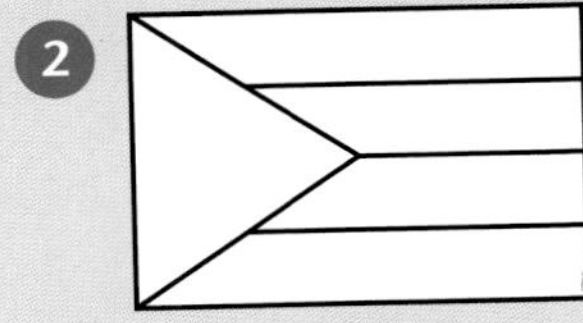
3. 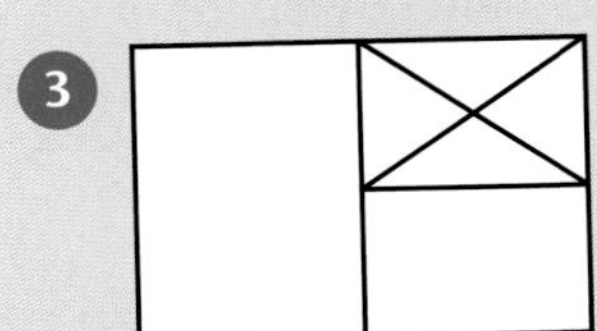
4. 

C

Copy each letter in a 4 × 4 grid.
Use a different colour for each of the following:

a) horizontal lines
b) vertical lines
c) diagonals of the 4 × 4 grid.
d) other lines.

1, 5. 

2, 6. 

3, 7. 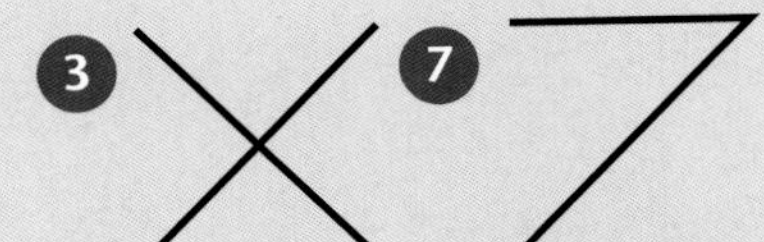

4, 8. 

9. Design each of the ten numerals in a 4 × 4 grid. Use the same colours to show the same types of lines.

I can give the position of a square on a labelled grid.

A

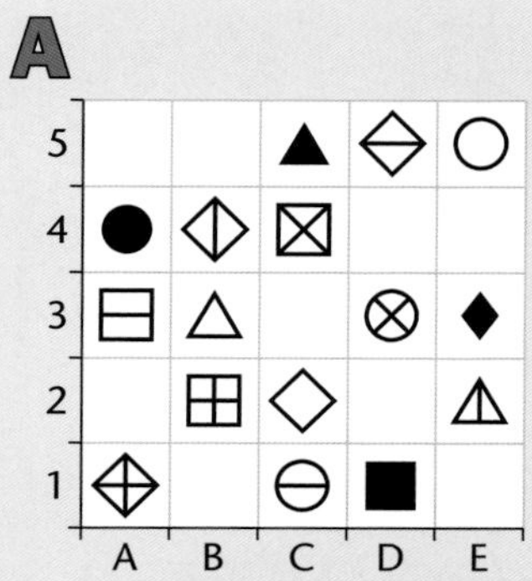

Give the position of each symbol.

4 ■

Draw the symbol found on each of these squares.

9 E2
10 C4
11 A3
12 D5
13 B3
14 C1
15 E3
16 A4

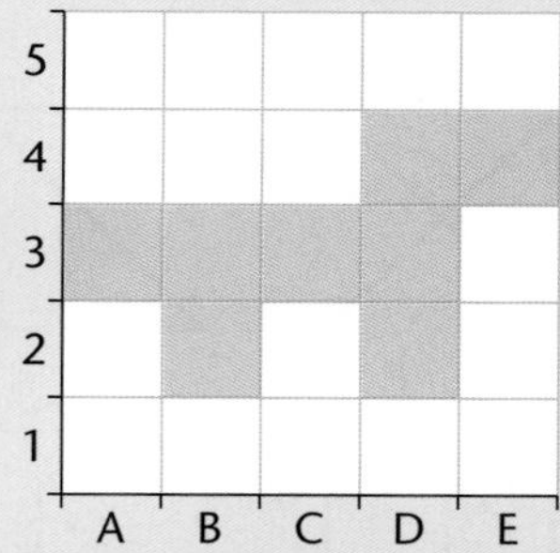

Look at the above grid picture. Give the position of:

17 the dog's back legs
18 the dog's head
19 the dog's tail
20 the dog's body.

B

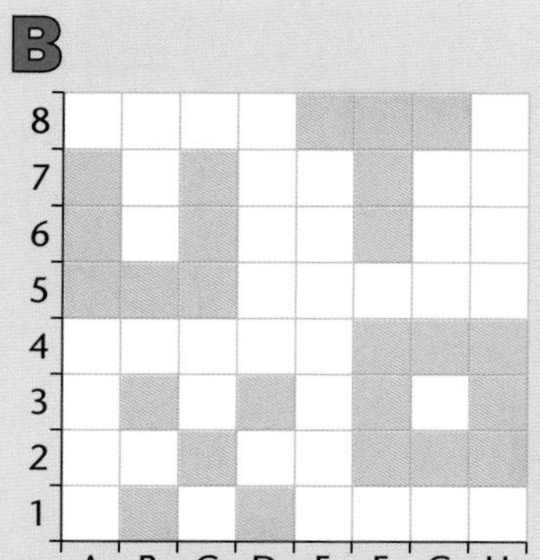

Give all the squares to describe the position of:

1 Letter U
2 Letter O
3 Letter T
4 Letter X.

Use an 8 × 8 grid like the one above. Shade in the following squares.

5 H2 H3 G3 F3
6 B4 B5 C4
7 C1 C2 D1 D2
8 C6 D6 E6 D7
9 G5 G6 G7 G8
10 For each of your shapes write down:
   a) the name of the shape
   b) whether the shape is symmetrical or not.
11 Design your initial letters in an 8 × 8 grid. Describe their position.

C

The position of a point on a grid is given by its co-ordinates. The across co-ordinate always comes first.

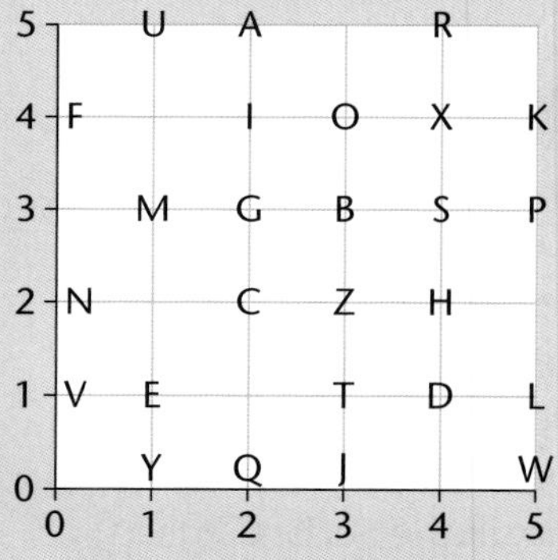

Examples
M is (1, 3) Q is (2, 0)
T is (3, 1) N is (0, 2)

Which letter is at point:

1 (0, 4)
2 (2, 3)
3 (1, 5)
4 (4, 2)
5 (1, 0)
6 (4, 4)
7 (3, 2)
8 (1, 3).

Give the position of:

9 B
10 N
11 R
12 Q
13 K
14 C
15 V
16 S.

17 Work out the author's childhood nickname.
(4, 2) (2, 5) (5, 1)
(0, 4) (5, 3) (2, 4)
(0, 2) (3, 1)

18 Write your name or nickname in co-ordinates.

D1 UNITS OF TIME

I can use the relationships between seconds, minutes, hours and days.

60 seconds = 1 minute
60 minutes = 1 hour
24 hours = 1 day

Example
How many minutes are left in the hour if the time is 3:25?
Answer *35 minutes* (60 − 25)

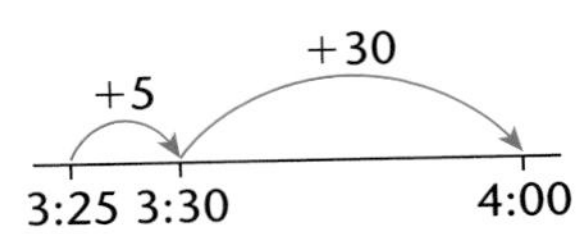

A

How many seconds make:

1. one minute
2. two minutes
3. one and a quarter minutes
4. three quarters of a minute?

How many minutes make:

5. one hour
6. one and one half hours
7. two and a quarter hours
8. five hours?

How many minutes are left in the hour if the time is:

9. half past the hour
10. quarter past the hour
11. 5 past the hour
12. quarter to the hour?

How many hours make:

13. one day
14. one and one half days
15. one quarter of a day
16. one third of a day?

B

How many minutes are:

1. 90 seconds
2. 600 seconds
3. 150 seconds
4. 240 seconds?

How many hours are:

5. 120 minutes
6. 75 minutes
7. 180 minutes
8. 300 minutes?

How many minutes are left in the hour if the time is:

9. 5:35
10. 10:10
11. 2:55
12. 9:20
13. 6:50
14. 3:05
15. 11:40
16. 7:25?

How many hours are left in the day if the time is:

17. 5:00 in the afternoon
18. 10:00 in the morning
19. 8:00 in the evening
20. 1:00 at night?
21. How many hours are there in November?

C

How many minutes are left in the hour if the time is:

1. 1:32
2. 4:07
3. 8:41
4. 2:19
5. 10:56
6. 5:23
7. 9:38
8. 3:04?

How many hours and minutes are left in the day if the time is:

9. 7:05 in the evening
10. 9:55 in the morning
11. 2:40 in the afternoon
12. 4:25 in the night?

Write as days.

13. 2 weeks
14. a 6 week holiday
15. 48 hours
16. 120 hours

Write as years.

17. 3 decades
18. half of one century
19. 60 months
20. 104 weeks
21. How many minutes are there in one day?

I can read the time to the nearest minute on an analogue clock and on a 12-hour digital clock.

Examples

Analogue clocks have faces.

Read the minutes as:
'past' before 30 minutes
'to' after 30 minutes.

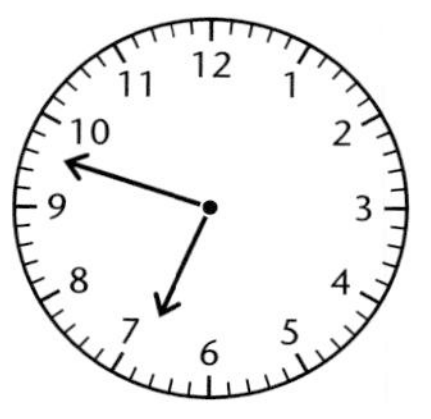

22 minutes past eight 12 minutes to seven

Digital clocks have figures only.
The minutes are always shown as minutes past the hour.

8:22 6:48

am means before 12 noon
pm means after 12 noon

morning 8:22 am

evening 6:48 pm

A

Write each time shown in words and figures.

1  3  5 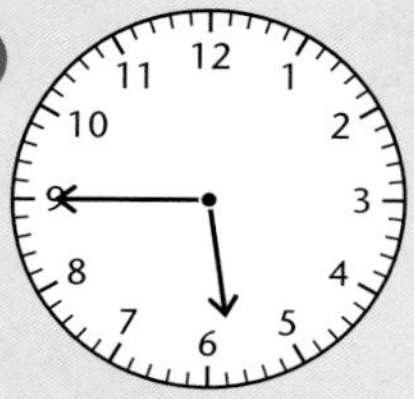 7  9

2  4  6  8  10

Write each time shown in words.

11 8:25
13 11:15
15 1:10
17 9:50
19 7:05

12 2:55
14 6:30
16 4:00
18 3:45
20 5:35

B

Write each time shown to the nearest minute:

a) in words

b) in figures using am or pm for all digital clocks.

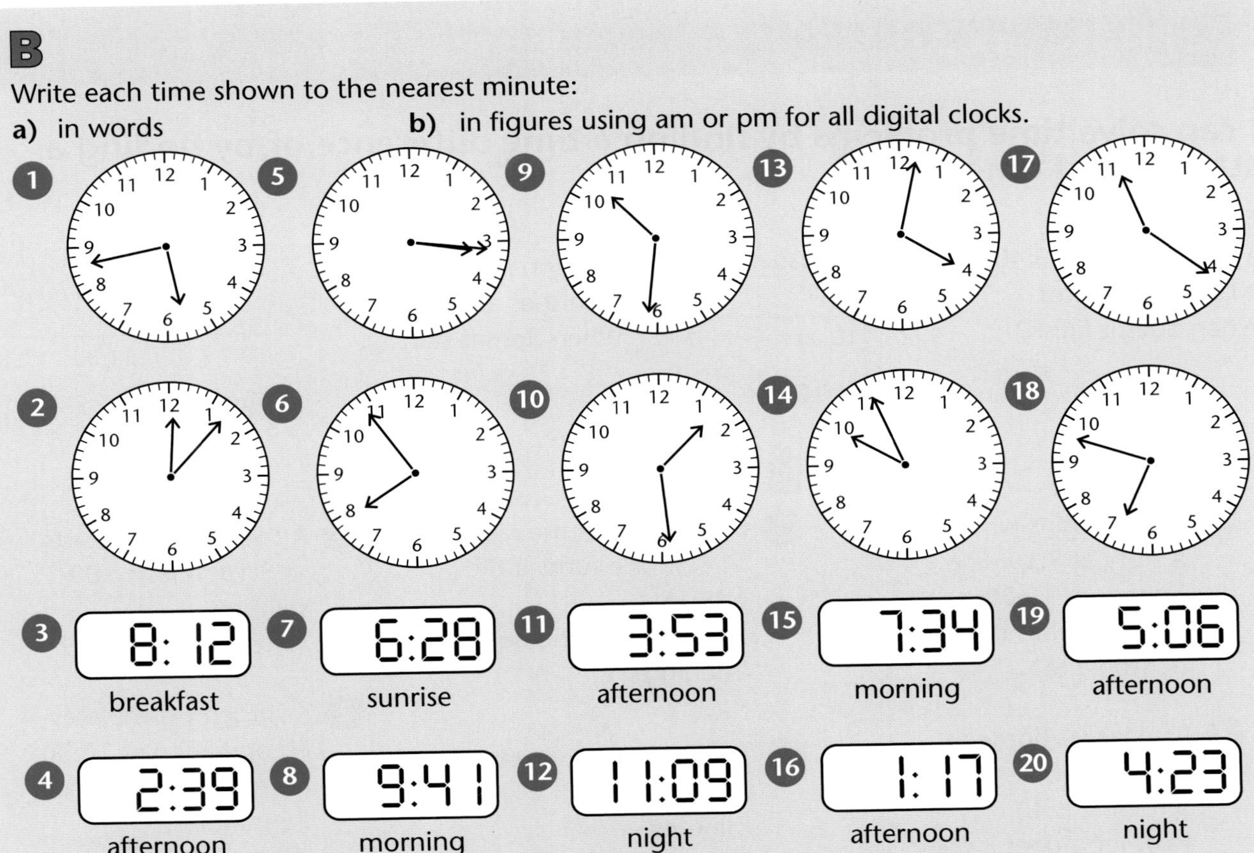

C

1 Copy and complete the table.

Time in words	12-hour clock	24-hour clock
half past eight	8:30 pm	20:30
		07:06
		11:47
		21:54
	4:25 am	
	3:43 pm	
	8:09 am	
		17:34
		13:11
		01:28
	4:32 pm	
	10:15 pm	
	9:56 am	

2 How many hours and minutes are there between each pair of times?

a) 8:30 am and 13:00

b) 2:30 am and 12:25

c) 22:15 and 2:05 am

d) 11:35 and 4:15 pm

e) 19:42 and 05:28

3 How many minutes make:

a) two thirds of an hour

b) seven tenths of an hour

c) three fifths of an hour

d) 3 hours

e) half a day?

4 Look at your table.
What would the 24-hour clock time be if the clocks were:

a) 16 minutes slow

b) 40 minutes fast?

D1 TIME PROBLEMS

I can solve time problems by finding a time difference or by finding a start or end time.

Examples

A lesson starts at 9:40.
It lasts 50 minutes.
When does it finish?

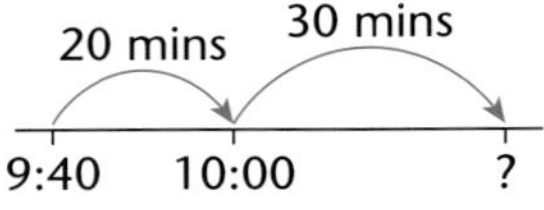

Answer 10:30

A lesson lasts 40 minutes.
If finishes at 11:15.
When does it start?

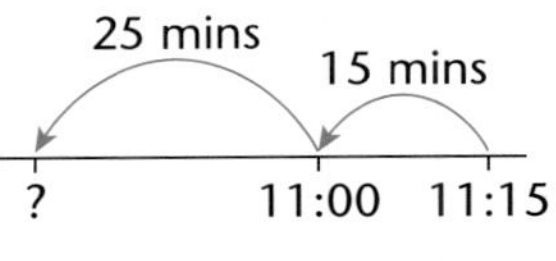

Answer 10:35

A

1. Lorna begins writing a story at 9:10. She finishes at 10:00. How long has it taken her to write?
2. Pete leaves home at 8:15. He arrives at school at 8:40. How long does it take him to get to school?
3. A cake is put into the oven at 2:50. It is taken out at 3:30. How long is it in the oven?
4. Playtime starts at 10:30. It finishes at 10:50. How long does it last?
5. Max is due at work at 8:45. He is held up by roadworks and is 40 minutes late. When does he arrive?

B

1. Baljit turns on the radio at 8:35. He turns it off at 9:15. How long has he been listening?
2. The Music lesson starts at 10:50. It lasts 45 minutes. When does it finish?
3. Football training finishes at 4:20. It has lasted for 50 minutes. When did it start?
4. Ruby puts on a CD at 1:10. It lasts 55 minutes. When will it finish?
5. Danni notices that the time is 8:20. She realises that she should have left for school half an hour ago. When should she have set off?
6. Robin starts doing his homework at 6:45. It takes him 40 minutes. When does he finish?

C

1. A cricket match starts at 3:10. It lasts 100 minutes. When does it finish?
2. A surgeon completes an operation at 11:30. He realises it has taken 75 minutes. When did the operation begin?
3. Gail arrives at the fete at 2:30. She leaves at 4:20. How long is she at the fete?
4. The class need to be at the castle by 10:30. The coach journey will take 80 minutes. What is the latest time they can leave school?
5. The car race starts at 12:20. It takes 95 minutes. When does it finish?
6. Lunchtime begins at 12:25. Anaf realises this is one and a half hours away. What is the time now?

I can find information in a timetable.

BBC1

2:15	Tennis
4:20	Doctor Who (Drama)
5:10	Newsround
5:20	Blue Peter
5:45	Local News
6:00	National News
6:25	Weather
6:30	Sports Quiz (Game Show)
6:55	Gardener's World
7:20	EastEnders (Soap)
7:50	Jane Eyre (Film)
9:30	Panorama

ITV1

2:30	Carry On Nurse (Film)
4:15	Heartbeat (Drama)
5:10	You've Been Framed
5:50	National News
6:28	Weather
6:30	Local News
6:50	Emmerdale (Soap)
7:15	Coronation Street (Soap)
7:45	Football
9:40	Millionaire (Game Show)
10:30	National News
11:00	The South Bank Show

A

Which programme starts at:

1. 6:25
2. 7:45
3. 2:15
4. 5:20
5. 9:30
6. 10:30
7. 5:45
8. 2:30?

How long is:

9. Blue Peter
10. Coronation Street
11. Sports Quiz
12. Gardener's World?

Which programme can you watch:

13. on BBC1 at 5:00
14. on ITV1 at 8:00
15. on BBC1 at 7:00
16. on ITV1 at 4:00?

B

Which programme *finishes* at:

1. 7:50
2. 6:28
3. 5:20
4. 4:15
5. 7:20
6. 4:20
7. 7:15
8. 5:45?

How long is:

9. Tennis
10. Millionaire
11. Doctor Who
12. Jane Eyre?

Which two programmes could you watch at:

13. 3:45
14. 6:15
15. 5:55
16. 4:35
17. 5:30
18. 7:10
19. 9:05
20. 6:40?

C

What is the total length of the following types of programmes?

1. Game Shows
2. Soaps
3. Dramas
4. Films
5. Local News
6. National News

Which programme would you be watching if you switched channels at the end of:

7. Doctor Who
8. Sports Quiz
9. Emmerdale
10. Carry On Nurse
11. You've Been Framed
12. Jane Eyre?

I know the multiplication facts for the 2, 3, 4, 5, 6 and 10 times-tables and can use them to solve problems.

A

Write the answer only.

1. 10×2
2. 3×4
3. 7×10
4. 6×3
5. 4×6
6. 2×5
7. 9×10
8. 5×3
9. 7×2
10. 3×5
11. 6×4
12. 9×6
13. 8×3
14. 0×2
15. 5×4
16. 10×5
17. 1×6
18. 6×10
19. 8×5
20. 9×2
21. 5×6
22. 4×3
23. 2×10
24. 9×4
25. $9 \div 3$
26. $25 \div 5$
27. $16 \div 2$
28. $40 \div 4$
29. $10 \div 10$
30. $42 \div 6$
31. $8 \div 2$
32. $32 \div 4$
33. $30 \div 5$
34. $21 \div 3$
35. $18 \div 6$
36. $100 \div 10$
37. $28 \div 4$
38. $10 \div 2$
39. $36 \div 6$
40. $20 \div 5$
41. $30 \div 10$
42. $27 \div 3$
43. $35 \div 5$
44. $80 \div 10$
45. $16 \div 4$
46. $12 \div 2$
47. $6 \div 3$
48. $48 \div 6$

B

Copy and complete.

1. $\square \times 4 = 24$
2. $\square \times 10 = 80$
3. $\square \times 2 = 18$
4. $\square \times 6 = 42$
5. $\square \times 5 = 25$
6. $\square \times 3 = 24$
7. $\square \div 2 = 10$
8. $\square \div 4 = 9$
9. $\square \div 5 = 7$
10. $\square \div 10 = 1$
11. $\square \div 3 = 6$
12. $\square \div 6 = 8$

Copy and complete the multiplication squares.

13.

×	2	3	4
10			
6			
4			

14.

×			
7			70
2	6		
9		54	

15.

×			
	12		15
			40
	20	30	

C

Copy and complete

1. $\square \times 10 = 500$
2. $\square \times 3 = 210$
3. $\square \times 5 = 400$
4. $\square \times 20 = 120$
5. $\square \times 60 = 540$
6. $\square \times 40 = 280$
7. $\square \div 3 = 90$
8. $\square \div 2 = 80$
9. $\square \div 10 = 100$
10. $\square \div 60 = 6$
11. $\square \div 40 = 8$
12. $\square \div 50 = 9$

Work out the brackets first. Write the answers only.

13. $(6 \times 2) + (3 \times 6)$
14. $(8 \times 10) + (9 \times 5)$
15. $(7 \times 6) + (4 \times 10)$
16. $(9 \times 3) + (8 \times 4)$
17. $(7 \times 4) + (3 \times 5)$
18. $(10 \times 10) + (6 \times 6)$
19. $(6 \times 4) - (9 \times 2)$
20. $(5 \times 6) - (8 \times 2)$
21. $(7 \times 5) - (8 \times 3)$
22. $(8 \times 6) - (7 \times 3)$
23. $(7 \times 10) - (6 \times 3)$
24. $(9 \times 6) - (9 \times 4)$

E1 WORD PROBLEMS

I can use my knowledge of multiplication facts to solve word problems.

A

1. Multiply 10 by 2.
2. Divide 40 by 5.
3. What is the product of 6 and 10?
4. Halve 18.
5. Find 4 lots of 5.
6. Share 100 between 10.
7. Double 6.
8. What number when multiplied by 5 gives an answer of 45?
9. How much is five 10ps?
10. There are seven pairs of socks and one sock left over. How many socks are there?
11. What number, when divided by 5, gives an answer of 7?
12. How many £10 notes make £70?
13. There are five pencils in each pack. How many pencils are there in 6 packs?

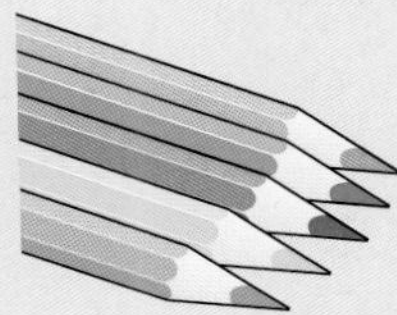

B

1. Divide 28 by 4.
2. Find 4 groups of 6.
3. What number, when multiplied by 6, gives an answer of 54?
4. How many straws are needed to make five squares?
5. What is the product of 7 and 3?
6. What number, when divided by 6, gives an answer of 7?
7. How many legs are needed for 9 chairs?
8. How many £3 tickets can I buy with a £20 note? How much change would I have?
9. There are 5 boxes of six eggs and four eggs left over. How many eggs are there?
10. I have 48 straws. How many hexagons can I make?
11. What number when divided by 3 gives an answer of 12?
12. How many teams of 4 can be made from 30 children?
13. Find the product of:
    a) 2, 3 and 4
    b) 3, 4 and 5

C

1. There are 7 players in each team. There are 8 teams. How many players are there?
2. Eight children can sit at one table. How many tables are needed for 48 children?
3. How many minutes are there in three hours?
4. Find one ninth of 36.
5. How many weeks is 42 days?
6. One drink costs 40p. How much do five drinks cost?
7. There are 9 apples in each bag. How many apples are there in eight bags?
8. How many 20ps make £1·20?
9. How many legs do eight octopuses have?
10. How many 30 cm lengths can be cut from 2 metres of string? How much string is left?
11. How much is nine 50ps?
12. Find the product of:
    a) 4, 5 and 6
    b) 5, 6 and 7

I can recognise multiples of 3 and find new facts from known facts.

A

1. Which of these numbers are multiples of 10?

   24 37 30 109 60 180 21

2. Explain how you know.
3. Make up a rule for recognising multiples of 10.
4. Which of these numbers are multiples of 5?

   90 235 56 140 502 83 65

5. Make up a rule for recognising multiples of 5.

Copy and complete.
Use the three given numbers only.

6. 8 × 3 = 24

   3 × 8 = □

   24 ÷ □ = □

   24 ÷ □ = □

7. 5 × 7 = 35

   □ × □ = □

   35 ÷ □ = □

   □ ÷ □ = □

B

A number is a multiple of 3 if the sum of its digits is divisible by 3.

Example 485
4 + 8 + 5 = 15 (divisible by 3)
485 is a multiple of 3.

1. Which of these numbers are multiples of 3.

   126 47 954 260 174 419 561

2. Use these digits

   2 4 5 7 6

   Make up as many two-digit and three-digit multiples of 3 as you can.

For each fact write four related × or ÷ facts.

3. 12 ÷ 6 = 2
4. 3 × 8 = 24
5. 36 ÷ 4 = 9
6. 7 × 5 = 35

Copy and complete.

7. 6 × □ = 54
8. 540 ÷ 6 = □
9. 540 ÷ □ = 60
10. 60 × □ = 540
11. 90 × 6 = □
12. 900 × 6 = □

C

A number is a multiple of 6 if it is a multiple of 3 and an even number.

Example 378
3 + 7 + 8 = 18 (divisible by 3)
378 is even.
378 is a multiple of 6.

1. Which of these numbers are multiples of:
   a) 3 **b)** 6?

   630 771 842 894 136 363 135

2. Use these digits

   1 3 4 7 8

   Make up as many three-digit and four-digit multiples of 6 as you can.

Write four related × or ÷ facts for each set of numbers.

3. 6, 8, 48
4. 72, 9, 8
5. 7, 63, 9
6. 60, 4, 15

Copy and complete.

7. □ × 7 = 560
8. □ × 70 = 5600
9. 5600 ÷ 7 = □
10. 5600 ÷ □ = 70

I can use my knowledge of multiples to solve problems.

Example

Chocko biscuits are sold in packs of 3.
Snacks biscuits are sold in packs of 5.
Naomi buys both types of biscuit.
She buys 39 biscuits altogether.
How many packs of each biscuit does she buy?

Write out multiples of 3 and of 5 to 39.
3 6 9 12 15 18 21 24 27 30 33 36 39
5 10 15 20 25 30 35
Taking one number from each list, look for pairs that add up to 39.

There are 2 possible solutions.
Naomi bought 30 Snacks biscuits in 6 packs and 3 Chocko biscuits in 3 packs. OR Naomi bought 15 Snacks biscuits in 3 packs and 24 Chocko biscuits in 8 packs.

A

1 Maurice has more than 20 books and less than 30 books. He can arrange his books in piles of 3 or in piles of 4. How many books does he have?

a) Write out the multiples of 3 to 30.
b) Write out the multiples of 4 to 30.
c) Which number appears in both lists?
d) Check that this answer makes sense. How many piles of 3 books would Maurice have? How many piles of 4 books?

B

1 Chloe has 29 books. Of course, unlike Maurice, she cannot arrange them exactly into piles of 3 or into piles of 4. She can, however, arrange them in piles of 3 *and* of 4. In fact, she has found two different ways of doing this.
Can you find both ways?

2 Chloe and Maurice's big brother, Simon, thinks he is clever.
He tells them:

I've got more books than either of you and I can arrange them exactly into piles of 2, or of 3 or of 5.

However, to Simon's surprise, Chloe and Maurice quickly work out how many books he has. Can you?

C

1 Tickets for a concert cost £7 for adults and £4 for children.
Mr. Green buys tickets for £54.
How many adult tickets and how many child tickets does he buy?
Can you find both possible solutions?

2 A shopkeeper has 100 eggs. The eggs can be put into boxes of 6 or 8. How can she put all the eggs into boxes so that there are no eggs left over?
Find all the possible solutions.

I can read and write fractions.

Example

3 equal parts

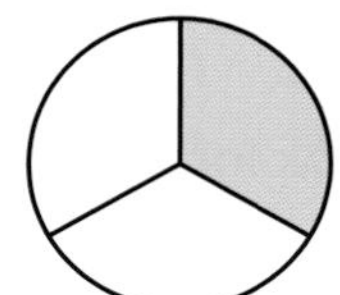

$\frac{1}{3}$ is shaded

$\frac{2}{3}$ unshaded

Here are some words that you may need.

$\frac{1}{2}$ half	$\frac{1}{5}$ fifth	$\frac{1}{9}$ ninth
$\frac{1}{3}$ third	$\frac{1}{6}$ sixth	$\frac{1}{10}$ tenth
$\frac{1}{4}$ quarter	$\frac{1}{8}$ eighth	$\frac{1}{12}$ twelfth

A

What fraction is shaded?
Write your answers:

a) in figures
b) in words.

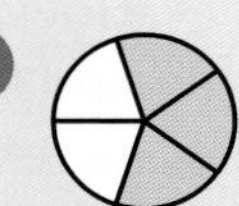

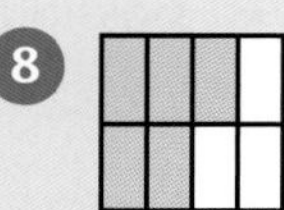

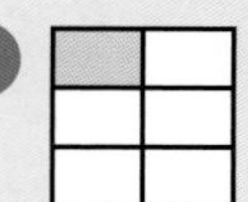

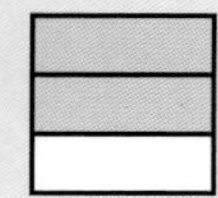

11 Draw a grid like this one.

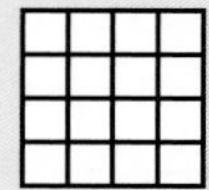

Colour $\frac{7}{16}$ red.

Colour $\frac{1}{4}$ yellow.

How many squares are left?

B

What fraction is shaded?
Write your answers:

a) in figures
b) in words.

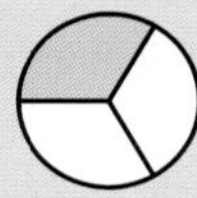

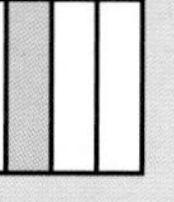

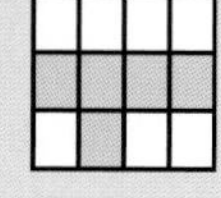

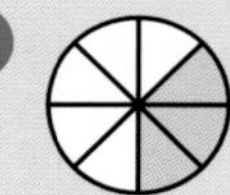

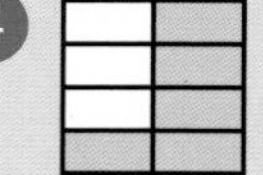

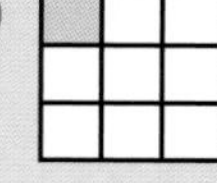

11 Draw a grid like this one.

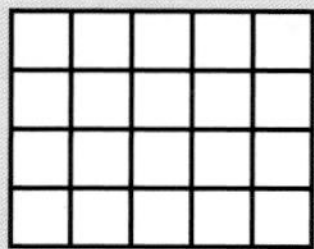

Colour $\frac{1}{2}$ red.

Colour $\frac{1}{4}$ yellow.

Colour $\frac{1}{10}$ blue.

How many squares are left?

C

Write in both figures and words what fraction is:

a) shaded
b) unshaded.

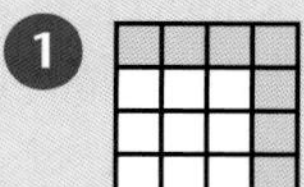

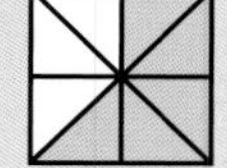

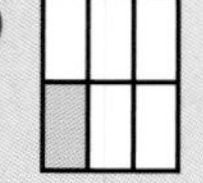

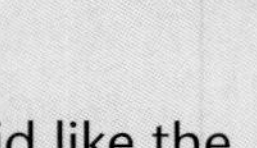

11 Draw a grid like the one shown.

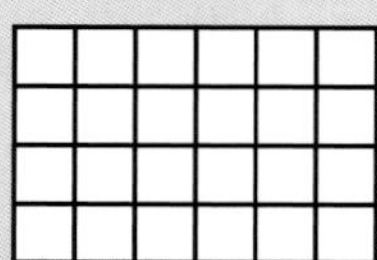

Colour $\frac{5}{12}$ red.

Colour $\frac{3}{8}$ yellow.

Colour $\frac{1}{6}$ blue.

What fraction of the grid is left?

E1 FRACTIONS OF AMOUNTS

I can find a fraction of an amount.

Examples

$\frac{1}{4}$ of 12 = 3

$\frac{1}{5}$ of 30 = 30 ÷ 5
= 6

$\frac{3}{10}$ of 40 = (40 ÷ 10) × 3
= 4 × 3
= 12

A

Use the diagram to help you find:

1. $\frac{1}{2}$ of 6
2. $\frac{1}{3}$ of 6
3. $\frac{1}{2}$ of 10
4. $\frac{1}{5}$ of 10
5. $\frac{1}{2}$ of 8
6. $\frac{1}{4}$ of 8
7. $\frac{1}{3}$ of 15
8. $\frac{1}{5}$ of 15
9. $\frac{1}{4}$ of 12
10. $\frac{1}{3}$ of 12
11. $\frac{1}{2}$ of 12
12. $\frac{1}{4}$ of 20
13. $\frac{1}{5}$ of 20
14. $\frac{1}{2}$ of 20
15. Draw a diagram to help you find:
    a) $\frac{1}{2}$ of 14
    b) $\frac{1}{7}$ of 14

B

Copy and complete.

1. $\frac{1}{5}$ of 35 = 35 ÷ 5
   = □
2. $\frac{1}{4}$ of 16 = □ ÷ 4
   = □
3. $\frac{1}{3}$ of 18 = 18 ÷ □
   = □
4. $\frac{1}{10}$ of 40 = □ ÷ 10
   = □
5. $\frac{1}{2}$ of 14 = □ ÷ □
   = □
6. $\frac{1}{6}$ of 30 = □ ÷ □
   = □

Work out

7. $\frac{1}{3}$ of 27
8. $\frac{1}{5}$ of 50
9. $\frac{1}{6}$ of 24
10. $\frac{1}{2}$ of 18
11. $\frac{1}{4}$ of 32
12. $\frac{1}{10}$ of 70
13. $\frac{1}{8}$ of 16
14. $\frac{1}{3}$ of 21
15. $\frac{1}{7}$ of 35
16. $\frac{1}{9}$ of 90

C

Copy and complete

1. $\frac{3}{10}$ of 60 = (60 ÷ 10) × 3
   = □ × 3
   = □
2. $\frac{2}{5}$ of 20 = (20 ÷ 5) × 2
   = □ × □
   = □
3. $\frac{3}{8}$ of 24 = (24 ÷ 8) × 3
   = □ × □
   = □
4. $\frac{2}{3}$ of 60 = (60 ÷ 3) × □
   = □ × 2
   = □

Work out

5. $\frac{3}{4}$ of £32
6. $\frac{7}{10}$ of 60p
7. $\frac{5}{6}$ of 4·8 cm
8. $\frac{3}{5}$ of 100 ml
9. $\frac{5}{8}$ of 40 kg
10. $\frac{9}{10}$ of £1
11. $\frac{2}{9}$ of 180 g
12. $\frac{4}{5}$ of 100 km
13. $\frac{3}{4}$ of 1 kg
14. $\frac{5}{7}$ of £2·80

I can find pairs of fractions that make one whole.

one	one	one
half	half	half
quarters	thirds	fifths
eighths	sixths	tenths

A

Use the fraction charts.
Copy and complete.

1. one = ☐ halves
2. one = ☐ thirds
3. one = ☐ tenths
4. one = ☐ quarters
5. one = ☐ sixths
6. one = ☐ fifths

Use the diagram to complete the pair of fractions that make one.

7.  $1 = \frac{\square}{5} + \frac{\square}{5}$
8.  $1 = \frac{\square}{8} + \frac{\square}{8}$
9.  $1 = \frac{\square}{\square} + \frac{\square}{\square}$
10. 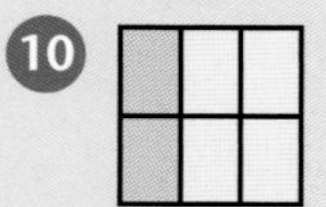 $1 = \frac{\square}{\square} + \frac{\square}{\square}$
11.  $1 = \frac{\square}{\square} + \frac{\square}{\square}$
12.  $1 = \frac{\square}{\square} + \frac{\square}{\square}$

B

Use the fraction charts.
Copy and complete.

1. $1 = \frac{1}{3} + \frac{\square}{3}$
2. $1 = \frac{7}{10} + \frac{\square}{10}$
3. $1 = \frac{6}{8} + \frac{\square}{8}$
4. $1 = \frac{1}{4} + \frac{\square}{4}$
5. $1 = \frac{3}{6} + \frac{\square}{6}$
6. $1 = \frac{2}{5} + \frac{\square}{5}$
7. $1 = \frac{7}{8} + \frac{\square}{8}$
8. $1 = \frac{4}{10} + \frac{\square}{10}$
9. Three eighths of the children on a bus are boys. What fraction are girls?
10. Nine tenths of the chocolates were eaten. What fraction was left?

C

Copy and complete.

1. $\frac{3}{4} + \frac{\square}{4} = 1\frac{1}{4}$
2. $\frac{4}{5} + \frac{3}{5} = 1\frac{\square}{5}$
3. $\frac{72}{100} + \frac{\square}{100} = 1\frac{22}{100}$
4. $\frac{\square}{7} + \frac{6}{7} = 1\frac{4}{7}$
5. $\frac{2}{3} + \frac{\square}{3} = 1\frac{1}{3}$
6. $\frac{7}{10} + \frac{\square}{10} = 1\frac{3}{10}$
7. $\frac{8}{9} + \frac{\square}{9} = 1\frac{7}{9}$
8. $\frac{64}{100} + \frac{\square}{100} = 1\frac{11}{100}$
9. $\frac{5}{8} + \frac{\square}{8} = 1\frac{4}{8}$
10. $\frac{\square}{12} + \frac{6}{12} = 1\frac{3}{12}$
11. One ninth of the people watching a film were men. Two ninths were women. What fraction were children?
12. Two tenths of the dogs in the park were corgis. One tenth were collies. What fraction were other breeds?

E1 EQUIVALENT FRACTIONS

I can recognise equivalent fractions.

Equivalent fractions are fractions that look different but are the same.

Examples

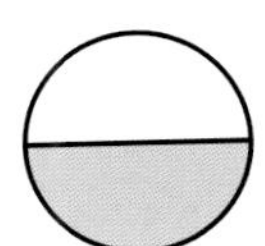 $\frac{1}{2} = \frac{2}{4}$ 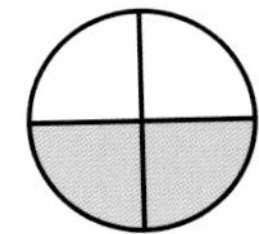

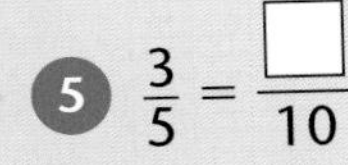 $\frac{2}{3} = \frac{4}{6}$ 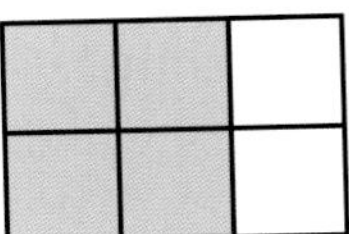

A

Use the fraction charts on page 42. Copy and complete.

1. $\frac{1}{2} = \frac{\square}{4}$
2. $\frac{1}{3} = \frac{\square}{6}$
3. $\frac{1}{2} = \frac{\square}{10}$
4. $\frac{1}{4} = \frac{\square}{8}$
5. $\frac{1}{2} = \frac{\square}{8}$
6. $\frac{1}{5} = \frac{\square}{10}$
7. $\frac{1}{2} = \frac{\square}{6}$
8. $\frac{2}{2} = \frac{\square}{10}$

Write the equivalent fractions shown in each pair of diagrams.

9. 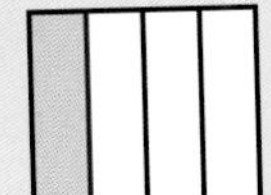 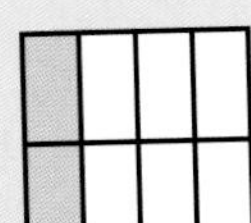
10. 
11. 
12.  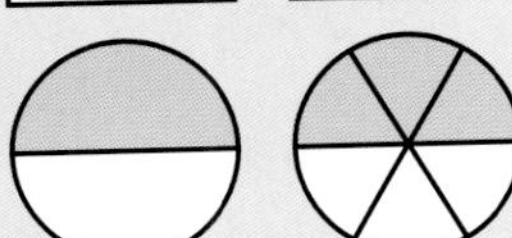
13. Draw a pair of diagrams to show $\frac{1}{2} = \frac{4}{8}$.

B

Use the fraction charts on page 42. Copy and complete.

1. $1 = \frac{\square}{5}$
2. $\frac{2}{4} = \frac{\square}{8}$
3. $\frac{4}{5} = \frac{\square}{10}$
4. $\frac{2}{3} = \frac{\square}{6}$
5. $\frac{3}{5} = \frac{\square}{10}$
6. $\frac{3}{4} = \frac{\square}{8}$
7. $\frac{3}{3} = \frac{\square}{6}$
8. $\frac{2}{5} = \frac{\square}{10}$

Write the equivalent fractions shown by each pair of diagrams.

9. 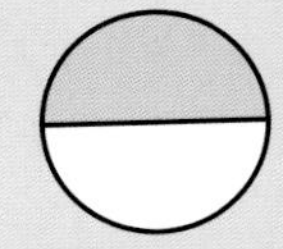 
10. 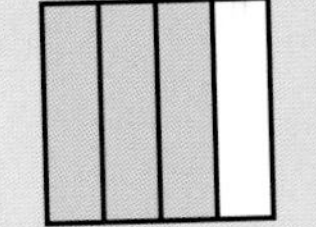 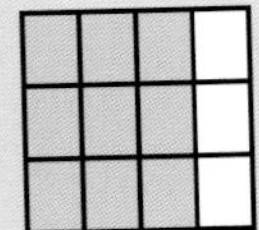
11. 
12.   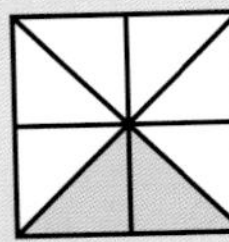
13. Draw a pair of diagrams to show $\frac{2}{3} = \frac{8}{12}$.

C

Draw 4 number lines of equal length showing $\frac{1}{2}$s, $\frac{1}{3}$s, $\frac{1}{6}$s and $\frac{1}{12}$s.
(Hint – make your number lines 6 cm or 12 cm long.)
Use your lines to complete these equivalent fractions.

1. $\frac{8}{12} = \frac{\square}{6}$
2. $\frac{1}{6} = \frac{\square}{12}$
3. $\frac{1}{2} = \frac{\square}{12}$
4. $\frac{10}{12} = \frac{\square}{6}$
5. $\frac{1}{3} = \frac{\square}{12}$
6. $\frac{3}{6} = \frac{\square}{12}$
7. $\frac{8}{12} = \frac{\square}{3}$
8. $\frac{4}{12} = \frac{\square}{6}$

Copy and complete by writing $>$, $<$ or $=$ in the box.

9. $\frac{1}{2} \square \frac{4}{10}$
10. $\frac{1}{3} \square \frac{4}{12}$
11. $\frac{1}{4} \square \frac{2}{8}$
12. $\frac{2}{5} \square \frac{5}{10}$
13. $\frac{1}{3} \square \frac{1}{6}$
14. $\frac{7}{10} \square \frac{70}{100}$
15. $\frac{3}{6} \square \frac{6}{12}$
16. $\frac{2}{3} \square \frac{4}{9}$
17. $\frac{1}{2} \square \frac{4}{8}$
18. $\frac{3}{4} \square \frac{8}{12}$
19. $\frac{1}{2} \square \frac{4}{6}$
20. $\frac{3}{5} \square \frac{14}{20}$
21. Draw a pair of diagrams to show $\frac{3}{4} = \frac{15}{20}$.

E1 DECIMAL FRACTIONS

I can write tenths and hundredths as fractions and as decimals.

Examples

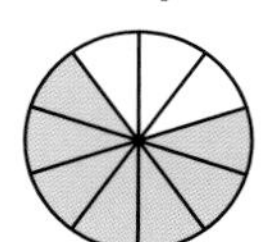

$\frac{7}{10} = 0{\cdot}7$

seven tenths

$\frac{3}{10} + \frac{4}{100} = 0{\cdot}34$

thirty-four hundredths

$£\frac{7}{10} = £0{\cdot}70 = 70p$

$£\frac{34}{100} = £0.34 = 34p$

A

Write the shaded part of each shape as:

a) a fraction

b) a decimal fraction.

1  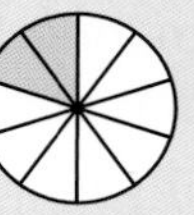 5  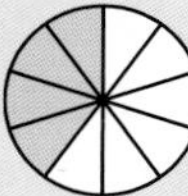

2 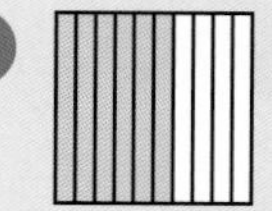 6 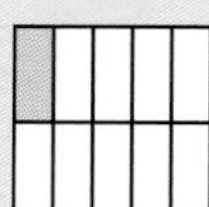

3  7 

4   8 

Copy and complete.

9. $£\frac{7}{10} = £\square = 70p$
10. $£\frac{3}{10} = £\square = \square p$
11. $£\frac{\square}{10} = £\square = 10p$
12. $£\frac{\square}{10} = £\square = 40p$
13. $£\frac{\square}{10} = £0{\cdot}90 = \square p$
14. $£\frac{\square}{10} = £0{\cdot}20 = \square p$

B

Write the shaded part of each shape as:

a) a fraction

b) a decimal fraction.

1 5 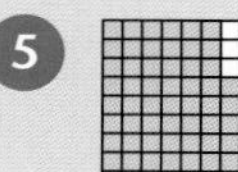

2 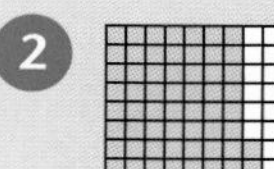 6 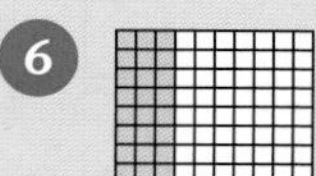

3 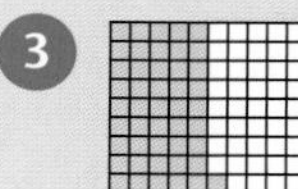 7 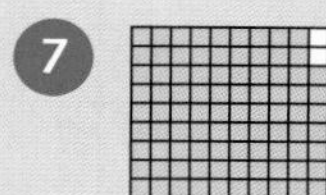

4 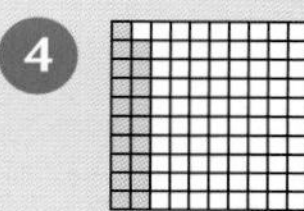 8 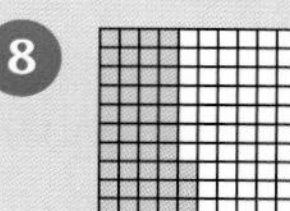

Copy and complete.

9. $\frac{3}{10} + \frac{2}{100} = \frac{\square}{100} = 0{\cdot}32$
10. $\frac{5}{10} + \frac{\square}{100} = \frac{58}{100} = 0{\cdot}58$
11. $\frac{2}{10} + \frac{7}{100} = \frac{\square}{100} = \square$
12. $\frac{\square}{10} + \frac{1}{100} = \frac{91}{100} = \square$
13. $\frac{\square}{10} + \frac{\square}{100} = \frac{\square}{100} = 0{\cdot}46$
14. $\frac{\square}{10} + \frac{\square}{100} = \frac{83}{100} = \square$

C

Write as fractions.

1. 0·67
2. 0·91
3. 0·2
4. 0·55
5. 0·03
6. 0·14
7. 0·3
8. 0·85
9. 0·47
10. 0·08
11. 0·99
12. 0·61

Write as decimals.

13. $\frac{36}{100}$
14. $\frac{9}{10}$
15. $\frac{19}{100}$
16. $\frac{81}{100}$
17. $\frac{45}{100}$
18. $\frac{5}{100}$
19. $\frac{72}{100}$
20. $\frac{29}{100}$
21. $\frac{8}{10}$
22. $\frac{18}{100}$
23. $\frac{4}{100}$
24. $\frac{65}{100}$

Write in order, smallest first.

25. $0{\cdot}01, \frac{1}{2}, 0{\cdot}1$
26. $0{\cdot}3, 0{\cdot}23, \frac{2}{3}$
27. $\frac{1}{5}, 0{\cdot}5, \frac{15}{100}$
28. $0{\cdot}4, \frac{1}{4}, \frac{14}{100}$

Give the answer as a decimal.

29. $\frac{1}{2} + 0{\cdot}1$
30. $0{\cdot}8 - \frac{7}{10}$
31. $\frac{4}{10} + 0{\cdot}35$
32. $0{\cdot}73 - \frac{2}{100}$

I can find pairs of numbers that sum to 100.

Example

26 + ☐ = 100

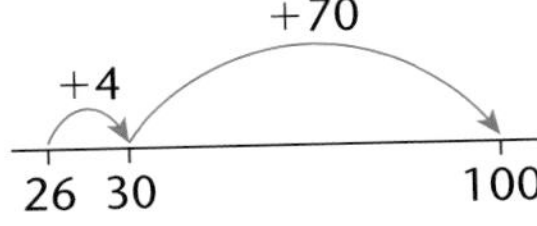

Answer = 74

A

Copy and complete.

1. 50 + ☐ = 100
2. 90 + ☐ = 100
3. 40 + ☐ = 100
4. 20 + ☐ = 100
5. 80 + ☐ = 100
6. 65 + ☐ = 100
7. 35 + ☐ = 100
8. 75 + ☐ = 100
9. 15 + ☐ = 100
10. 55 + ☐ = 100

B

Copy and complete.

1. 100 − 48 = ☐
2. 100 − 69 = ☐
3. 100 − 91 = ☐
4. 100 − 37 = ☐
5. 100 − 84 = ☐
6. 100 − ☐ = 16
7. 100 − ☐ = 72
8. 100 − ☐ = 45
9. 100 − ☐ = 28
10. 100 − ☐ = 53

C

Copy and complete.

1. ☐ + 760 = 1000
2. ☐ + 340 = 1000
3. ☐ + 230 = 1000
4. ☐ + 610 = 1000
5. ☐ + 480 = 1000
6. 970 + ☐ = 1000
7. 520 + ☐ = 1000
8. 190 + ☐ = 1000
9. 850 + ☐ = 1000
10. 360 + ☐ = 1000

I can find a difference by counting up.

Examples

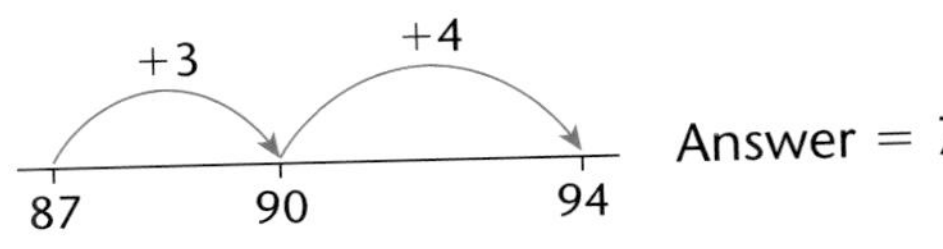

Answer = 7

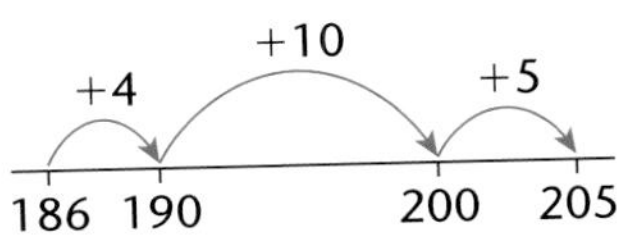

Answer = 19

A

Work out

1. 32 − 26
2. 51 − 47
3. 64 − 55
4. 85 − 78
5. 40 − 22
6. 50 − 27
7. 100 − 86
8. 200 − 192
9. 400 − 381
10. 103 − 90

B

Work out

1. 63 − 58
2. 300 − 188
3. 74 − 66
4. 5000 − 4992
5. 306 − 199
6. 705 − 495
7. 6000 − 5983
8. 2000 − 1942
9. 3002 − 2970
10. 107 − 88

C

Copy and complete.

1. 604 − ☐ = 186
2. 703 − ☐ = 274
3. 6000 − ☐ = 3875
4. 512 − ☐ = 197
5. 915 − ☐ = 498
6. 6018 − ☐ = 3993
7. 9012 − ☐ = 4998
8. 9000 − ☐ = 5693
9. 7000 − ☐ = 3876
10. 3008 − ☐ = 1985

I can use decimals when I work with money and measurements.

Decimals are a way of expressing fractions. The decimal point separates the whole number from the fractions.

Examples

$\frac{1}{10} = 0{\cdot}1$

$\frac{1}{100} = 0{\cdot}01$

$2\frac{3}{10} = 2{\cdot}3$

$1\frac{57}{100} = 1{\cdot}57$

Decimals are used to show amounts of money.

Examples

1p = £0·01	107p = £1·07
5p = £0·05	238p = £2·38
10p = £0·10	440p = £4·40
78p = £0·78	200p = £2·00

Decimals are also used to show metric measurements, including lengths.

Examples

10 cm = 0·1 m	1 cm = 0·01 m
62 cm = 0·62 m	31 cm = 0·31 m
318 cm = 3·18 m	160 cm = 1·6 m

The value of a digit depends upon its position in a number.

Examples

U	·	$\frac{1}{10}$	$\frac{1}{100}$	
£3	·	<u>8</u>	4	$£\frac{8}{10}$ = 80p
£2	·	5	<u>7</u>	$£\frac{7}{100}$ = 7p
1	·	<u>6</u>	5 m	$\frac{6}{10}$ m = 60 cm
0	·	3	<u>2</u> m	$\frac{2}{100}$ m = 2 cm

A

Copy and complete

1. 10p = $£\frac{1}{10}$ = £☐
2. 20p = £☐ = £0·20
3. ☐ = $£\frac{3}{10}$ = £0·30
4. 40p = $£\frac{4}{10}$ = £☐
5. 50p = £☐ = £0·50
6. ☐ = $£\frac{6}{10}$ = £0·60
7. 70p = £☐ = £☐
8. ☐ = £☐ = £0·80
9. ☐ = $£\frac{9}{10}$ = £☐
10. ☐ = £☐ = £1·00

Change these amounts to pounds and pence.

11. 230p
12. 591p
13. 104p
14. 25p
15. 659p
16. 42p
17. 817p
18. 403p

Change these measurements to metres.

19. 120 cm
20. 85 cm
21. 496 cm
22. 30 cm
23. 638 cm
24. 217 cm
25. 56 cm
26. 740 cm

Write the numbers shown by each of the arrows on the 0 to 1 number line as:

a) a fraction.

b) a decimal fraction.

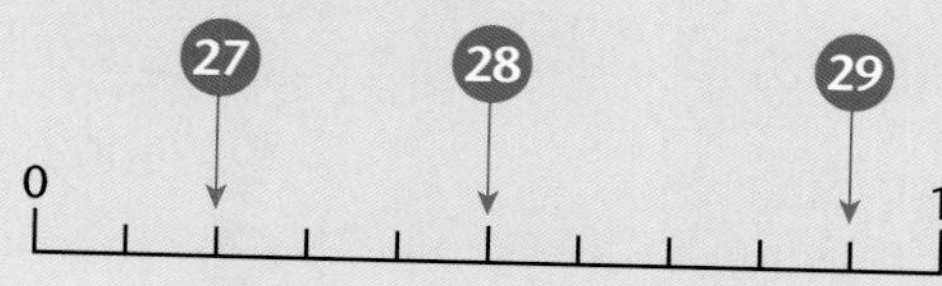

B

Write the measurements shown by the arrows in:

a) centimetres b) metres.

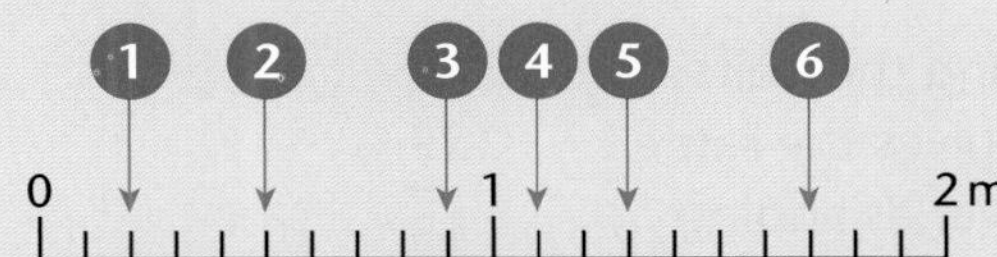

Give the value of the underlined figure in each of these numbers.

7. £6·80
8. £14·90
9. £0·72
10. £5·36
11. £18·20
12. £24·19
13. 3·1 m
14. 8·6 m
15. 20·3 m
16. 12·46 m
17. 0·52 m
18. 16·8 m

Give the next four terms in each of these sequences.

19. 0·1 m 0·2 m 0·3 m 0·4 m
20. 0·2 m 0·4 m 0·6 m 0·8 m
21. 0·5 m 1·0 m 1·5 m 2·0 m
22. £0·10 £0·30 £0·50 £0·70
23. £0·05 £0·10 £0·15 £0·20
24. £0·02 £0·04 £0·06 £0·08

Write the answers only.

25. 0·6 m + 0·1 m
26. 0·3 m + 0·2 m
27. 1·4 m + 0·4 m
28. 1·2 m + 0·5 m
29. 0·7 m − 0·3 m
30. 0·9 m − 0·6 m
31. 1·7 m − 0·5 m
32. 1·6 m − 0·4 m
33. £0·50 + £0·30
34. £0·40 + £0·20
35. £1·10 + £0·80
36. £1·30 + £0·40
37. £0·60 − £0·40
38. £0·70 − £0·20
39. £1·90 − £0·50
40. £1·80 − £0·60

C

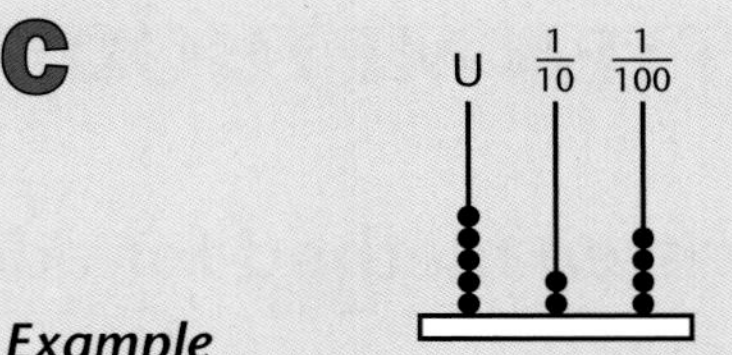

Example

5 units 2 tenths 4 hundredths

The number shown is 5·24.

Write the decimal fraction shown on each abacus.

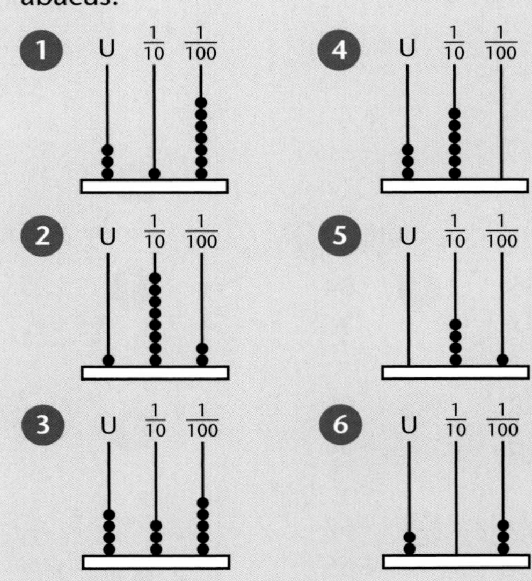

Give the value of the underlined figure in each of these numbers.

7. 0·9
8. 10·4
9. 24·7
10. 18·76
11. 13·91
12. 26·58
13. 2·96
14. 35·42
15. 41·78
16. 17·49
17. 7·34
18. 32·57
19. 16·23
20. 25·04
21. 5·13
22. 78·06
23. 100·83
24. 136·59

Write the answer only.

25. 1·5 + 0·4
26. 2·3 + 0·7
27. 1·3 − 0·3
28. 1·6 − 0·7
29. 3·8 + 0·5
30. 1·5 + 1·9
31. 2·4 − 0·6
32. 1·7 − 0·9
33. 0·2 + 0·8
34. 0·6 + 1·1
35. 1·8 − 1·4
36. 2·1 − 0·8
37. 1·8 + 1·6
38. 2·3 + 0·9
39. 3·2 − 0·8
40. 4·5 − 0·6

I can use a written method for addition calculations.

Examples

```
 384 = 300 +  80 +  4
+129 = 100 +  20 +  9
       400 + 100 + 13 = 513
```

```
 384
+129
 400
 100
  13
 513
```

Adding the units first gives the same answer as adding the hundreds first.

```
 384
+129
  13
 100
 400
 513
```

A

Copy and complete.

1. 65 + 27
2. 58 + 36
3. 92 + 25
4. 74 + 52
5. 66 + 48
6. 84 + 36
7. 95 + 58
8. 67 + 65
9. 76 + 47
10. 89 + 94
11. Heather has 68 story books and 93 non-fiction books. How many books does she have altogether?

B

Copy and complete.

1. 125 + 147
2. 342 + 138
3. 257 + 175
4. 439 + 154
5. 606 + 178
6. 342 + 194
7. 256 + 287
8. 438 + 273
9. 507 + 382
10. 215 + 579
11. A supermarket sells 182 bottles of white wine and 167 bottles of red wine. How many bottles of wine are sold altogether?
12. During the afternoon 145 people watch a film at a cinema. In the evening 238 people see the film. What is the total audience?

C

Set out as in the examples.

1. 573 + 248
2. 868 + 47
3. 749 + 355
4. 908 + 296
5. 795 + 438
6. 685 + 69
7. 807 + 673
8. 943 + 528
9. 876 + 95
10. 782 + 429
11. A school library has 686 non-fiction books and 578 story books. How many books are there in the library?
12. The Peters family went touring in their camper van. They travelled 386 miles in the first week and 278 miles in the second week. How far did they travel altogether?

I can subtract three-digit numbers using a written method.

Example

Estimate first

427 − 185 427 rounds to 400

185 rounds to 200

400 − 200 = 200

Answer is about 200

200 + 20 + 10 + 7 + 5

200 + 30 + 12

200 + 42

242

```
  427
 −185
    5 → 190
   10 → 200
  200 → 400
   27 → 427
  242
```

A

Copy and complete.

1. 47 − 24
2. 63 − 45
3. 92 − 56
4. 67 − 29
5. 51 − 25
6. 36 − 17
7. 61 − 34
8. 72 − 44
9. 85 − 38
10. 57 − 18
11. Lewis is 27. His grandfather is 83. What is the difference in their ages?

B

Copy and complete.

1. 263 − 191
2. 371 − 186
3. 542 − 267
4. 437 − 351
5. 755 − 242
6. 482 − 279
7. 796 − 445
8. 812 − 283
9. 345 − 262
10. 563 − 338
11. There are 182 children in a school. 95 are boys. How many girls are there?
12. A plane carries 317 passengers to New York and 243 passengers when it returns to London. How many fewer passengers are on the return journey?

C

Set out as in the example.

1. 1231 − 145
2. 1562 − 386
3. 1748 − 1263
4. 1483 − 1138
5. 1819 − 1679
6. 1443 − 929
7. 2476 − 1287
8. 3837 − 1552
9. 2352 − 2176
10. 3928 − 2463
11. In one week 724 people use a Leisure Centre. 569 are adults. How many are children?
12. A play is seen by 346 people on Friday and 470 people on Saturday. How many fewer people were in the audience on Friday?

A2 MULTIPLICATION FACTS

I know the multiplication facts for the 2, 3, 4, 5, 6 and 10 times-tables.

A

What is

1. 3×4
2. 5×3
3. 6×5
4. 4×10
5. 7×2
6. 8×6
7. 4×5
8. 9×3
9. 5×2
10. 7×4
11. 3×6
12. 6×10
13. $4 \div 2$
14. $15 \div 5$
15. $20 \div 4$
16. $90 \div 10$
17. $18 \div 3$
18. $24 \div 6$
19. $35 \div 5$
20. $80 \div 10$
21. $36 \div 4$
22. $12 \div 6$
23. $16 \div 2$
24. $12 \div 3$

B

Copy and complete.

1. $\square \times 5 = 25$
2. $\square \times 2 = 18$
3. $\square \times 4 = 8$
4. $\square \times 3 = 21$
5. $\square \times 6 = 36$
6. $\square \times 10 = 30$
7. $\square \div 3 = 8$
8. $\square \div 5 = 2$
9. $\square \div 4 = 6$
10. $\square \div 10 = 7$
11. $\square \div 6 = 9$
12. $\square \div 2 = 4$

Write the answer only

13. 4×40
14. 7×60
15. 9×50
16. 6×20
17. 3×30
18. 10×100
19. 80×4
20. 60×3
21. 80×2
22. 90×5
23. 80×10
24. 50×6
25. $100 \div 2$
26. $500 \div 5$
27. $200 \div 10$
28. $360 \div 4$
29. $120 \div 3$
30. $480 \div 6$
31. $500 \div 10$
32. $300 \div 5$
33. $280 \div 4$
34. $60 \div 2$
35. $240 \div 6$
36. $270 \div 3$

C

Copy and complete.

1. $\square \times 20 = 180$
2. $\square \times 40 = 240$
3. $\square \times 30 = 150$
4. $\square \times 6 = 540$
5. $\square \times 10 = 400$
6. $\square \times 5 = 350$
7. $\square \div 40 = 5$
8. $\square \div 20 = 8$
9. $\square \div 30 = 10$
10. $\square \div 5 = 30$
11. $\square \div 10 = 10$
12. $\square \div 6 = 50$

Write the answer only

13. 3×7
14. 10×7
15. 6×7
16. 7×7
17. 5×8
18. 9×8
19. 2×8
20. 6×8
21. 3×9
22. 7×9
23. 4×9
24. 8×9
25. $35 \div 7$
26. $56 \div 7$
27. $28 \div 7$
28. $63 \div 7$
29. $24 \div 8$
30. $56 \div 8$
31. $64 \div 8$
32. $32 \div 8$
33. $45 \div 9$
34. $90 \div 9$
35. $54 \div 9$
36. $81 \div 9$

I can multiply and divide numbers by 10 and 100.

Examples

37 × 10 = 370 37 × 100 = 3700 2420 ÷ 10 = 242 5100 ÷ 100 = 51

A Work out

1. 7 × 10
2. 62 × 10
3. 45 × 10
4. 820 ÷ 10
5. 490 ÷ 10
6. 1000 ÷ 10
7. 3 × 100
8. 7 × 100
9. 10 × 100
10. 500 ÷ 100
11. 400 ÷ 100
12. 1000 ÷ 100

B

Multiply by:

10		100	
1	29	5	28
2	572	6	65
3	400	7	100
4	138	8	79

Divide by

10		100	
9	900	13	2000
10	3580	14	1300
11	2400	15	500
12	7610	16	3800

C Copy and complete.

1. 147 × 100 = □
2. 8260 × 10 = □
3. 439 × □ = 43 900
4. 160 × □ = 1600
5. □ × 100 = 38 700
6. □ × 10 = 71 250
7. 94 600 ÷ 10 = □
8. 2000 ÷ 100 = □
9. 5200 ÷ □ = 52
10. 35 100 ÷ □ = 3510
11. □ ÷ 100 = 478
12. □ ÷ 10 = 690

I can multiply single-digit numbers by multiples of 10/100

A Work out

1. 20 × 3
2. 40 × 2
3. 50 × 4
4. 30 × 5
5. 40 × 3
6. 20 × 5
7. 50 × 2
8. 30 × 3
9. 40 × 4
10. 30 × 2
11. 50 × 5
12. 30 × 4

B Copy and complete.

1. 50 × 3 = □
2. 30 × 8 = □
3. 90 × □ = 360
4. 70 × □ = 350
5. □ × 30 = 90
6. □ × 20 = 100
7. 280 ÷ 7 = □
8. 210 ÷ 3 = □
9. 180 ÷ □ = 20
10. 400 ÷ □ = 80
11. □ ÷ 4 = 60
12. □ ÷ 6 = 50

C Copy and complete.

1. 800 × 4 = □
2. 500 × 9 = □
3. 700 × □ = 4200
4. 200 × □ = 1600
5. □ × 6 = 5400
6. □ × 7 = 2100
7. 4800 ÷ 8 = □
8. 3600 ÷ 9 = □
9. 2400 ÷ □ = 800
10. 6300 ÷ □ = 900
11. □ ÷ 8 = 700
12. □ ÷ 6 = 600

I can multiply two-digit numbers by one-digit numbers.

Example

27 × 6

Approximate first
27 rounds to 30
30 × 6 = 180
27 × 6 is less than 180

×	6
20	120
7	42
	162

	20 + 7
×	6
20	120
7	42
	162

```
   20 + 7
 ×      6
   ------
      120    20 × 6
       42     7 × 6
   ------
      162
```

A

Work out

1. 14 × 2
2. 15 × 3
3. 17 × 5
4. 13 × 4
5. 29 × 2
6. 33 × 5
7. 36 × 3
8. 25 × 4

9. There are 23 crayons in one packet. How many crayons are there in three packets?
10. Each tile is 18 cm long. How long is a row of 5 tiles?
11. One bar of chocolate costs 29p. How much will four bars cost?
12. What is double 34p?

B

Work out

1. 24 × 2
2. 26 × 5
3. 13 × 6
4. 21 × 7
5. 28 × 4
6. 47 × 3
7. 35 × 7
8. 68 × 5
9. 23 × 8
10. 32 × 9
11. 43 × 7
12. 33 × 8
13. 67 × 4
14. 45 × 9
15. 27 × 7
16. 36 × 6
17. Cartons of milk come in packets of 24. How many cartons are there in six packets?
18. One lolly costs 55p. How much will nine lollies cost?
19. One spider has eight legs. How may legs do 48 spiders have altogether?

C

Work out

1. 127 × 4
2. 129 × 5
3. 214 × 7
4. 153 × 8
5. 224 × 6
6. 164 × 9
7. 138 × 7
8. 257 × 8
9. 162 × 6
10. 325 × 9
11. 248 × 6
12. 167 × 9
13. 288 × 5
14. 469 × 8
15. 196 × 7
16. 285 × 9
17. Wendy buys a printer for £149. Her new computer costs three times as much. How much does she spend altogether?
18. A production of *Oliver* plays to full houses of 458 for all of its seven performances. How many people see the show altogether?
19. One can weighs 245 g. What is the weight of eight cans?
20. One glass holds 175 ml. How much drink is needed to fill six glasses?

I can divide a two-digit number by a one-digit number.

Example

$86 \div 5$

Estimate

$5 \times 10 = 50$

$5 \times 20 = 100$

$50 < 86 < 100$

$10 < 86 \div 5 < 20$

$$86 \div 5 = (50 \div 5) + (36 \div 5)$$
$$= 10 + 7\text{R}1$$
$$= 17\text{R}1$$

$$\begin{array}{rrl} & 86 & \\ - & 50 & (5 \times 10) \\ \hline & 36 & \\ - & 35 & (5 \times 7) \\ \hline & 1 & \end{array}$$

Answer 17R1

$186 \div 5$

$$\begin{array}{rrl} & 186 & \\ - & 150 & (5 \times 30) \\ \hline & 36 & \\ - & 35 & (5 \times 7) \\ \hline & 1 & \end{array}$$

Answer 37R1

A

Work out

1. $26 \div 2$
2. $36 \div 3$
3. $64 \div 4$
4. $75 \div 5$
5. $56 \div 4$
6. $65 \div 5$
7. $34 \div 2$
8. $48 \div 3$
9. $90 \div 5$
10. $76 \div 4$
11. $45 \div 3$
12. $38 \div 2$
13. $52 \div 4$
14. $57 \div 3$
15. $85 \div 5$
16. $72 \div 4$
17. Divide 27 by 2.
18. Share 49 by 3.
19. How many 4s are there in 67?
20. What is 83 divided by 5?

B

Work out

1. $36 \div 2$
2. $95 \div 5$
3. $96 \div 6$
4. $98 \div 7$
5. $69 \div 3$
6. $96 \div 8$
7. $136 \div 4$
8. $126 \div 9$
9. $120 \div 5$
10. $108 \div 6$
11. $102 \div 3$
12. $136 \div 8$
13. $112 \div 4$
14. $153 \div 9$
15. $145 \div 5$
16. $154 \div 7$
17. The bill for a meal is £102. It is shared between six friends. How much do they each pay?

18. Cakes are sold in packets of 8. How many packets are made up from 168 cakes?

C

Work out

1. $114 \div 6$
2. $147 \div 7$
3. $176 \div 8$
4. $162 \div 9$
5. $126 \div 6$
6. $105 \div 7$
7. $149 \div 8$
8. $225 \div 9$
9. $162 \div 6$
10. $161 \div 7$
11. $232 \div 8$
12. $198 \div 9$
13. $144 \div 6$
14. $217 \div 7$
15. $191 \div 8$
16. $306 \div 9$
17. A packet of sweets weighs 224 g. Each sweet weighs 8 g. How many sweets are there in the packet?
18. Nine oil drums contain 315 litres. How much oil is there in each drum?
19. One seventh of the 308 children in a school come by bus. How many children come to school in other ways?

A2 NUMBER PUZZLES

I can use my knowledge of calculations to solve problems and puzzles.

Examples

Find 2 consecutive numbers with a product of 20. Answer = 4, 5

Find 3 consecutive numbers with a total of 18. Answer = 5, 6, 7

Find 2 consecutive numbers which add up to:

1. 23
2. 17
3. 39
4. 51.

Find a pair of numbers with:

5. a sum of 14 and a difference of 6
6. a sum of 20 and a difference of 8
7. a sum of 30 and a difference of 4
8. a sum of 100 and a difference of 2.

Find a pair of numbers with:

9. a sum of 5 and a product of 6
10. a sum of 9 and a product of 14
11. a sum of 9 and a product of 20
12. a sum of 12 and a product of 20.
13. Find different ways to complete this calculation.

   1☐ + 1☐ = 2☐

B

Find 3 consecutive numbers with a total of:

1. 12
2. 27
3. 39
4. 90.
5. Ramiz says
   The sum of three consecutive numbers is always a multiple of 3.
   Is he correct? Investigate by finding all the numbers to 50 which are the total of 3 consecutive numbers.

Find 2 consecutive numbers with a product of:

6. 12
7. 90
8. 42
9. 72.

Find the number.

10. It is below 50. It is a multiple of 4. The sum of its digits is 5.
11. It is a 2-digit number. It is a multiple of 7. The product of its digits is 9.
12. Find different ways to complete this calculation.

    6☐ + 7☐ = 14☐

C

1. Lucie says
   The total of 4 consecutive numbers is always a multiple of 4.
   Is she correct? Find three examples to match or disprove Lucie's statement.

You may use a calculator. Find 2 consecutive numbers with a product of:

2. 132
3. 210
4. 306
5. 156
6. 380
7. 240
8. 506
9. 420
10. 600
11. 702
12. 930
13. 812.

You may use a calculator. Find 3 consecutive numbers with a total of:

14. 15
15. 27
16. 45
17. 60
18. 99
19. 333
20. 126
21. 303
22. 261
23. 111
24. 450
25. 237.
26. Find all the possible solutions.

    1☐☐ − 1☐☐ = 9☐

B2 MULTIPLICATION FACTS

I know the multiplication and division facts for the 2, 3, 4, 5, 6, and 10 times-tables and can use them to solve problems.

A

Write the answer only.

1. 4×5
2. 8×3
3. 5×2
4. 2×6
5. 9×4
6. 3×10
7. 7×2
8. 9×5
9. 6×10
10. 8×6
11. 1×3
12. 5×4
13. 10×10
14. 4×2
15. 7×4
16. 3×5
17. 6×3
18. 9×6
19. 0×4
20. 7×5
21. 8×2
22. 3×6
23. 4×10
24. 5×3
25. $16 \div 4$
26. $18 \div 2$
27. $30 \div 6$
28. $21 \div 3$
29. $80 \div 10$
30. $15 \div 5$
31. $54 \div 6$
32. $2 \div 2$
33. $70 \div 10$
34. $24 \div 4$
35. $40 \div 5$
36. $30 \div 3$
37. $50 \div 10$
38. $24 \div 6$
39. $27 \div 3$
40. $12 \div 4$
41. $25 \div 5$
42. $12 \div 2$
43. $100 \div 10$
44. $30 \div 5$
45. $32 \div 4$
46. $12 \div 3$
47. $6 \div 2$
48. $36 \div 6$

B

Copy and complete.

1. $\square \times 5 = 35$
2. $\square \times 2 = 12$
3. $\square \times 4 = 32$
4. $\square \times 3 = 27$
5. $\square \times 10 = 20$
6. $\square \times 6 = 42$
7. $\square \div 2 = 8$
8. $\square \div 3 = 6$
9. $\square \div 5 = 9$
10. $\square \div 6 = 6$
11. $\square \div 10 = 5$
12. $\square \div 4 = 7$
13. $7 \times \square = 21$
14. $9 \times \square = 45$
15. $8 \times \square = 16$
16. $6 \times \square = 24$
17. $9 \times \square = 90$
18. $6 \times \square = 36$
19. $28 \div \square = 7$
20. $18 \div \square = 6$
21. $30 \div \square = 6$
22. $18 \div \square = 9$
23. $70 \div \square = 7$
24. $48 \div \square = 8$

C

Copy and complete.

1. $\square \times 30 = 240$
2. $\square \times 60 = 540$
3. $\square \times 20 = 140$
4. $\square \times 4 = 360$
5. $\square \times 5 = 400$
6. $\square \times 10 = 1000$
7. $\square \div 20 = 9$
8. $\square \div 50 = 6$
9. $\square \div 40 = 5$
10. $\square \div 10 = 30$
11. $\square \div 3 = 70$
12. $\square \div 6 = 80$
13. How many seconds are there in 4 minutes?
14. How much is nine 50ps?
15. One cup of coffee costs 90p. How much do 3 cups cost?
16. Carly takes 40 ml of medicine each day. How much does she take in one week?
17. There are 160 chairs arranged in rows of 20. How many chairs are in each row?

B2 WORD PROBLEMS

I can use my knowledge of multiplication facts to solve word problems.

A

1. Multiply 8 by 2.
2. Share 21 by 3.
3. Find 5 lots of 4.
4. Divide 45 by 5.
5. How many is 4 times 10?
6. Halve 12.
7. What is 4 times as big as 3?
8. How many 4s make 36?
9. Find 7 groups of 5.
10. What is 80 shared by 10?
11. Double 9.
12. What is 18 divided by 3?
13. What is the product of 7 and 4?
14. How many 5ps make 40p?
15. How much is three 10ps?
16. How many horseshoes are needed for 6 horses?

B

1. How many faces are there on six dice?
2. A netball team has seven players. How many teams can be made from 28 children?
3. How many packs of 8 can be made from 24 sausages?
4. There are 9 sweets in each packet. How many are there in 7 packets?
5. There are 52 cards in a pack. Four players are each dealt 8 cards. How many cards are left in the pack?

6. How many hexagons can be made with 48 straws?
7. How many days are there in 6 weeks?
8. One sweet costs 9p. How much do 4 sweets cost?
9. Six children can sit at one table. How many tables are needed for 30 children?
10. What is one eighth of 40?

C

1. Each class has 30 children. How many children are there in 8 classes?
2. How many hours is 420 minutes?
3. One loaf has 20 slices. How many loaves are needed for 120 slices.
4. There are 80 tea bags in each box. How many are there in 9 boxes?
5. Each necklace needs 40 beads. How many necklaces can be made from 200 beads?
6. One egg weighs 70 g. What is the weight of 6 eggs?
7. One water bottle holds 500 ml. How much water is needed to fill eight bottles?
8. Each day Petra earns £90. How much does she earn in six days?
9. How many 80p cakes can be bought for £5?
10. One lap of a running track is 400 metres. How far is 7 laps?

I know the 8 times-table.

A

Double and double again to multiply by 4.

1. 6
2. 3
3. 10
4. 1
5. 5
6. 8
7. 2
8. 7
9. 4
10. 9

Double, double and double again to multiply by 8.

11. 4
12. 1
13. 8
14. 5
15. 2
16. 10
17. 7
18. 3
19. 9
20. 6

21. Copy and complete by doubling.

TIMES TABLES		
TWOS	FOURS	EIGHTS
2		
4		
6		
8		
10		
12		
14		
16		
18		
20		

B

Write the answers only.

1. 3×8
2. 10×8
3. 6×8
4. 0×8
5. 9×8
6. 4×8
7. 7×8
8. 1×8
9. 8×8
10. 5×8
11. $80 \div 8$
12. $24 \div 8$
13. $72 \div 8$
14. $48 \div 8$
15. $8 \div 8$
16. $64 \div 8$
17. $32 \div 8$
18. $56 \div 8$
19. $40 \div 8$
20. $16 \div 8$

Copy and complete.

21. $\square \times 8 = 40$
22. $\square \times 8 = 24$
23. $\square \times 8 = 48$
24. $\square \times 8 = 16$
25. $\square \times 8 = 72$
26. $\square \times 8 = 56$
27. $\square \times 8 = 32$
28. $\square \times 8 = 64$
29. $\square \div 8 = 3$
30. $\square \div 8 = 7$
31. $\square \div 8 = 1$
32. $\square \div 8 = 4$
33. $\square \div 8 = 8$
34. $\square \div 8 = 6$
35. $\square \div 8 = 5$
36. $\square \div 8 = 9$

C

Write the answers only.

1. 40×8
2. 20×8
3. 70×8
4. 50×8
5. 80×8
6. 60×8
7. 30×8
8. 90×8
9. $320 \div 8$
10. $160 \div 8$
11. $480 \div 8$
12. $240 \div 8$
13. $640 \div 8$
14. $560 \div 8$
15. $720 \div 8$
16. $400 \div 8$

Work out by multiplying by 8 and doubling.

17. 2×16
18. 5×16
19. 7×16
20. 3×16
21. 9×16
22. 6×16
23. 8×16
24. 4×16
25. 20×16
26. 30×16

27. A lorry travels the same route eight times every day. The route is 29 miles long. How far does the lorry travel in one day?
28. There are 36 chocolates in one box. How many chocolates are there in eight boxes?

I can double and halve two-digit numbers.

Examples

Double 17	Double 68	Half of 18	Half of 76		Half of 76
10 + 7	60 + 8	10 + 8	70 + 6		60 + 16
↓ ↓ ×2	↓ ↓ ×2	↓ ↓ ÷2	↓ ↓ ÷2	or	↓ ↓ ÷2
20 + 14 = 34	120 + 16 = 136	5 + 4 = 9	35 + 3 = 38		30 + 8 = 38

A

Double each number.

1. 2
2. 3
3. 8
4. 5
5. 7
6. 9
7. 4
8. 6
9. 40
10. 60
11. 90
12. 10
13. 80
14. 30
15. 70
16. 50
17. 15
18. 17
19. 12
20. 18
21. 13
22. 16
23. 14
24. 19

Copy and complete.

25. 16 ÷ 2 = (10 + 6) ÷ 2 = □
26. 12 ÷ 2 = (10 + 2) ÷ 2 = □
27. 18 ÷ 2 = (10 + 8) ÷ 2 = □
28. 14 ÷ 2 = (10 + 4) ÷ 2 = □

Halve each number.

29. 60
30. 100
31. 80
32. 40
33. 30
34. 70
35. 50
36. 90

B

Work out

1. 23 × 2
2. 31 × 2
3. 22 × 2
4. 35 × 2
5. 44 × 2
6. 29 × 2
7. 25 × 2
8. 38 × 2
9. 27 × 2
10. 45 × 2
11. 36 × 2
12. 49 × 2
13. 24 × 2
14. 37 × 2
15. 28 × 2
16. 46 × 2
17. 22 ÷ 2
18. 46 ÷ 2
19. 84 ÷ 2
20. 68 ÷ 2
21. 42 ÷ 2
22. 26 ÷ 2
23. 64 ÷ 2
24. 88 ÷ 2
25. 34 ÷ 2
26. 58 ÷ 2
27. 72 ÷ 2
28. 36 ÷ 2
29. 94 ÷ 2
30. 52 ÷ 2
31. 76 ÷ 2
32. 96 ÷ 2

Work out by partitioning.

33. 64 × 2
34. 56 × 2
35. 78 × 2
36. 93 × 2
37. 67 × 2
38. 59 × 2
39. 162 ÷ 2
40. 134 ÷ 2
41. 158 ÷ 2
42. 178 ÷ 2
43. 116 ÷ 2
44. 174 ÷ 2

C

Copy and complete

1. □ × 2 = 62
2. □ × 2 = 76
3. □ × 2 = 136
4. □ × 2 = 184
5. □ × 2 = 1520
6. □ × 2 = 1380
7. □ × 2 = 7800
8. □ × 2 = 1160
9. □ ÷ 2 = 92
10. □ ÷ 2 = 76
11. □ ÷ 2 = 59
12. □ ÷ 2 = 54
13. □ ÷ 2 = 770
14. □ ÷ 2 = 980
15. □ ÷ 2 = 7300
16. □ ÷ 2 = 8600

Double by partitioning.

17. 143
18. 156
19. 167
20. 174
21. 138
22. 179
23. 185
24. 197

Halve by partitioning.

25. 244
26. 338
27. 256
28. 354
29. 392
30. 296
31. 318
32. 376

I can describe the properties of 2-D shapes and recognise symmetrical polygons.

3 SIDES	4 SIDES	4+ SIDES	CONVEX POLYGON	CONCAVE POLYGON
triangle	quadrilateral	5 pentagon	all angles $< 180^\circ$	1 angle $> 180^\circ$
equilateral triangle	square	6 hexagon		
isosceles triangle	rectangle	7 heptagon		
right-angled triangle		8 octagon	regular hexagon	irregular pentagon

A

1 Write the name of each shape. (e.g. square, regular pentagon, etc.)

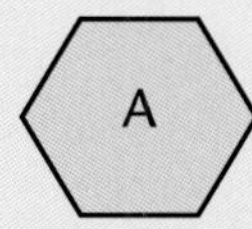

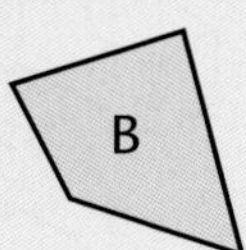

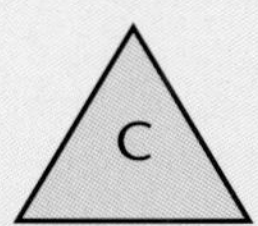

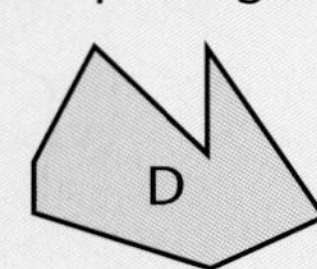

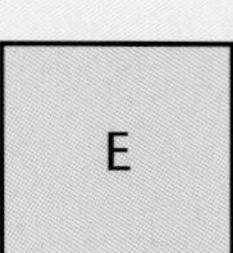

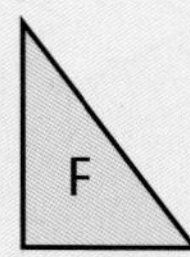

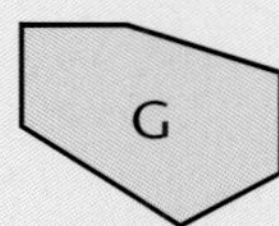

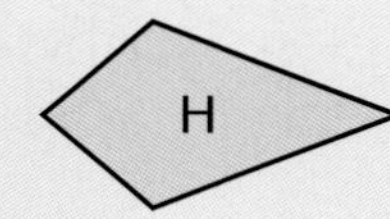

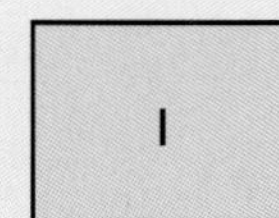

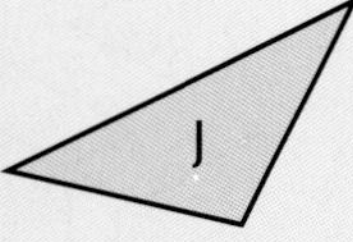

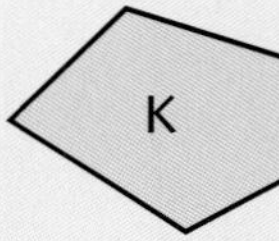

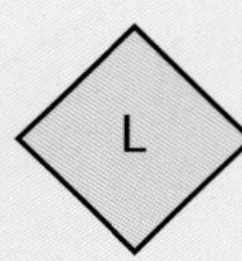

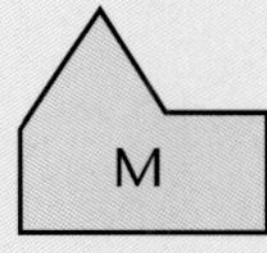

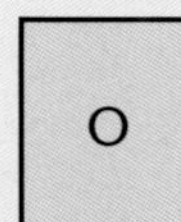

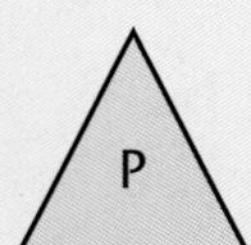

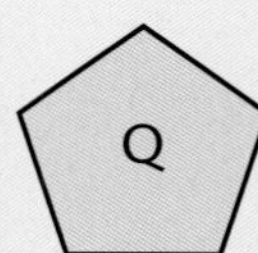

2 Which of the above shapes have a right angle?

B

1 Which of the above shapes A–R are concave?

2 Draw and label:

a) a concave pentagon

b) a convex pentagon

c) a concave quadrilateral

d) a convex quadrilateral.

3 Which of the above shapes A–R have one or more lines of symmetry?

4 Copy or trace the symmetrical shapes and draw on the lines of symmetry.

C

1 Draw a concave quadrilateral with one line of symmetry.

2 Draw a concave hexagon with two lines of symmetry.

3 Draw a concave octagon with:

a) two lines of symmetry

b) four lines of symmetry.

4 Find three examples to match this statement.

The number of lines of symmetry in a regular polygon is equal to the number of sides of the polygon.

I can visualise 3-D shapes from 2-D drawings.

A

Use cubes to build these shapes.

1 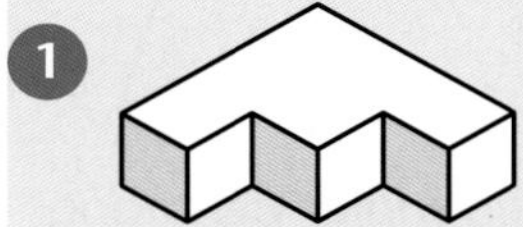

2 

3 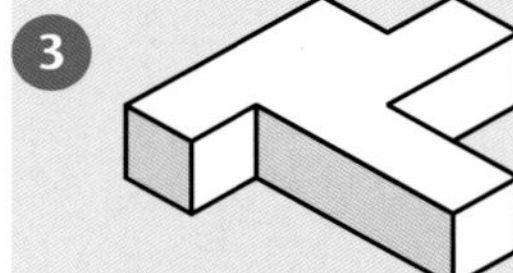

4 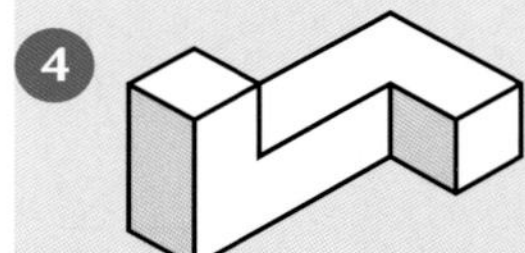

5 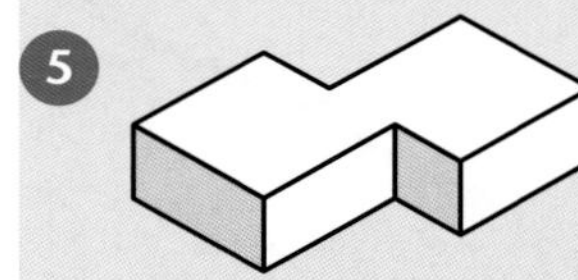

6 

7 

8 

9 

10 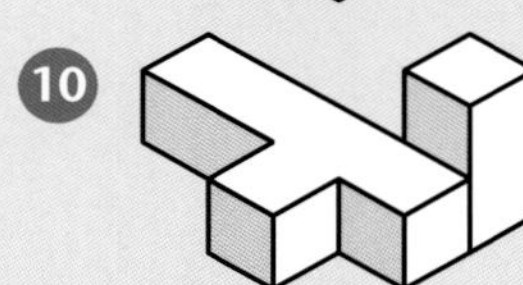

11 

12 

13 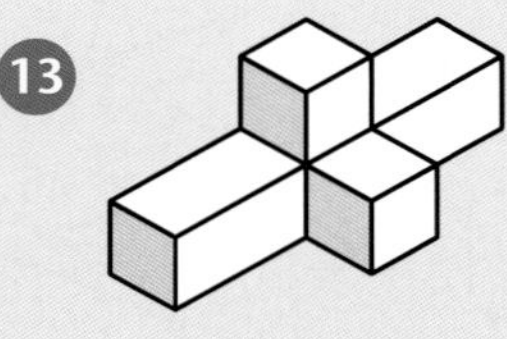

14 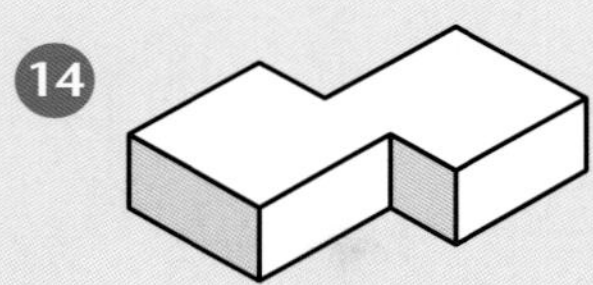

15 

B

Without using cubes, work out how many cubes are needed to build the above shapes.

C

How many more cubes are needed to make each of the above shapes into a cuboid?

Examples

1 3 cubes are needed.

2 6 cubes are needed.

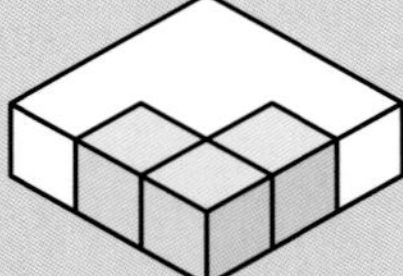

I can describe 3-D shapes and make a net of a cuboid.

SHAPES WITH:	CURVED FACES	STRAIGHT EDGES	
	sphere	cube	triangular prism
	hemisphere	cuboid	pentagonal prism
	cone	triangular based pyramid	hexagonal prism
	cylinder	square based pyramid	octagonal prism

Write the name of each shape.

1 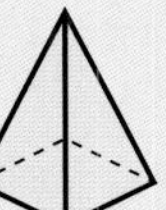

7 

2 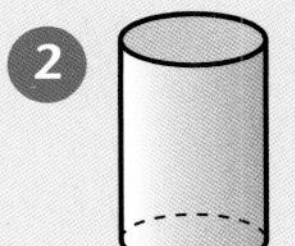

8 

3 

9 

4 

10 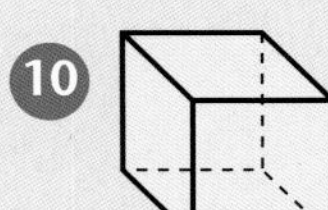

5 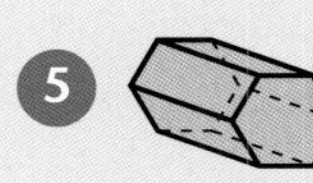

11 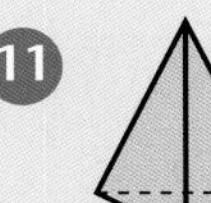

6 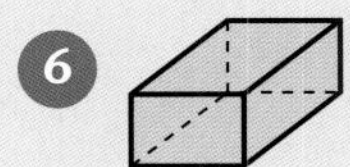

12 

13. Copy these nets onto squared paper. Cut them out and fold them to make open cubes.

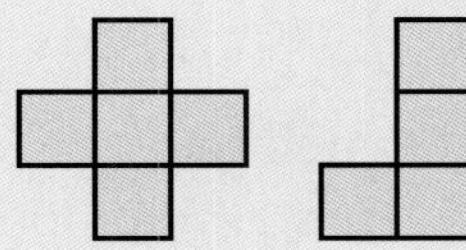

B

Describe the faces of:

1. a triangular based pyramid
2. a pentagonal prism
3. a cube
4. a hexagonal prism.

Which 3-D shape has:

5. rectangular faces only
6. 5 vertices
7. 8 faces
8. 2 curved edges
9. 16 vertices
10. 9 edges?

11. Use a set square and a ruler. Draw a net for an open cube with 3 cm edges.

12. Draw a net for this open cuboid.

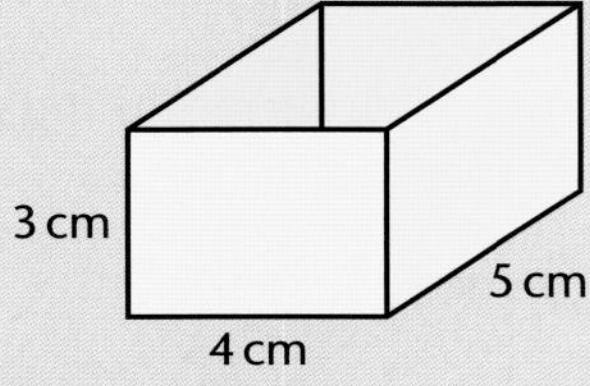

C

1. Which two shapes have 8 vertices?

2. Give the names of three shapes with:
   a) circular faces
   b) triangular faces

3. Name a shape with straight edges which does not have a face with a right angle.

4. How many faces are there in:
   a) an heptagonal pyramid
   b) an heptagonal prism?

5. Construct a net for a closed cube with 2·5 cm edges.

6. Construct nets for these closed cuboids.

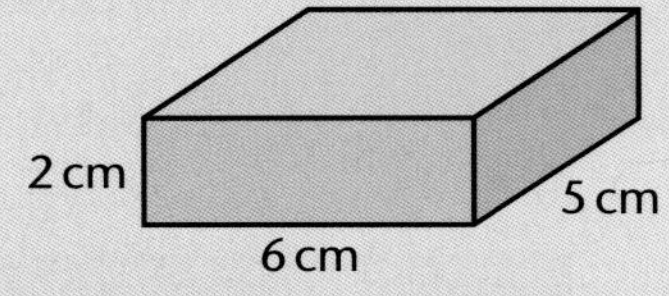

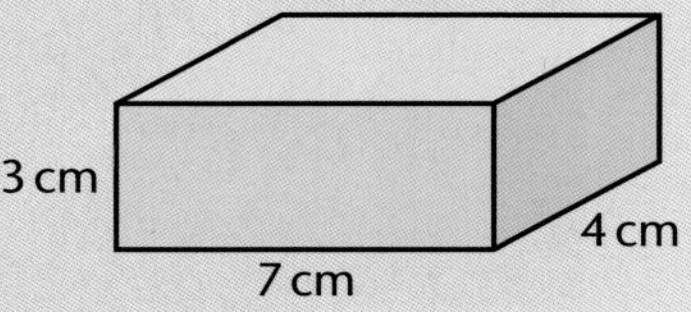

I can choose and use metric units to measure lengths, weights or capacities.

Examples

LENGTH	10 mm = 1 cm	57 mm = 5 cm 7 mm = 5·7 cm
	100 cm = 1 m	130 cm = 1 m 30 cm = 1·3 m
	1000 m = 1 km	2300 m = 2 km 300 m = 2·3 km
WEIGHT	1000 g = 1 kg	1600 g = 1 kg 600 g = 1·6 kg
CAPACITY	1000 ml = 1 litre	2500 ml = 1 ℓ 500 ml = 2·5 ℓ

A

Copy and complete.

1. 200 cm = ☐ m
2. 150 cm = ☐ m ☐ cm
3. 3 m = ☐ cm
4. 5 m 50 cm = ☐ cm
5. 1000 m = ☐ km
6. 3500 m = ☐ km ☐ m
7. 5 km = ☐ m
8. 4 km 500 m = ☐ m
9. 3000 g = ☐ kg
10. 1500 g = ☐ kg ☐ g
11. 4000 ml = ☐ litres
12. 2500 ml = ☐ ℓ ☐ ml

Which metric unit would you use to measure:

13. the height of a church
14. the weight of a phone
15. the length of a bus ride
16. the capacity of an ocean?

B

Copy and complete.

1. 47 mm = ☐ cm ☐ mm
2. 24 mm = ☐ cm ☐ mm
3. 5 cm 9 mm = ☐ mm
4. 1 cm 1 mm = ☐ mm
5. 120 cm = ☐ m ☐ cm
6. 34 cm = ☐ m ☐ cm
7. 8 m 20 cm = ☐ cm
8. 6 m 70 cm = ☐ cm
9. 1600 g = ☐ kg ☐ g
10. 3200 ml = ☐ ℓ ☐ ml
11. 1 kg 400 g = ☐ g
12. 2 ℓ 700 ml = ☐ ml

Which metric unit would you use to measure:

13. the capacity of a sponge
14. the width of a brick
15. the length of a woodlice
16. the weight of a bicycle?

Think of two more things you would measure using:

17. mm
18. kg
19. ml
20. litres
21. grams
22. km

C

Copy and complete

1. 1·8 cm = ☐ mm
2. 4·3 cm = ☐ mm
3. 26 mm = ☐ cm
4. 32 mm = ☐ cm
5. 1·15 m = ☐ cm
6. 0·6 m = ☐ cm
7. 220 cm = ☐ m
8. 75 cm = ☐ m
9. 6300 m = ☐ km
10. 2700 m = ☐ km
11. 7·25 km = ☐ m
12. 5·6 km = ☐ m

Copy the sentence choosing the most sensible estimate.

13. A baby weighs (30 g, 300 g, 3 kg).
14. A saucepan holds (200 ml, 2 litres, 20 litres).
15. A balloon weighs (1 g, 10 g, 100 g).
16. A match is (5 mm, 50 mm, 50 cm) long.

I can read a scale accurately by counting on from the last numbered interval.

For each of the scales work out the measurement shown by each arrow.

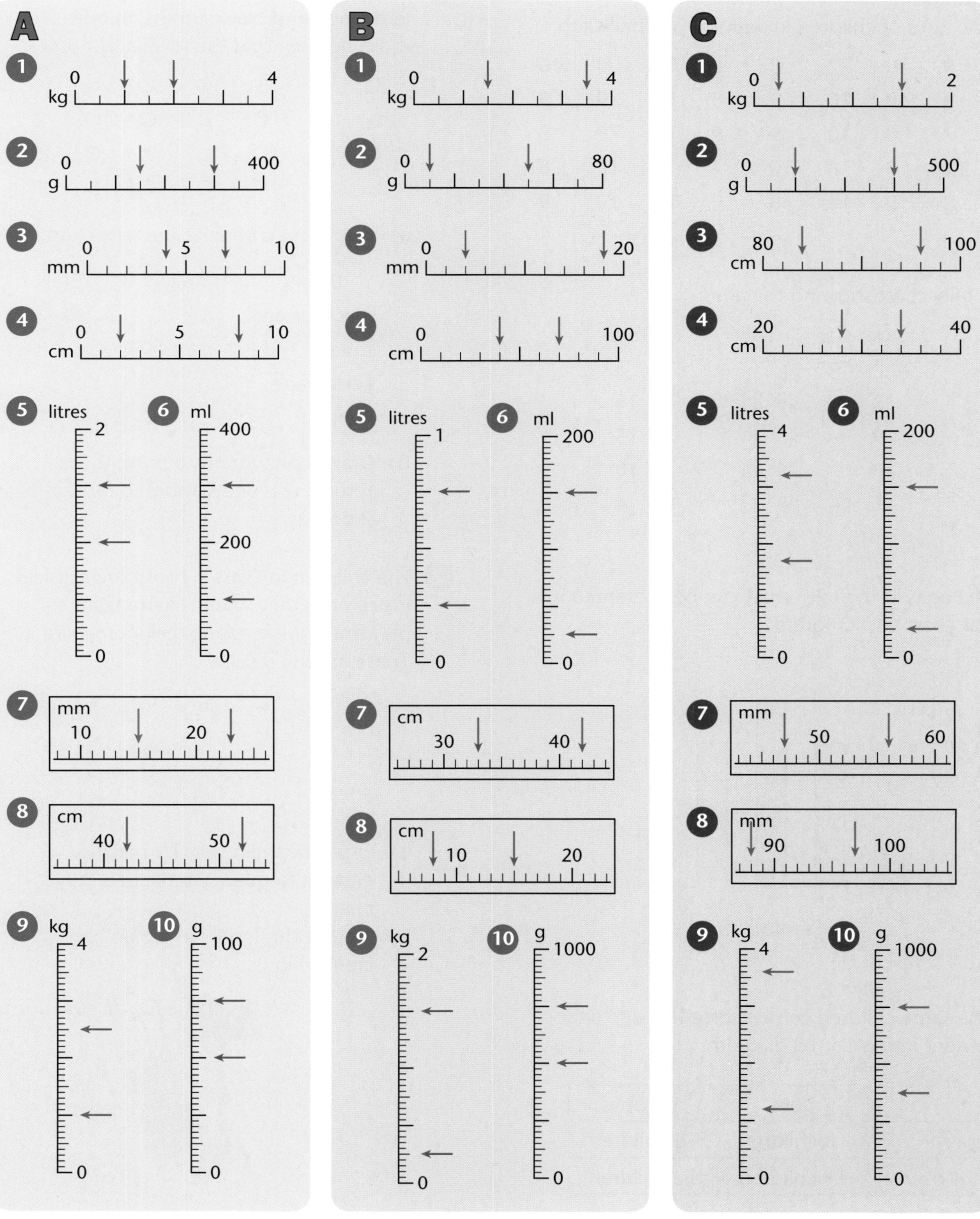

I can collect, organise and present data.

Example

The ages of children in a Junior Football Club.

9	10	7	8	8	11	9	10
9	10	10	9	8	10	9	9
7	8	10	9	9	10	9	8
11	9	8	10	7	8	10	8
8	9	11	8	9	11	10	9

A tally chart showing the ages:

Age		Tally	Total
7	–	|||	3
8	–	~~||||~~ ~~||||~~	10
9	–	~~||||~~ ~~||||~~ |||	13
10	–	~~||||~~ ~~||||~~	10
11	–	||||	4

The ages in the tally chart can be presented in a bar chart or pictogram.

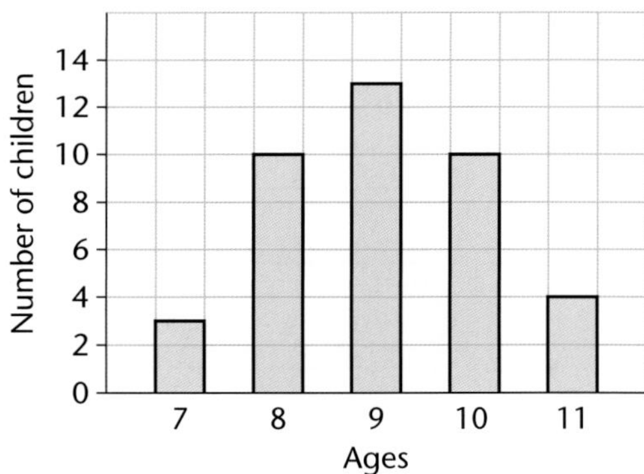

The same children can be sorted by age and gender into a Carroll diagram.

	boys	not boys
over 9	8 children	6 children
not over 9	14 children	12 children

A

1 A cafe sold bottles of orange, cola, lemonade and blackcurrant. In one morning they sold the following bottles.

O	C	B	O	L	C	O
B	O	C	L	C	O	B
O	C	O	L	B	O	C
L	B	C	O	C	B	O

a) Copy and complete the tally chart.

Drinks	Tally	Total
Blackcurrant	~~||||~~ |	6
Cola		
Lemonade		
Orange		

b) Draw a pictogram to present the results. Use one symbol to represent 2 bottles.

2 The children in Class 4 chose the musical instrument they would like to learn to play from guitar, piano, cello or violin. These are the results.

C	P	C	G	C	V	P
P	G	C	P	V	C	C
V	C	P	V	C	G	P
P	C	V	C	G	P	C

a) Organise the results by making either a frequency table or a tally chart.

b) Present the results in a bar chart labelled in 2s.

Class 4 collected the following information for each child:

a) height in cm **b)** how they travel to school **c)** favourite pet (mammals only)

Name	Height	Travel	Pet
Ami	129	car	dog
Brad	138	walk	rabbit
Cath	121	bus	cat
Del	133	walk	dog
Ella	135	car	hamster
Finn	126	walk	cat
Gaby	137	car	rabbit
Hugh	143	walk	dog
Inga	131	car	cat
Jack	140	car	dog
Kyrah	128	walk	dog
Levi	124	walk	dog
Mani	136	walk	dog
Neil	132	car	rabbit
Olga	135	walk	dog

Name	Height	Travel	Pet
Phil	130	bus	hamster
Queeny	141	walk	cat
Ray	139	walk	dog
Sita	134	car	dog
Theo	125	car	rabbit
Usha	142	walk	dog
Vinod	131	walk	dog
Wendy	127	car	rabbit
Xeno	137	walk	cat
Yitzi	135	walk	dog
Zak	126	bus	cat
Anita	144	walk	dog
Ben	142	car	cat
Cleo	140	walk	dog
David	132	car	rabbit

B

1 Make a frequency table or a tally chart to find the totals for each type of pet and then present the results in a bar chart labelled in 2s.

2 Hugh thought that taller children were more likely to walk. This is the Carroll diagram he drew to investigate.

	walk	not walk
over 133 cm		
not over 133 cm		

a) Copy and complete the diagram by writing each name (or initial letter) in the right place.

b) Was Hugh right? Are taller children in Class A more likely to walk? Explain how the Carroll diagram helps you decide.

C

1 Copy and complete this tally chart organising the heights of the children into 5 cm groups.

Height (cm)	Tally	Total
121–125	|||	3
126–130		
131–135		
136–140		
141–145		

2 Ami thought that girls in Class 4 were more likely than boys to have a dog.

a) Use a Venn diagram to investigate her theory.

b) Write a conclusion.

3 Kyrah wondered if children in Class 4 who had dogs were more likely to walk to school.

a) Draw a Carroll diagram to investigate.

b) Write a conclusion.

I can interpret data shown in tables and graphs and describe the effect of using different scales on bar charts showing the same data.

Examples

Blue group	Height (cm)	Weight (kg)
Jacob	122	25
Elly	143	38
Nicola	131	30
Zilan	128	34
Andrew	136	33

What information is shown in the table?
Look at the table headings.
The height and weight of children in Blue Group.
How tall is Nicola? *131 cm*

Who weighs 34 kg? *Zilan*

Who is tallest? *Elly*

This bar chart shows the number of cans of cola sold in a shop each day in 6 days.

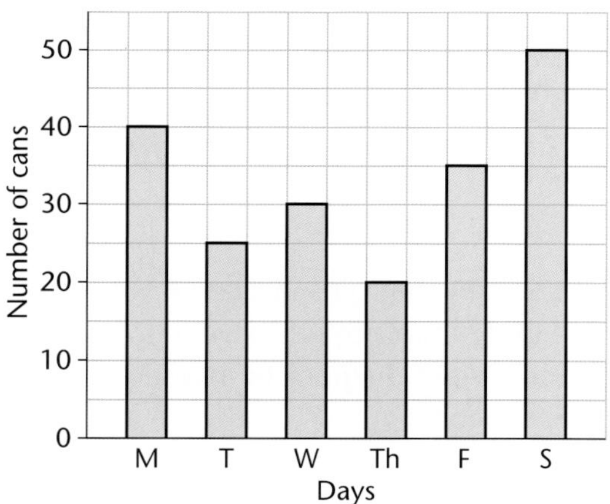

How many cans were sold on Thursday? *20*

On which day were 35 cans sold? *Friday*

How many more cans were sold on Monday than Tuesday? *15*

A

1 This pictogram shows the numbers of apples sold at playtime.

a) How many apples were sold on Thursday?
b) How many apples were sold on Monday?
c) On which day were most apples sold?
d) On which day were least apples sold?
e) On which day were 8 apples sold?
f) How many more apples were sold on Monday than on Tuesday?
g) How many fewer apples were sold on Tuesday than on Wednesday?
h) How many apples were sold during the week?
i) How many apples would need to be drawn on the pictogram if 24 apples were sold?
j) How many apples would have been sold if there were 15 apples on the pictogram?

2 Show the information in the pictogram in a table.

3 Compare the pictogram and the table. Which do you think shows the information better? Give a reason for your answer.

B

1 This pictogram shows the flavours of ice creams sold in a cafe.

Chocolate 

Coffee 

Mint

Pistachio 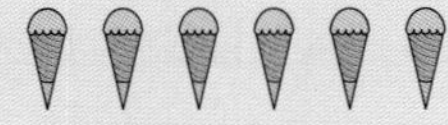

Strawberry 

Vanilla 

represents 5 ice creams.

a) How many coffee ice creams were sold?

b) Of which flavour were 30 ice creams sold?

c) How many more vanilla ice creams were sold than strawberry?

d) How many fewer mint ice creams were sold than chocolate?

e) Which were the most popular flavours?

f) Which was the least popular flavour?

g) How many ice creams were sold altogether?

2 Draw a vertical bar chart to show the ice cream flavours sold. Use a scale of one square for 5 ice creams.

3 Draw another vertical bar chart to show the same data, but this time use a scale of one square for 10 ice creams.

4 Compare the two bar charts. What is the effect of changing the scale?

C

1 The pictogram shows the size of the audience for *Toy Story 3*.

1 pm

3 pm

5 pm

7 pm

9 pm

represents 50 people.

a) How many people saw the 1 pm performance?

b) How many people saw the 9 pm performance?

c) How many more people saw the 3 pm performance than the 7 pm performance?

d) How many fewer people saw the 3 pm performance than the 5 pm performance?

e) Which performance had the smallest audience? Explain why.

f) How many people saw the film during the day?

g) Do you think it was the weekend or a week day? Give a reason for your answer.

h) How many symbols would need to be drawn if there were 425 people in the audience?

2 Show the above data in a horizontal bar chart. Use a scale of 1 square for every 100 people.

3 Show the same data in another horizontal bar chart, but this time use a scale of 1 square for every 20 people.

4 Compare the two bar charts. What is the effect of changing the scale?

D2 MEASURING LENGTH

I can use a ruler to measure and draw lines to the nearest millimetre.

Start measuring from 0, not from the end of the ruler, and read the scale.

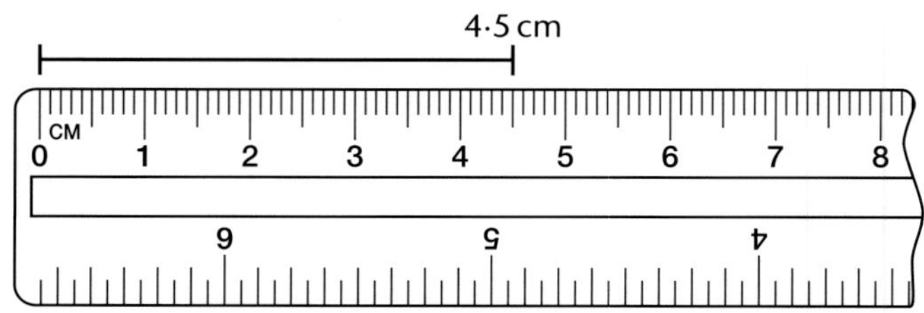

Examples

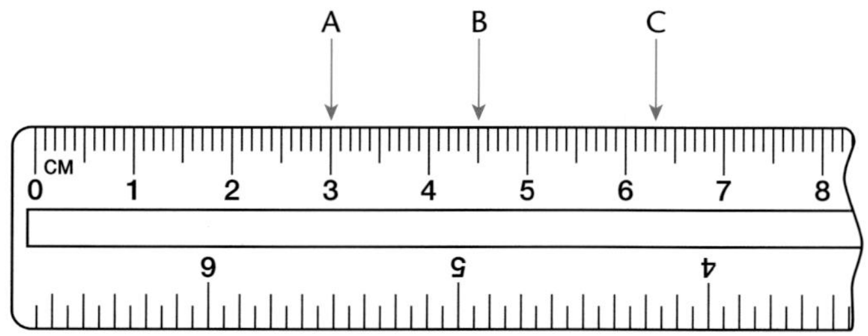

A = 3 cm

B = $4\frac{1}{2}$ cm
= 4·5 cm

C = 6 cm 3 mm
= 6·3 cm

A

1 Read the measurements shown on the ruler.

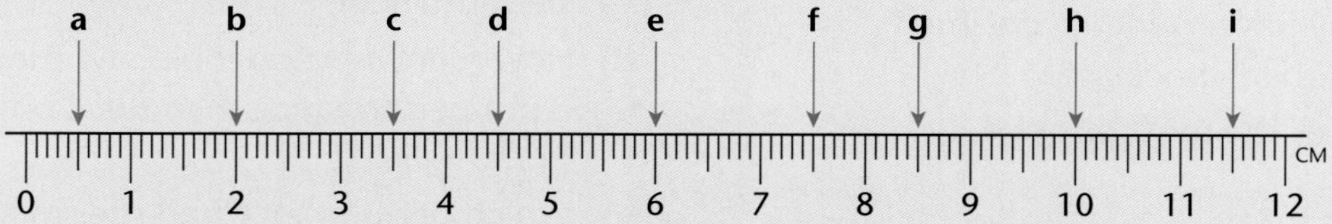

a b c d e f g h i

0 1 2 3 4 5 6 7 8 9 10 11 12 CM

Measure these lines to the nearest half centimetre.

2

3

4

5

6

7

8

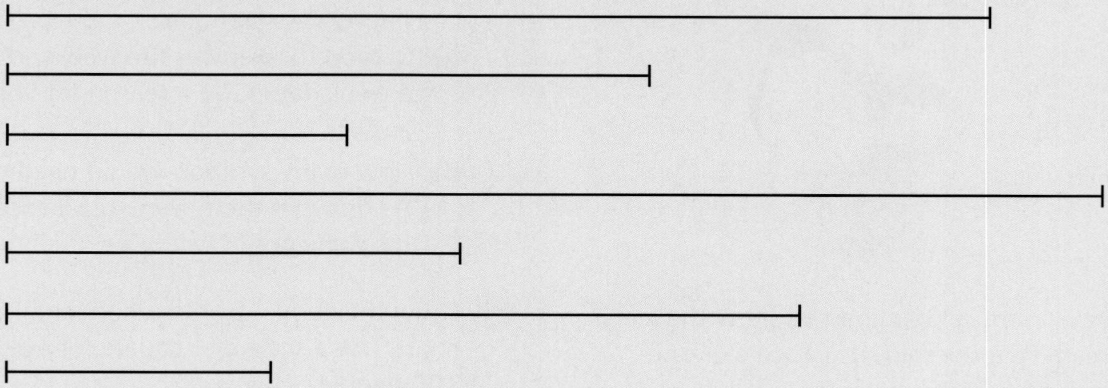

9 Draw lines of the following lengths.

a) 7·5 cm **b)** 12·5 cm **c)** 9 cm **d)** 5·5 cm **e)** 11·5 cm

10 Use a set square and ruler.

a) Draw a square with sides of 3·5 cm.

b) Draw a rectangle with sides of 1·5 cm and 4·5 cm.

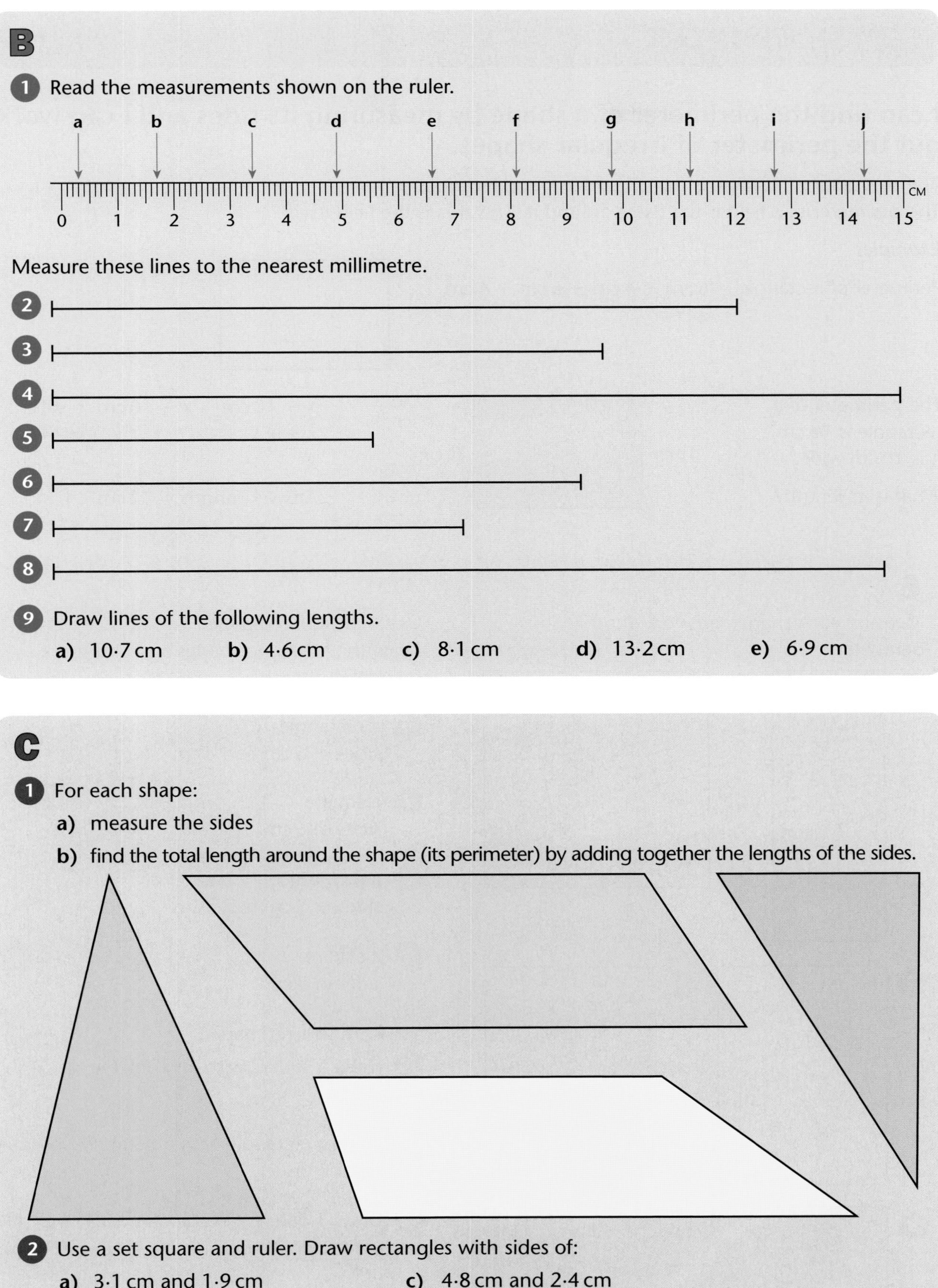

B

1. Read the measurements shown on the ruler.

Measure these lines to the nearest millimetre.

2.
3.
4.
5.
6.
7.
8.
9. Draw lines of the following lengths.

a) 10·7 cm **b)** 4·6 cm **c)** 8·1 cm **d)** 13·2 cm **e)** 6·9 cm

C

1. For each shape:
   a) measure the sides
   b) find the total length around the shape (its perimeter) by adding together the lengths of the sides.

2. Use a set square and ruler. Draw rectangles with sides of:
   a) 3·1 cm and 1·9 cm
   b) 2·7 cm and 5·2 cm
   c) 4·8 cm and 2·4 cm
   d) 3·3 cm and 4·6 cm.

I can find the perimeter of a shape by measuring its sides and I can work out the perimeter of irregular shapes.

The perimeter of a shape is the distance around its edges.
The perimeter of a field is the fence around it. The area is the field itself.

Examples

Perimeter of rectangle = 6 cm + 4 cm + 6 cm + 4 cm
= 24 cm

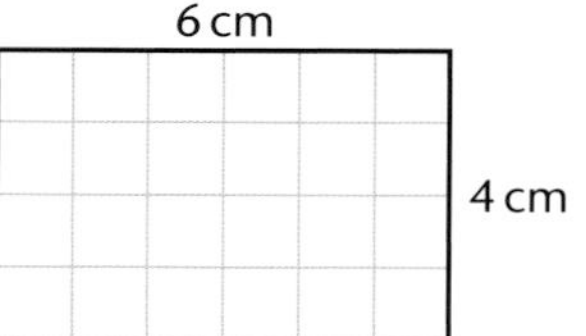

The perimeter of a rectangle is 44 cm. It is 10 cm wide.

What is its length?

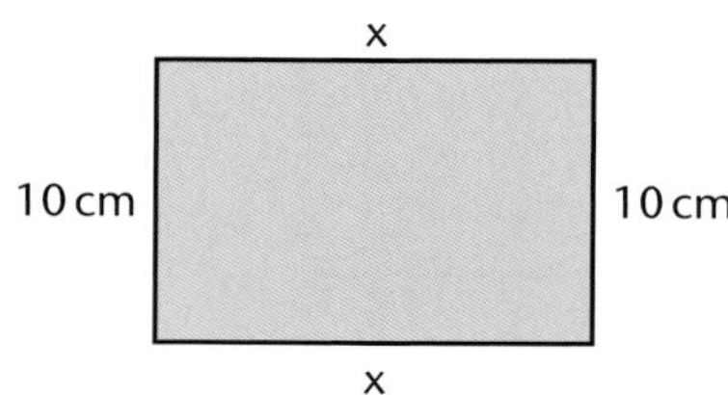

$x + 10\text{ cm} + x + 10\text{ cm} = 44\text{ cm}$
$x + x = 24\text{ cm}$
$x = 12\text{ cm}$

Answer length = 12 cm

Measure each shape and work out the perimeter.

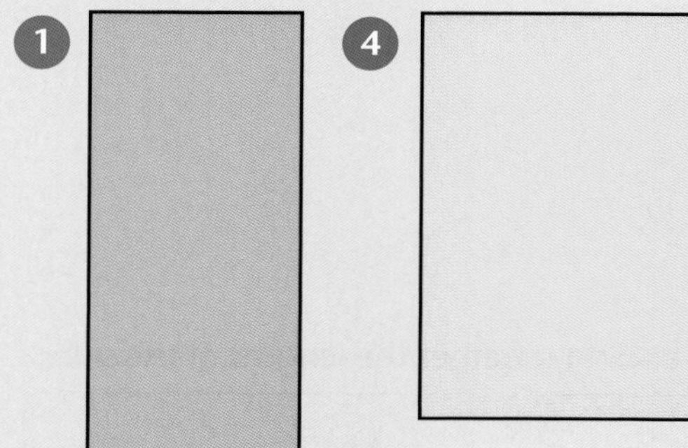

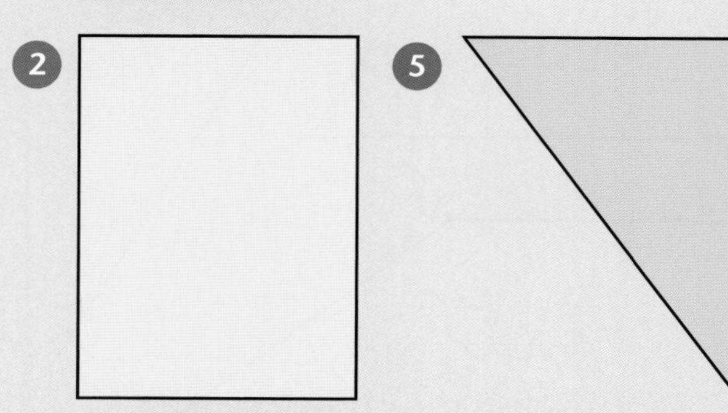

Use 1 cm squared paper.
Draw the following shapes and find the perimeter of each.

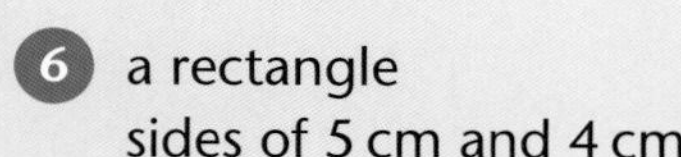

6. a rectangle
sides of 5 cm and 4 cm

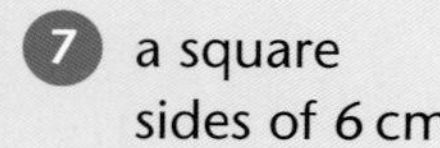

7. a square
sides of 6 cm

8. a rectangle
sides of 8 cm and 3 cm

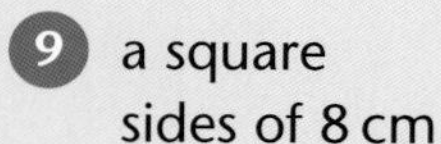

9. a square
sides of 8 cm

Use 1 cm squared paper.

10. Draw a square with a perimeter of 20 cm.

11. Draw a rectangle with a perimeter of 20 cm.

12. Draw 3 different rectangles, each with a perimeter of 16 cm.

B

Measure the edges of each shape to the nearest millimetre. Work out their perimeters.

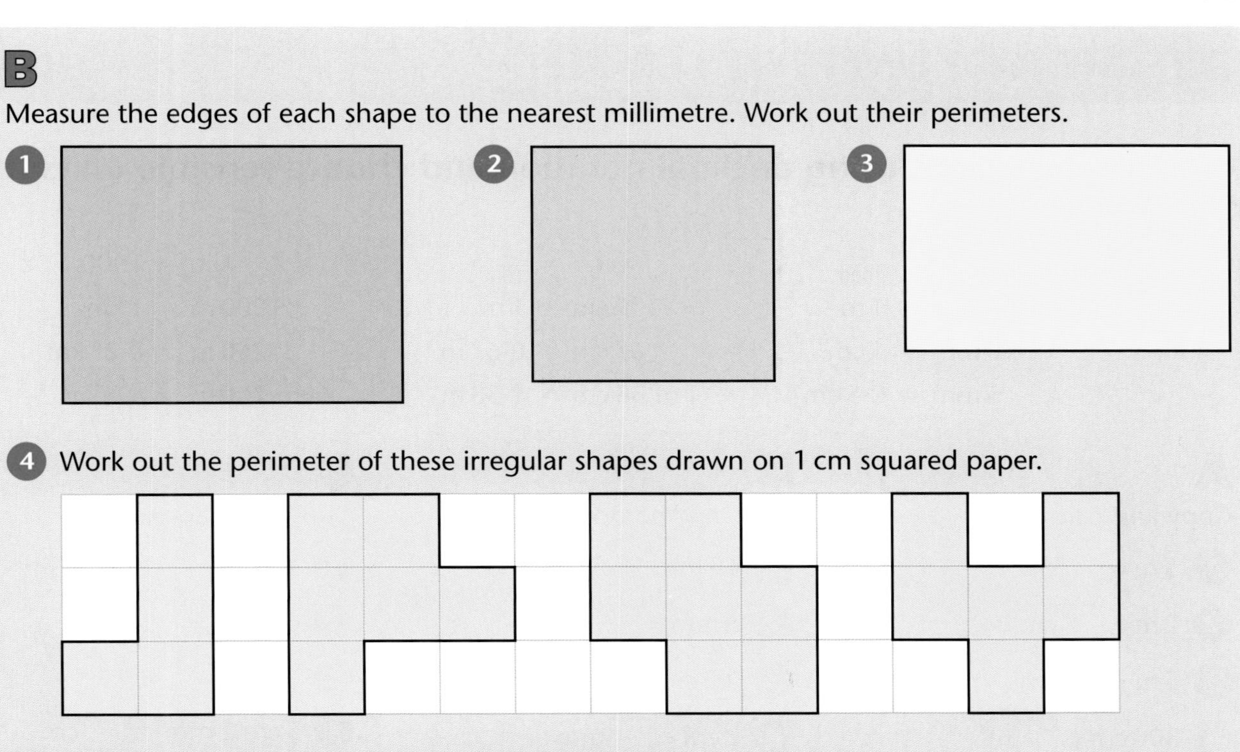

1 **2** **3**

4 Work out the perimeter of these irregular shapes drawn on 1 cm squared paper.

5 Use squared paper. Draw different rectangles with a perimeter of:

a) 18 cm **b)** 28 cm.

C

1 Copy and complete this table showing measurements of rectangles.

Length (cm)	3	7		6	6		18		20	
Width (cm)	4		8	5		9		5		7
Perimeter (cm)		20	36		16	48	60	32	48	30

Work out the perimeter of each shape. All the lengths are in centimetres.

2

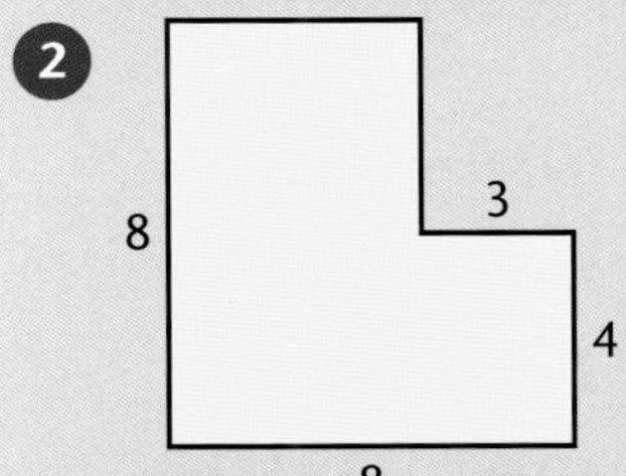

3

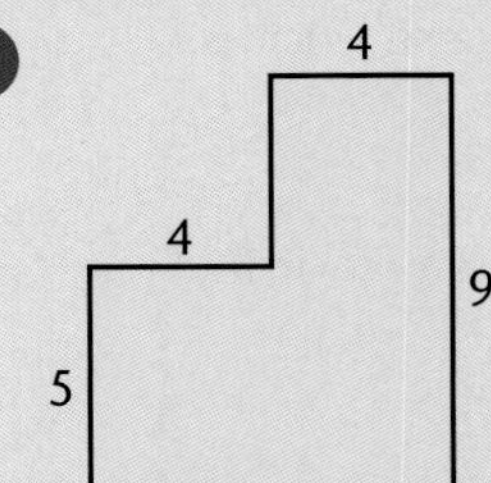

4

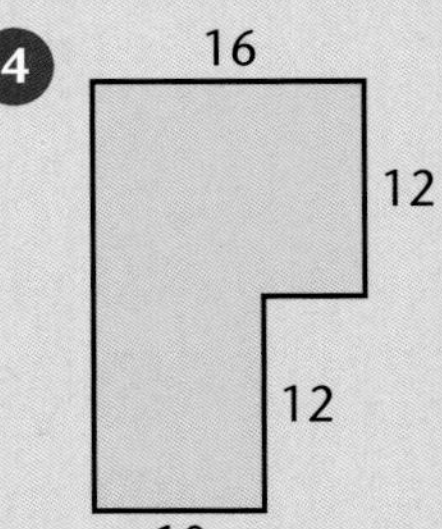

5

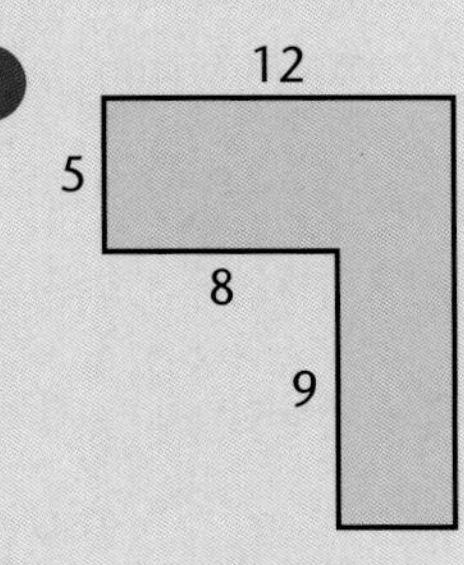

Use a set square and ruler.
Draw the following rectangles and work out their perimeters.

6 4·8 cm by 2·7 cm

7 7·1 cm by 3·9 cm

8 2·5 cm by 6·2 cm

9 5·3 cm by 3·6 cm

D2 METRIC UNITS OF LENGTH

I can record lengths using decimal notation and choose sensible units to measure lengths.

Remember

milli = $\frac{1}{1000}$	centi = $\frac{1}{100}$	kilo = 1000
1000 mm = 1 m	100 cm = 1 m	1000 m = 1 km
10 mm = 1 cm	67 cm = 0·67 m	250 m = 0·25 km
5 mm = 0·5 cm	1 m 38 cm = 1·38 m	4 km 700 m = 4·7 km

A

Copy and complete.

1. 5 m = □ cm
2. 2 m = □ cm
3. 6 m = □ cm
4. 300 cm = □ m
5. 100 cm = □ m
6. 400 cm = □ m
7. 3 km = □ m
8. 7 km = □ m
9. 4 km = □ m
10. 6000 m = □ km
11. 1000 m = □ km
12. 10 000 m = □ km

Choose the longer length from each pair.

13. 500 m 5 km
14. 20 cm $\frac{1}{2}$ m
15. 40 cm $\frac{1}{4}$ m
16. $\frac{1}{2}$ km 400 m

Think of three things you would measure using:

17. centimetres
18. metres.

B

Copy and complete.

1. 60 mm = □ cm
2. 5 mm = □ cm
3. 3·5 cm = □ cm □ mm
4. 2 cm = □ mm
5. 41 cm = □ m
6. 1 m 93 cm = □ m
7. 7·6 m = □ m □ cm
8. 0·58 m = □ cm
9. 500 m = □ km
10. 2 km 750 m = □ km
11. 0·25 km = □ m
12. 1·3 km = □ km □ m

Suggest a suitable metric unit to measure these lengths.

13. a smartie
14. a motorway journey
15. a banana
16. an ant

Think of three more things you would measure using:

17. millimetres
18. kilometres.

C

Copy and complete.

1. 1·8 cm = □ cm □ mm
2. 0·9 cm = □ mm
3. 4 mm = □ cm
4. 5 cm 2 mm = □ cm
5. 3·67 m = □ m □ cm
6. 0·83 m = □ cm
7. 4 m 90 cm = □ m
8. 9 cm = □ m
9. 0·738 km = □ m
10. 2·1 km = □ km □ m
11. 960 m = □ km
12. 1 km 450 m = □ km

Copy and complete by writing >, < or = in the box.

13. 0·04 km □ 200 m
14. 10 mm □ 0·5 cm
15. 17 cm □ 1·7 m
16. 50 m □ 0·05 km
17. 0·1 cm □ 2 mm
18. 0·8 m □ 80 cm
19. 0·3 km □ 30 m
20. 27 mm □ 2·7 cm

MATHS ON TARGET

Year 4

Answers

Stephen Pearce

Elmwood Education Limited

First published 2008 by
Elmwood Education
Unit 5 Mallow Park
Watchmead
Welwyn Garden City
Herts. AL7 1GX.
Tel. 01707 333232

ISBN 9781 902 214 962

Printed by Face Communications
www.facecommunications.co.uk

Maths on Target Year 4 provides a simple, manageable structure to help teachers plan and teach all the objectives set out in the yearly programme in the renewed Primary Framework for Mathematics, each lesson clearly differentiated at three levels of ability.

In the renewed Framework the mathematics curriculum has been organised into seven strands.

- Using and applying mathematics
- Counting and understanding number
- Knowing and using number facts
- Calculating
- Understanding shape
- Measuring
- Handling data

For planning purposes the curriculum is structured around five blocks of work, each block drawing on three of the strands.

The five blocks are:

- Block A – Counting, partitioning and calculating
- Block B – Securing number facts, understanding shape
- Block C – Handling data and measures
- Block D – Calculating, measuring and understanding shape
- Block E – Securing number facts, relationships and calculating

Each block is further organised into three units of work. Each unit provides two or three weeks of learning. To ensure progression throughout the year the units are best taught in the following order.

	Block A	Block B	Block C	Block D	Block E
Term 1	Unit 1	Unit 1	Unit 1	Unit 1	Unit 1
Term 2	Unit 2	Unit 2	Unit 2	Unit 2	Unit 2
Term 3	Unit 3	Unit 3	Unit 3	Unit 3	Unit 3

The structure of **Maths on Target** matches that of the renewed Framework, with fifteen units arranged in the above order. Each unit in **Maths on Target** consists of lessons based upon the learning overview for that unit in the renewed Framework, with the learning intention for each lesson expressed as an *I can* statement.

All lessons in **Maths on Target** are divided into three sections, each providing material at a different level of ability. Section A: activities based upon work previously covered, generally matching the objectives for Year 3 pupils.

Section B: activities based upon the objectives for Year 4 pupils. Most children should be able to work successfully at this level.

Section C: activities providing extension material for faster workers and those needing more challenging tasks, generally matching the objectives for Year 5 pupils.

Maths on Target – Year 4 Answers

Page 2

A

1 211 **2** 196 **3** 304 **4** 832 **5** 478 **6** 298
7 628 **8** 253 **9** 515 **10** 209
11 one hundred and eighty-eight kilometres
12 two hundred and ninety-one kilometres
13 three hundred and twenty-five kilometres
14 four hundred and sixty kilometres
15 three hundred and thirty-three kilometres
16 eighty-seven kilometres
17 eight hundred and eighty-five kilometres
18 one hundred and thirty-nine kilometres
19 three hundred and sixty-four kilometres
20 seven hundred and twenty-one kilometres
21 (a) 459, 495, 549, 594, 945, 954
(b) four hundred and fifty-nine
four hundred and ninety-five
five hundred and forty-nine
five hundred and ninety-four
nine hundred and forty-five
nine hundred and fifty-four

Page 3

B

1

River	Length (km)
Amazon	6750
Nile	6670
Yangtze	6300
Mississippi	6020
Yenisey	5540
Hwang He	5464
Ob	5409
Parana	4880
Congo	4700
Lena	4400

2 four thousand one hundred and ninety-four miles
3 four thousand one hundred and forty-five miles
4 three thousand nine hundred and fifteen miles
5 three thousand seven hundred and forty-one miles
6 three thousand four hundred and forty-two miles
7 three thousand three hundred and ninety-five miles
8 three thousand three hundred and sixty-one miles
9 three thousand and thirty-two miles
10 two thousand nine hundred and twenty miles
11 two thousand seven hundred and thirty-four miles

C

1 250 000 **2** 500 000 **3** 100 000
4 750 000 **5** 1 000 000 000 **6** 1 500 000
7 (a) 25 079 25 097 25 709 25 790 25 907 25 970
27 059 27 095 27 509 27 590 27 905 27 950
(b) twenty-five thousand and seventy-nine
twenty-five thousand and ninety-seven
twenty-five thousand seven hundred and nine
twenty-five thousand seven hundred and ninety
twenty-five thousand nine hundred and seven
twenty five thousand nine hundred and seventy
twenty-seven thousand and fifty-nine
twenty-seven thousand and ninety-five
twenty-seven thousand five hundred and nine
twenty-seven thousand five hundred and ninety
twenty-seven thousand nine hundred and five
twenty-seven thousand nine hundred and fifty

Page 4

A

1 100 + 20 + 8 **2** 300 + 60 + 9 **3** 400 + 20 + 7
4 500 + 80 + 4 **5** 300 + 90 + 2 **6** 600 + 50 + 5
7 700 + 10 + 6 **8** 900 + 20 + 5
9 20 **10** 9 **11** 800 **12** 80 **13** 400 **14** 60
15 4 **16** 300 **17** 390 **18** 528 **19** 881 **20** 119
21 161 **22** 586 **23** 214 **24** 152

B

1 30 **2** 500 **3** 2000 **4** 5 **5** 600 **6** 40
7 7000 **8** 2 **9** 1000 + 600 + 30 + 7
10 2000 + 400 + 50 + 2 **11** 3000 + 900 + 80 + 5
12 2000 + 100 + 70 + 4 **13** 4000 + 500 + 30 + 8
14 5000 + 800 + 40 + 3 **15** 7000 + 200 + 90 + 6
16 8000 + 300 + 10 **17** –30 **18** –500 **19** +6000 **20** –400
21 +2000 **22** +70 **23** +500 **24** –5000 **25** +80 **26** –600

C

1 6137 **2** 473 **3** 1208 **4** 4690 **5** 25 851
6 2917 **7** 1369 **8** 56 434 **9** 5227 **10** 608
11 414 **12** 23 236 **13** 4980 **14** 92 342 **15** 1675
16 7317 **17** 5815 **18** 5036 **19** 100 423 **20** 52 840
21 +13 000 **22** –40 **23** +1100 **24** +99 000 **25** 12 500 + 94
26 16 300 + 50 **27** 7006 + 930 **28** 20 017 + 8500

Page 5

A

1 68 **2** 39 **3** 315 **4** 428 **5** 932 **6** 584
7 162 **8** 654 **9** 238, 283, 382, 823
10 174, 417, 471, 714 **11** 325, 352, 523, 532
12 469, 496, 649, 694 **13** True **14** True **15** False **16** False

B

1 < **2** > **3** > **4** < **5** < **6** >
7 > **8** < **9** 2536, 2635, 3256, 3526
10 1498, 1849, 1948, 4189 **11** 6472, 6724, 7246, 7462
12 3478, 3748, 3784, 3874 **13** +40 **14** –300
15 +6000 **16** –700 **17** +20 **18** –4000

C

1 3560 **2** 2250 **3** 4570 **4** 20 500 **5** 1000 **6** 2110
7 1470 **8** 17 285 **9** –168 **10** –130 **11** +70 **12** –1600
13 (a) Hundreds are 7, 9 Tens are 4, 5 Units are 2, 3
(b) Hundreds are 2, 3 Tens are 4, 5 Units are 7, 9
(c) 234, 975 (d) 497, 523

Page 6

A

1 –6 **2** –2 **3** 5 **4** 0 **5** 1 **6** 1
7 2 **8** 6 **9** –5, –4, –3, –2, –1, 0, 1, 2, 3, 4, 5
10 –10, –8, –6, –4, –2, 0, 2, 4, 6, 8, 10
11 5, 4, 3, 2, 1, 0, –1, –2, –3, –4, –5
12 10, 8, 6, 4, 2, 0, –2, –4, –6, –8, –10
13 A = –1°C B = –4°C C = 3°C **14** B **15** (a) 3°C
(b) 7°C (c) 4°C **16** (a) –1°C (c) 1°C (b) 1°C
(d) –3°C

Page 7

B

1 1 **2** –2 **3** 4 **4** 2 **5** –3 **6** –7
7 –7 **8** –9 **9** 3, 2, 1, 0, –1, –2, –3
10 –2, –1, 0, 1, 2, 3, 4 **11** 0, –2, –4, –6, –8, –10, –12
12 –10, –9, –8, –7, – 6, –5, –4 **13** –10, –8, –6, –4, –2, 0, 2
14 –7, –5, –3, –1, 1, 3, 5 **15** 6, 4, 2, 0, –2, –4, –6
16 5, 3, 1, –1, –3, –5, –7
17 A = –1°C B = –7°C C = 6°C **18** B
19 (a) 6°C (b) 7°C (c) 13°C **20** (a) – 8°C (b) 2°C
21 > **22** < **23** > **24** > **25** < **26** <
27 > **28** <

C

1 2 **2** 4 **3** 8 **4** 4 **5** 6 **6** 6
7 4 **8** 5 **9** –3, –1, 0, 2, 5 **10** –5, –3, –1, 1, 4
11 –4, –2, 0, 1, 3 **12** –4, –1, 0, 2, 4

13

Monday	3°C	–1°C	0°C	4°C	–6°C	–2°C
Change	–4°C	+3°C	–5C	–7°C	+2°C	+4°C
Tuesday	–1°C	2°C	–5°	–3°C	–4°C	2°C

14

Monday	7°C	–2°C	–4°C	1°C	0°C	–3°C
Change	–4°C	+5°C	+3°C	–4°C	–6°C	+7°C
Tuesday	3°C	3°C	–1°C	–3°C	–6°C	4°C

Page 8

A

1 160 **2** 200 **3** 580 **4** 1000 **5** 5 **6** 91
7 60 **8** 73 **9** 400 **10** 700 **11** 200 **12** 60
13 3 **14** 8 **15** 5 **16** 10 **17** 10 **18** 300
19 60 **20** 120 **21** 420 **22** 500 **23** 100 **24** 500
25 1000 **26** 1200 **27** 300 **28** 2000 **29** 20 m

B

1 1760 **2** 490 **3** 3000 **4** 2200 **5** 900 **6** 1700
7 6000 **8** 4800 **9** 755 **10** 500 **11** 644 **12** 409
13 32 **14** 7 **15** 90 **16** 83 **17** 63 **18** 28
19 4000 **20** 5100 **21** (a) 2 km (b) 15 cm

C

1 386 **2** 6320 **3** 70 **4** 600 **5** 4 **6** 21 000
7 9500 **8** 3500 **9** 280 **10** 19 400 **11** 60 **12** 11 000
13 1000 **14** 3000 **15** 10 000 **16** 500 **17** 2500 **18** 14 000
19 (a) 12 m (b) 7.5 m

Page 9

A

1 14 **2** 32 **3** 30 **4** 18 **5** 24 **6** 45
7 24 **8** 24 **9** 35 **10** 40 **11** 18 **12** 30
13 8 **14** 5 **15** 9 **16** 3 **17** 7 **18** 6
19 6 **20** 7 **21** 8 **22** 9 **23** 6 **24** 10

B

1 5 **2** 4 **3** 6 **4** 8 **5** 5 **6** 7
7 10 **8** 24 **9** 70 **10** 16 **11** 28 **12** 24
13 180 **14** 400 **15** 100 **16** 540 **17** 120 **18** 200
19 160 **20** 270 **21** 150 **22** 480 **23** 1000 **24** 240
25 50 **26** 70 **27** 40 **28** 90 **29** 40 **30** 60
31 50 **32** 90 **33** 80 **34** 50 **35** 30 **36** 60

C

1 7 **2** 6 **3** 4 **4** 100 **5** 20 **6** 60
7 350 **8** 360 **9** 120 **10** 420 **11** 240 **12** 400
13 14 **14** 63 **15** 35 **16** 49 **17** 24 **18** 64
19 32 **20** 48 **21** 45 **22** 18 **23** 63 **24** 81
25 3 **26** 6 **27** 8 **28** 4 **29** 2 **30** 9
31 5 **32** 7 **33** 4 **34** 6 **35** 3 **36** 8

Page 10 (top half)

A

1 71 **2** 29 **3** 57 **4** 38 **5** 73 **6** 46
7 94 **8** 63 **9** 67 **10** 37

B

1 102 **2** 48 **3** 145 **4** 56 **5** 79 **6** 42
7 136 **8** 115 **9** 107 **10** 105

C

1 256 + 68 **2** 232 + 39 **3** 765 + 52 **4** 179 + 59
5 468 – 99 **6** 486 + 61 **7** 191 + 72 **8** 315 – 48
9 418 + 96 **10** 69 + 78

Page 10 (bottom half)

A

1 78 **2** 67 **3** 33 **4** 44 **5** 88 **6** 79
7 53 **8** 64 **9** 89 **10** 45

B

1 83 **2** 83 **3** 44 **4** 28 **5** 95 **6** 95
7 42 **8** 38 **9** 84 **10** 29

C

1 326 + 252 **2** 438 + 256 **3** 428 + 108 **4** 174 – 148
5 283 – 219 **6** 857 – 505 **7** 649 – 583 **8** 736 – 222
9 462 – 321 **10** 525 – 307

Page 11

A

1 41 p **2** 62 p **3** 61 p **4** 83 p **5** 53 p **6** 24 p
7 41 p **8** 37 p **9** 54 p **10** 63 p **11** £10.50 **12** 60 p
13 £6.00

B

1 £4.08 **2** £3.15 **3** £5.53 **4** £5.83 **5** £23.70 **6** £20.80
7 £3.70 **8** £3.60 **9** £6.01 **10** £11.75 **11** £9.40 **12** £1.80

C

1 £4.31 **2** £3.40 **3** £8.87 **4** £11.21 **5** £142.50 **6** £159.60
7 £1.10 **8** £2.40 **9** £61.25 **10** £2.80 **11** £567

Page 12

A

1 ○, Δ are 17, 18 or 18, 17 ◇ is 16 □ is 15
2 □, ◇ are 25, 45 or 45, 25 ○ is 55 Δ is 35
3 23 + 14 **4** 31 + 25 **5** 16 + 19 **6** 28 + 33 **7** 46 – 33
8 42 – 35 **9** 75 – 57 **10** 30 – 14 **11** 17

B

1 □ is 78 ○ is 34 ◇, Δ are 48, 68 or 68, 48
2 □, ○ are 26, 29 or 29, 26 ◇ is 28 Δ is 27
3 42 + 12 **4** 45 + 28 **5** 26 + 15 **6** 38 – 17 **7** 57 – 41
8 68 – 34 **9** 30 – 21 **10** 61 – 36 **11** 74

C

1 □ is 66 ◇ is 80 ○ is 27 Δ is 39
2 □ is 28 ◇ is 35 ○ is 63 Δ is 98

3 32   **4** 45   **5** 58   **6** 58
+ 27   + 34   + 12   + 38
59   79   70   96

7 58   **8** 67   **9** 85   **10** 53
− 23   − 16   − 39   − 28
25   51   46   25

11 (a) 19, 26 (b) 41, 59

Page 13

A

1 24 **2** (a) 8, Double 4 (b) 2, Double 1 (c) 2, Double 2 (d) Double 6, Treble 4 **3** 6
4 (a) Treble 3 (b) Double 7 (c) Treble 7 (d) Double 5 (e) Treble 5 (f) Double 8 **5** 11, 13, 17, 19

B

1 48 **2** (a) D5 + T8 D8 + T6 (b) T5 + T8 T6 + T7
3 (a) T8 + D6 T8 + T4 T7 + T5 T6 + T6
(b) T8 + T3 T7 + D6 T7 + T4 T6 + T5
(c) T8 + 8 T8 + D4 T6 + D7 D8 + D8
(d) T8 + 5 T7 + 8 T7 + D4 T5 + D7
4 (a) T7 + D7 (b) T7 + D8 (c) T8 + D7 (d) T8 + D8

C

1 72 **2** T8 + T7 + D7
3 T8 + T8 + D5 T7 + T7 + D8 T8 + T6 + D8 **4** 65, 67, 68

Page 14

A

1 14 **2** 14 **3** 13 **4** 16 **5** 17 **6** 13
7 15 **8** 18 **9** 14 **10** 15 **11** 16 **12** 17
13 13 **14** 16 **15** 15 **16** 8 **17** 9 **18** 8
19 6 **20** 7 **21** 7 **22** 9 **23** 8 **24** 8
25 9 **26** 8 **27** 7 **28** 7 **29** 6 **30** 9
31 23 + 16 = 39 16 + 23 = 39 39 − 23 = 16 39 − 16 = 23
32 46 + 17 = 63 17 + 46 = 63 63 − 17 = 46 63 − 46 = 17

B

1 170 **2** 140 **3** 140 **4** 140 **5** 160 **6** 80
7 80 **8** 80 **9** 90 **10** 90 **11** 1300 **12** 1500
13 1700 **14** 1200 **15** 1300 **16** 700 **17** 900 **18** 700
19 900 **20** 400
21 16 + 48 = 64 64 − 48 = 16 64 − 16 = 48
22 67 − 38 = 29 38 + 29 = 67 29 + 38 = 67
23 38 + 45 = 83 83 − 38 = 45 83 − 45 = 38
24 58 − 32 = 26 32 + 26 = 58 26 + 32 = 58

C

1 80 **2** 70 **3** 80 **4** 90 **5** 60 **6** 70
7 90 **8** 60 **9** 90 **10** 90 **11** 400 **12** 9000
13 800 **14** 9000 **15** 700 **16** 7000 **17** 600 **18** 7000
19 800 **20** 8000
21 123 + 214 = 337 214 + 123 = 337 337 − 214 = 123 337 − 123 = 214
22 72 + 37 = 109 37 + 72 = 109 109 − 72 = 37 109 − 37 = 72
23 430 + 170 = 600 170 + 430 = 600 600 − 430 = 170 600 − 170 = 430
24 360 + 340 = 700 340 + 360 = 700 700 − 360 = 340 700 − 340 = 360

Page 15

A

1

5	4	9
10	6	2
3	8	7

2

10	3	8
5	7	9
6	11	4

3

2	7	6
9	5	1
4	3	8

4

9	10	5
4	8	12
11	6	7

B

1

8	7	12
13	9	5
6	11	10

2

12	2	16
14	10	6
4	18	8

3

9	16	11
14	12	10
13	8	15

4

12	13	8
7	11	15
14	9	10

C

1

2	11	7	14
13	8	12	1
16	5	9	4
3	10	6	15

2

5	16	15	2
10	7	8	13
6	11	12	9
17	4	3	14

3

3	14	10	15
16	9	13	4
17	8	12	5
6	11	7	18

Page 16

A

1 20 **2** 40 **3** 50 **4** 80 **5** 70 **6** 50
7 80 **8** 40 **9** 30 **10** 100 **11** 200 **12** 400
13 500 **14** 600 **15** 900 **16** 900 **17** 800 **18** 500
19 400 **20** 700 **21** £3 **22** £9 **23** £5 **24** £2
25 £9 **26** £6 **27** £4 **28** £2 **29** £8 **30** £5

B

1 120 **2** 130 **3** 100 **4** 40 **5** 90 **6** 80
7 90 **8** 100 **9** 80 **10** 300 **11** 800 **12** 700
13 600 **14** 300 **15** 500 **16** £15 **17** £45 **18** £21
19 £10 **20** £48

C

1 About 3000 **2** About 1000 **3** About 135 000
4 About 30 000 **5** 260 **6** 810 **7** 200 **8** 610
9 £90 **10** £184 **11** £56 **12** £195

Page 17

A

1 14 **2** 40 **3** 18 **4** 45 **5** 80 **6** 5
7 4 **8** 2 **9** 10 **10** 3 **11** 7 **12** 8
13 10 **14** 6 **15** 9 **16** 6 **17** 8 **18** 10
19 5 **20** 7 **21** 175 **22** 900 **23** 81 **24** 128
25 8

B

1 18 **2** 60 **3** 42 **4** 54 **5** 36 **6** 12
7 30 **8** 0 **9** 48 **10** 6 **11** 1 **12** 10
13 4 **14** 8 **15** 5 **16** 9 **17** 3 **18** 7
19 3 × 6 **20** 7 × 6 **21** 4 × 6 **22** 6 × 6 **23** 0 × 6 **24** 8 × 6
25 5 × 6 **26** 9 × 6 **27** 30 ÷ 6 **28** 48 ÷ 6 **29** 60 ÷ 6 **30** 24 ÷ 6
31 42 ÷ 6 **32** 6 ÷ 6 **33** 54 ÷ 6 **34** 36 ÷ 6

C

1 240 **2** 1200 **3** 3000 **4** 420 **5** 180 **6** 4800
7 2400 **8** 4200 **9** 540 **10** 3600 **11** 20 **12** 100
13 40 **14** 1000 **15** 600 **16** 50 **17** 800 **18** 300
19 70 **20** 900 **21** 36 **22** 120 **23** 60 **24** 24
25 96 **26** 72 **27** 48 **28** 108 **29** 84 **30** 240
31 144 **32** 16

Page 18

A

1 35 **2** 8 **3** 160 g **4** 40 **5** 96

B

1 145 **2** 20 **3** 84 **4** 45 **5** 1 m 44 cm **6** £1.75

C

1 487 **2** 25 **3** 672 **4** 295 **5** 2 m 36 m **6** 90 p

Page 19

A

A hexagonal based prism
B hemisphere
C square based pyramid
D cube
E cone
F pentagonal based prism
G triangular based pyramid
H cylinder
I cuboid
J triangular based prism
K sphere
L octagonal based prism

B

1 4 triangles, 1 square
2 3 rectangles, 2 triangles
3 6 rectangles
4 8 rectangles, 2 octagons
5 cylinder
6 pentagonal based prism
7 sphere
8 cube

C

1

Name	Faces	Edges	Vertices
cuboid	6	12	8
hexagonal prism	8	18	12
square based pyramid	5	8	5
triangular prism	5	9	6
cube	6	12	8
octagonal prism	10	24	16
triangular pyramid	4	6	4
pentagonal prism	7	15	10

Page 20

A

1

	symmetrical	not symmetrical
triangles	B C H	A F
not triangles	E	D G

2 A triangle
B equilateral triangle
C right angled isosceles triangle
D quadrilateral
E regular pentagon
F right angled triangle
G quadrilateral
H isosceles triangle

5 (a) B E (b) B C D E H (c) C H (d) E

Page 21

B

1

	has a right angle	no right angle
regular	N	J K Q
not regular	I M P	L O

2 I quadrilateral
J equilateral triangle
K regular octagon
L irregular pentagon
M irregular hexagon
N square
O isosceles triangle
P irregular heptagon
Q regular hexagon

3 (a) J K L M N O P Q (b) I M N P **6** 2

C

1

	2 or more equal angles	not 2 or more equal angles
5 or more sides	E K L M P Q	
not 5 or more sides	B C D H I J N O	A F G

2 square
3 equilateral triangle
6 e.g. The angles of an equilateral triangle are equal. A triangle cannot have more than one right angle.
7 (a) 3 (b) 5

Page 22

A

1

Games	Netball	Football	Rounders	Hockey
Total	5	9	4	6

2

Goals	0	1	2	3	4
Matches	5	3	9	5	2

Page 23

B

1 (a) cm or cm^2 (b) cm (c) g (d) m (e) seconds
2 (a) weight attached (c) (b) drop time (e)
(c) size of cotton square (a) length of string (b)
drop height (d)
3 weight attached, drop time **4** e.g...... the longer the drop time
5 (a) 32
(b)

No. of children	1	2	3	4	5
Total	6	12	9	3	2

C

4

No. of letters	2	3	4	5	6	7	8
Total	14	9	9	6	4	6	2

5

No. of letters	1	2	3	4	5	6	7	8	9	10	11	12	13
Total	9	17	27	27	20	4	14	5	4	1	1	0	2

Page 24

A

1 Monday **2** Friday **3** 28 **4** 5
5 62 **6** red **7** 5 **8** 4 **9** 30
10 16 children chose red or yellow. 16 is more than half of 30. Kevin is right.

Page 25

B

1 (a) 1 (b) 3 (c) 1
2 (a) Rovers (b) United (c) United
3

Team	United	Town	City	Rovers
Points	8	7	6	3

4 E **5** U **6** (a) A (b) 1 **7** 235

C

1 metres, seconds **2** Drop height **3** Drop time
4 e.g. Did drop height affect drop time.
5 .... the greater the drop time. **6** 250 **7** 150 **8** 75 **9** 1775

Page 26

A

1 1000 m **2** 200 cm **3** 3000 g **4** 2000 ml **5** 3000 m
6 300 cm **7** 1000 g **8** 3000 ml **9** 2000 m **10** 100 cm
11 2000 g **12** 1000 ml **13** 1 g **14** 100 ml **15** 25 cm
16 2 kg

B

1 500 g **2** 5000 ml **3** 2 m **4** 500 m
5 6000 g **6** 3 litres **7** 50 cm **8** 2 km
9 4 kg **10** 500 ml **11** 400 cm **12** 7000 m
13 metres **14** grams **15** centimetres **16** kilograms
17 litres **18** grams **19** kilometres **20** kilograms

C

1 750 ml **2** 6 cm **3** 420 m **4** 610 g
5 890 ml **6** 24 cm **7** 910 m **8** 180 g
9 330 ml **10** 54 cm **11** 470 m **12** 790 g
13 150 g **14** 4000 m **15** 200 ml **16** $\frac{3}{4}$ kg

Page 27

A

1 15 kg, 35 kg **2** 45 g, 55 g **3** 2 kg, 8 kg
4 40 g, 90 g **5** 0.5 kg, 1.5 kg **6** 100 g, 300 g
7 53 kg, 65 kg **8** 440 g, 520 g **9** 0.5 kg
10 250 kg **11** 2.5 kg **12** 22.5 kg

B

1 2 kg, 8 kg **2** 30 g, 70 g **3** 100 g, 160 g
4 150 g, 450 g **5** 150 g, 700 g **6** 60 g, 170 g
7 280 g, 370 g **8** 17 kg, 28 kg **9** $1\frac{3}{10}$ kg or 1 kg 300 g
10 275 kg **11** 18 kg **12** $1\frac{3}{4}$ kg or 1 kg 750 g

C

1 1 kg, 2.5 kg **2** 22.5 kg, 24.5 kg **3** 2 kg, 600 g, 3 kg, 600 g
4 70 g, 90 g **5** 800 g, 2 kg 200 g **6** 280 g, 640 g
7 4 kg 600 g, 5 kg 800 g **8** 140 g, 180 g **9** 2 kg 400 g
10 60 kg **11** 5 kg 600 g **12** 125 kg

Page 28

A

1 58 **2** 69 **3** 67 **4** 32 **5** 24 **6** 64
7 43 **8** 24 **9** 35 **10** 27 **11** 41 **12** 34
13 62 minutes **14** 42 cm **15** 57 kg

B

1 81 **2** 93 **3** 75 **4** 19 **5** 45 **6** 31
7 26 **8** 45 **9** 23 **10** 56 **11** 29 **12** 35
13 59 cm **14** 83 km **15** 27 kg **16** 76 litres

C

1 121 **2** 123 **3** 142 **4** 84 **5** 76 **6** 79
7 68 **8** 77 **9** 29 **10** 68 **11** 84 **12** 99
13 82 ml **14** 163 g **15** 69 cm **16** 86 mm

Page 30

A

1 E5 **2** B4 **3** C5 **4** D1 **5** C2 **6** D3
7 A1 **8** B2 **9** ⚠ **10** ⊠ **11** ⊟ **12** ⟠
13 Δ **14** ⊖ **15** ◆ **16** ● **17** B2 **18** D4 E4
19 A3 **20** B3 C3 D3

B

1 A7 A6 A5 B5 C5 C6 C7 **2** F4 F3 F2 G2 H2 H3 H4 G4
3 E8 F8 G8 F7 F6 **4** B3 C2 D1 B1 D3
5 (a) hexagon (b) no **6** (a) hexagon (b) yes
7 (a) square (b) yes **8** (a) octagon (b) yes
9 (a) rectangle (b) yes

C

1 F **2** G **3** U **4** H **5** Y **6** X
7 Z **8** M **9** (3, 3) **10** (0, 2) **11** (4, 5) **12** (2, 0)
13 (5, 4) **14** (2, 2) **15** (0, 1) **16** (4, 3) **17** half pint

Page 31

A

1 60 **2** 120 **3** 75 **4** 45 **5** 60 **6** 90
7 135 **8** 300 **9** 30 **10** 45 **11** 55 **12** 15
13 24 **14** 36 **15** 6 **16** 8

B

1 $1\frac{1}{2}$ **2** 10 **3** $2\frac{1}{2}$ **4** 4 **5** 2 **6** $1\frac{1}{4}$
7 3 **8** 5 **9** 25 **10** 50 **11** 5 **12** 40
13 10 **14** 55 **15** 20 **16** 35 **17** 7 **18** 14
19 4 **20** 23 **21** 720

C

1 28 **2** 53 **3** 19 **4** 41 **5** 4 **6** 37
7 22 **8** 56 **9** 4 h 55 mins. **10** 14 h 5 mins.
11 9 h 20 mins. **12** 19 h 35 mins. **13** 14 days
14 42 days **15** 2 days **16** 5 days **17** 30 years **18** 50 years
19 5 years **20** 2 years **21** 1440

Page 32

A

1 20 part 7, 7:20 **2** 4 o'clock, 4:00 **3** 5 part 9, 9:05
4 10 to 1, 12:50 **5** $\frac{1}{4}$ to 6, 5:45 **6** $\frac{1}{2}$ part 11, 11:30
7 10 part 6, 6:10 **8** 20 to 2, 1:40 **9** $\frac{1}{4}$ part 10, 10:15
10 25 to 4, 3:35 **11** 25 part 8 **12** 5 to 3 **13** $\frac{1}{4}$ part 11
14 $\frac{1}{2}$ part 6 **15** 10 part 1 **16** 4 o'clock **17** 10 to 10
18 $\frac{1}{4}$ to 4 **19** 5 part 7 **20** 25 to 6

Page 33

B

1 (a) 17 mins. to 6 (b) 5:43
2 (a) 7 mins. part 12 (b) 12:07
3 (a) 12 mins. part 8 (b) 8:12 am
4 (a) 21 mins. to 3 (b) 2:39 pm
5 (a) 16 mins. part 3 (b) 3:16
6 (a) 6 mins. to 8 (b) 7.54
7 (a) 28 mins. part 6 (b) 6:28 am
8 (a) 19 mins. to 10 (b) 9:41 am
9 (a) 29 mins. to 11 (b) 10:31
10 (a) 29 mins. part 1 (b) 1:29
11 (a) 7 mins. to 4 (b) 3:53 pm
12 (a) 9 mins. part II (b) 11:09 pm
13 (a) 2 mins. part 4 (b) 4:02
14 (a) 4 mins. to 10 (b) 9:56
15 (a) 26 mins. to 8 (b) 7:34 am
16 (a) 17 mins. part I (b) 1:17 pm
17 (a) 21 mins. part II (b) 11:21
18 (a) 12 mins. to 7 (b) 6:48
19 (a) 6 mins. part 5 (b) 5:06 pm
20 (a) 23 mins. part 4 (b) 4:23 am

C

1

Time in words	12-hour clock	24-hour clock
$\frac{1}{2}$ part 8	8:30 pm	20:30
6 mins. part 7	7:06 am	07:06
13 mins. to 12	11:47 am	11:47
6 mins. to 10	9:54 pm	21:54
25 part 4	4:25 am	04:25
17 mins. to 4	3:43 pm	15:43
9 mins. part 8	8:09 am	08:09
26 mins. to 6	5:34 pm	17:34
11 mins. part I	1:11 pm	13:11
28 mins. part I	1:28 am	01:28
28 mins. to 5	4:32 pm	16:32
$\frac{1}{4}$ part 10	10:15 pm	22:15
4 mins. to 10	9:56 am	09:56

2 (a) 4 h. 30 mins. (b) 9 h. 55 mins. (c) 3 h. 50 mins.
(d) 4 h. 40 mins. (e) 9 h. 46 mins.
3 (a) 40 (b) 42 (c) 36 (d) 180 (e) 720
4 (a) 20:14 (b) 21:10

(a)	(b)
20:14	21:10
06:50	07:46
11:31	12:27
21:38	22:34
04:09	05:05
15:27	16:23
07:53	08:49
17:18	18:14
12:55	13:51
01:12	02:08
16:16	17:12
21:59	22:55
09:40	10:36

Page 34

A

1 50 mins. 2 25 mins. 3 40 mins. 4 20 mins. 5 9:25

B

1 40 mins. 2 11:35 3 3:30 4 2:05 5 7:50 6 7:25

C

1 4:50 2 10:15 3 1h. 50 mins. 4 9:10 5 1:55 6 10:55

Page 35

A

1 Weather 2 Football 3 Tennis
4 Blue Peter 5 Panorama 6 National News
7 Local News 8 Carry On Nurse 9 25 mins.
10 30 mins. 11 25 mins. 12 25 mins.
13 Doctor Who 14 Football 15 Gardener's World
16 Carry On Nurse

B

1 EastEnders 2 National News 3 Newsround
4 Carry On Nurse 5 Gardener's World 6 Tennis
7 Emmerdale 8 Blue Peter 9 2 h 5 mins.
10 50 mins. 11 50 mins. 12 1 h 40 mins.
13 Tennis, Carry On Nurse 14 National News, National News
15 Local News, National News 16 Doctor Who, Heartbeat
17 Blue Peter, You've Been Framed
18 Gardener's World, Emmerdale
19 Jane Eyre, Football 20 Sports Quiz, Local News

C

1 1 h 15 mins. 2 1 h 25 mins. 3 1 h 45 mins.
4 3 h 25 mins. 5 35 mins. 6 1 h. 33 mins.
7 You've Been Framed 8 Emmerdale 9 Gardener's World
10 Tennis 11 Local News 12 Football

Page 36

A

1 20 2 12 3 70 4 18 5 24 6 10
7 90 8 15 9 14 10 15 11 24 12 54
13 24 14 0 15 20 16 50 17 6 18 60
19 40 20 18 21 30 22 12 23 20 24 36
25 3 26 5 27 8 28 10 29 1 30 7
31 4 32 8 33 6 34 7 35 3 36 10
37 7 38 5 39 6 40 4 41 3 42 9
43 7 44 8 45 4 46 6 47 2 48 8

B

1 6 2 8 3 9 4 7 5 5 6 8
7 20 8 36 9 35 10 10 11 18 12 48
13

×	2	3	4
10	20	30	40
6	12	18	24
4	8	12	16

×	3	6	10
7	21	42	70
2	6	12	20
9	27	54	90

×	4	6	5
3	12	18	15
8	32	48	40
5	20	30	25

C

1 50 2 70 3 80 4 6 5 9 6 7
7 270 8 160 9 1000 10 360 11 320 12 450
13 30 14 125 15 82 16 59 17 43 18 136
19 6 20 14 21 11 22 27 23 52 24 18

Page 37

A

1 20 2 8 3 60 4 9 5 20 6 10 7 12
8 9 9 50 p 10 15 11 35 12 7 13 30

B

1 7 2 24 3 9 4 20 5 21 6 42
7 36 8 6, £2 change 9 34 10 8 11 36
12 7 13 (a) 24 (b) 60

C

1 56 2 6 3 180 4 4 5 6 6 £2.00
7 72 8 6 9 64 10 6, 20 cm left 11 £4.50
12 (a) 120 (b) 210

Page 38

A

1 30, 60, 180 3 e.g. All multiples of 10 end in 0.
4 90, 235, 140, 65 5 e.g. All multiples of 5 end in 0 or 5.
6 $8 \times 3 = 24$ $3 \times 8 = 24$ $24 \div 3 = 8$ $24 \div 8 = 3$
7 $5 \times 7 = 35$ $7 \times 5 = 35$ $35 \div 7 = 5$ $35 \div 5 = 7$

B

1 126, 954, 174, 561
2 24, 27, 42, 45, 54, 57, 72, 75, 246, 264, 426, 462, 624, 642, 456, 465, 546, 564, 645, 654, 567, 576, 657, 675, 756, 765, 267, 276, 627, 672, 726, 762
3 $12 \div 6 = 2$ $12 \div 2 = 6$ $2 \times 6 = 12$ $6 \times 2 = 12$
4 $3 \times 8 = 24$ $8 \times 3 = 24$ $24 \div 3 = 8$ $24 \div 8 = 3$
5 $36 \div 4 = 9$ $36 \div 9 = 4$ $9 \times 4 = 36$ $4 \times 9 = 36$
6 $7 \times 5 = 35$ $5 \times 7 = 35$ $35 \div 5 = 7$ $35 \div 7 = 5$
7 $6 \times 9 = 54$ 8 $540 \div 6 = 90$ 9 $540 \div 9 = 60$
10 $60 \times 9 = 540$ 11 $90 \times 6 = 540$ 12 $900 \times 6 = 5400$

C

1 (a) 630, 771, 894, 363, 135 (b) 630, 894
2 138, 174, 318, 348, 378, 384, 438, 714, 738, 1374, 1734, 3174, 3714, 7134, 7314
3 $6 \times 8 = 48$ $8 \times 6 = 48$ $48 \div 6 = 8$ $48 \div 8 = 6$
4 $72 \div 9 = 8$ $72 \div 8 = 9$ $8 \times 9 = 72$ $9 \times 8 = 72$
5 $7 \times 9 = 63$ $9 \times 7 = 63$ $63 \div 9 = 7$ $63 \div 7 = 9$
6 $60 \div 4 = 15$ $60 \div 15 = 4$ $15 \times 4 = 60$ $4 \times 15 = 60$
7 $80 \times 7 = 560$ 8 $80 \times 70 = 5600$
9 $5600 \div 7 = 800$ 10 $5600 \div 80 = 70$

Page 39

A

1 (c) 24 (d) 8 piles of 3 books 6 piles of 4 books

B

1 3 piles of 3 and 5 piles of 4 7 piles of 3 and 2 piles of 4
2 30 (accept 60, 90, etc.)

C

1 2 adult and 10 child tickets 6 adult and 3 child tickets

2 2 boxes of 6, 11 boxes of 8 6 boxes of 6, 8 boxes of 8
10 boxes of 6, 5 boxes of 8 14 boxes of 6, 2 boxes of 8

Page 40

A

1 (a) $\frac{1}{2}$ (b) one half **2** (a) $\frac{1}{8}$ (b) one eighth
3 (a) $\frac{1}{4}$ (b) one quarter **4** (a) $\frac{1}{10}$ (b) one tenth
5 (a) $\frac{1}{6}$ (b) one sixth **6** (a) $\frac{3}{4}$ (b) three quarters
7 (a) $\frac{3}{5}$ (b) three fifths **8** (a) $\frac{5}{8}$ (b) five eighths
9 (a) $\frac{2}{6}$ (b) two sixths **10** (a) $\frac{2}{3}$ (b) two thirds
11 5

B

1 (a) $\frac{1}{3}$ (b) one third **2** (a) $\frac{1}{4}$ (b) one quarter
3 (a) $\frac{3}{8}$ (b) three eighths **4** (a) $\frac{5}{8}$ (b) five eighths
5 (a) $\frac{4}{5}$ (b) four fifths **6** (a) $\frac{3}{4}$ (b) three quarters
7 (a) $\frac{5}{12}$ (b) five twelfths **8** (a) $\frac{4}{6}$ (b) four sixths
9 (a) $\frac{1}{9}$ (b) one ninth **10** (a) $\frac{6}{10}$ (b) six tenths
11 3

C

1 (a) $\frac{7}{16}$, seven sixteenths (b) $\frac{9}{16}$, nine sixteenths
2 (a) $\frac{3}{8}$, three eighths (b) $\frac{5}{8}$, five eighths
3 (a) $\frac{1}{4}$, one quarter (b) $\frac{3}{4}$, three quarters
4 (a) $\frac{7}{12}$, seven twelfths (b) $\frac{5}{12}$, five twelfths
5 (a) $\frac{4}{9}$, four ninths (b) $\frac{5}{9}$, five ninths
6 (a) $\frac{5}{8}$, five eighths (b) $\frac{3}{8}$, three eighths
7 (a) $\frac{3}{10}$, three tenths (b) $\frac{7}{10}$, seven tenths
8 (a) $\frac{1}{6}$, one sixth (b) $\frac{5}{6}$, five sixths
9 (a) $\frac{9}{16}$, nine sixteenths (b) $\frac{7}{16}$, seven sixteenths
10 (a) $\frac{4}{12}$, four twelfths (b) $\frac{8}{12}$, eight twelfths
11 $\frac{1}{24}$

Page 41

A

1 3 **2** 2 **3** 5 **4** 2 **5** 4 **6** 2 **7** 5
8 3 **9** 3 **10** 4 **11** 6 **12** 5 **13** 4 **14** 10

B

1 7 **2** 4 **3** 6 **4** 4 **5** 7 **6** 5
7 9 **8** 10 **9** 4 **10** 9 **11** 8 **12** 7
13 2 **14** 7 **15** 5 **16** 10

C

1 18 **2** 8 **3** 9 **4** 40 **5** £24 **6** 42 p
7 4.0 cm **8** 60 ml **9** 25 kg **10** 90 p **11** 40 g **12** 80 km
13 750 g **14** £2.00

Page 42

A

1 2 **2** 3 **3** 10 **4** 4 **5** 6 **6** 5
7 $\frac{4}{5}+\frac{1}{5}$ **8** $\frac{5}{8}+\frac{3}{8}$ **9** $\frac{2}{3}+\frac{1}{3}$ **10** $\frac{4}{6}+\frac{2}{6}$ **11** $\frac{3}{4}+\frac{1}{4}$ **12** $\frac{3}{5}+\frac{2}{5}$

B

1 $\frac{2}{3}$ **2** $\frac{3}{10}$ **3** $\frac{2}{8}$ **4** $\frac{3}{4}$ **5** $\frac{3}{6}$ **6** $\frac{3}{5}$
7 $\frac{1}{8}$ **8** $\frac{6}{10}$ **9** $\frac{5}{8}$ **10** $\frac{1}{10}$

C

1 $\frac{3}{4}+\frac{2}{4}$ **2** $1\frac{2}{5}$ **3** $\frac{72}{100}+\frac{50}{100}$ **4** $\frac{5}{7}+\frac{6}{7}$
5 $\frac{2}{3}+\frac{2}{3}$ **6** $\frac{7}{10}+\frac{6}{10}$ **7** $\frac{8}{9}+\frac{8}{9}$ **8** $\frac{64}{100}+\frac{47}{100}$
9 $\frac{5}{8}+\frac{7}{8}$ **10** $\frac{9}{12}+\frac{6}{12}$ **11** $\frac{6}{9}$ **12** $\frac{7}{10}$

Page 43

A

1 $\frac{2}{4}$ **2** $\frac{2}{6}$ **3** $\frac{5}{10}$ **4** $\frac{2}{8}$ **5** $\frac{4}{8}$ **6** $\frac{2}{10}$
7 $\frac{3}{6}$ **8** $\frac{10}{10}$ **9** $\frac{1}{4}=\frac{2}{8}$ **10** $\frac{1}{3}=\frac{2}{6}$ **11** $\frac{1}{2}=\frac{2}{4}$ **12** $\frac{1}{2}=\frac{3}{6}$

B

1 $\frac{5}{5}$ **2** $\frac{4}{8}$ **3** $\frac{8}{10}$ **4** $\frac{4}{6}$ **5** $\frac{6}{10}$ **6** $\frac{6}{8}$
7 $\frac{6}{6}$ **8** $\frac{4}{10}$ **9** $\frac{1}{2}=\frac{6}{12}$ **10** $\frac{3}{4}=\frac{9}{12}$ **11** $\frac{3}{5}=\frac{6}{10}$ **12** $\frac{1}{4}=\frac{2}{8}$

C

1 $\frac{4}{16}$ **2** $\frac{2}{12}$ **3** $\frac{6}{12}$ **4** $\frac{5}{6}$ **5** $\frac{4}{12}$ **6** $\frac{6}{12}$
7 $\frac{2}{3}$ **8** $\frac{2}{6}$ **9** $>$ **10** $=$ **11** $=$ **12** $<$
13 $>$ **14** $=$ **15** $=$ **16** $>$ **17** $=$ **18** $>$
19 $<$ **20** $<$

Page 44

A

1 (a) $\frac{2}{10}$ (b) 0.2 **2** (a) $\frac{6}{10}$ (b) 0.6 **3** (a) $\frac{3}{10}$ (b) 0.3
4 (a) $\frac{9}{10}$ (b) 0.9 **5** (a) $\frac{4}{10}$ (b) 0.4 **6** (a) $\frac{1}{10}$ (b) 0.1
7 (a) $\frac{8}{10}$ (b) 0.8 **8** (a) $\frac{5}{10}$ (b) 0.5 **9** £$\frac{7}{10}$ = £0.70 = 70 p
10 £$\frac{3}{10}$ = £0.30 = 30 p **11** £$\frac{1}{10}$ = £0.10 = 10 p **12** £$\frac{4}{10}$ = £0.40 = 40 p
13 £$\frac{9}{10}$ = £0.90 = 90 p **14** £$\frac{2}{10}$ = £0.20 = 20 p

B

1 (a) $\frac{25}{100}$ (b) 0.25 **2** (a) $\frac{74}{100}$ (b) 0.74
3 (a) $\frac{52}{100}$ (b) 0. 52 **4** (a) $\frac{19}{100}$ (b) 0.19
5 (a) $\frac{67}{100}$ (b) 0.67 **6** (a) $\frac{31}{100}$ (b) 0.31
7 (a) $\frac{98}{100}$ (b) 0.98 **8** (a) $\frac{43}{100}$ (b) 0.43
9 $\frac{3}{10}+\frac{2}{100}=\frac{32}{100}=0.32$ **10** $\frac{5}{10}+\frac{8}{100}=\frac{58}{100}=0.58$
11 $\frac{2}{10}+\frac{7}{100}=\frac{27}{100}=0.27$ **12** $\frac{9}{10}+\frac{1}{100}=\frac{91}{100}=0.91$
13 $\frac{4}{10}+\frac{6}{100}=\frac{46}{100}=0.46$ **14** $\frac{8}{10}+\frac{3}{100}=\frac{83}{100}=0.83$

C

1 $\frac{67}{100}$ **2** $\frac{91}{100}$ **3** $\frac{2}{10}$ **4** $\frac{55}{100}$ **5** $\frac{3}{100}$ **6** $\frac{14}{100}$
7 $\frac{3}{10}$ **8** $\frac{85}{100}$ **9** $\frac{47}{100}$ **10** $\frac{8}{100}$ **11** $\frac{99}{100}$ **12** $\frac{61}{100}$
13 0.36 **14** 0.9 **15** 0.19 **16** 0.81 **17** 0.45 **18** 0.05
19 0.72 **20** 0.29 **21** 0.8 **22** 0.18 **23** 0.04 **24** 0.65

Page 45 (top half)

A

1 50 **2** 10 **3** 60 **4** 80 **5** 20 **6** 35
7 65 **8** 25 **9** 85 **10** 45

B

1 52 **2** 31 **3** 9 **4** 63 **5** 16 **6** 84
7 28 **8** 55 **9** 72 **10** 47

C

1 240 **2** 660 **3** 770 **4** 390 **5** 520 **6** 30
7 480 **8** 810 **9** 150 **10** 640

Page 45 (bottom half)

A

1 6 **2** 4 **3** 9 **4** 7 **5** 18 **6** 23
7 14 **8** 8 **9** 19 **10** 13

B

1 5 **2** 112 **3** 8 **4** 8 **5** 107 **6** 210
7 17 **8** 58 **9** 32 **10** 19

C

1 604 – 418 **2** 703 – 429 **3** 6000 – 2125
4 512 – 315 **5** 915 – 417 **6** 6018 – 2025
79012 – 4014 **8** 9000 – 3307 **9** 7000 – 3124
10 3008 – 1023

Page 46

A

1 10p = £$\frac{1}{10}$ = £0.10 **2** 20p = £$\frac{2}{10}$ = £0.20
3 30p = £$\frac{3}{10}$ = £0.30 **4** 40p = £$\frac{4}{10}$ = £0.40
5 50p = £$\frac{5}{10}$ = £0.50 **6** 60p = £$\frac{6}{10}$ = £0.60
7 70p = £$\frac{7}{10}$ = £0.70 **8** 80p = £$\frac{8}{10}$ = £0.80
9 90p = £$\frac{9}{10}$ = £0.90 **10** 100p = £$\frac{10}{10}$ = £1.00
11 £2.30 **12** £5.91 **13** £1.04 **14** £0.25 **15** £6.59
16 £0.42 **17** £8.17 **18** £4.03 **19** 1.2 m **20** 0.85 m
21 4.96 m **22** 0.3 m **23** 6.38 m **24** 2.17 m **25** 0.56 m
26 7.4 m **27** (a) $\frac{2}{10}$ (b) 0.2 **28** (a) $\frac{5}{10}$ (b) 0.5
29 (a) $\frac{9}{10}$ (b) 0.9

Page 47

B

1 (a) 20 cm (b) 0.2 m **2** (a) 50 cm (b) 0.5 m
3 (a) 90 cm (b) 0.9 m **4** (a) 110 cm (b) 1.1 m
5 (a) 130 cm (b) 1.3 m **6** (a) 170 cm (b) 1.7 m
7 80 p **8** £4 **9** 2 p **10** £5 **11** £10 **12** 10 p
13 3 m **14** 60 cm **15** 20 m **16** 6 cm **17** 50 cm **18** 6 m
19 0.5 m 0.6 m 0.7 m 0.8 m
20 1.0 m 1.2 m 1.4 m 1.6 m
21 2.5 m 3.0 m 3.5 m 4.0 m
22 £0.90 £1.10 £1.30 £1.50
23 £0.25 £0.30 £0.35 £0.40
24 £0.10 £0.12 £0.14 £0.16
25 0.7 m **26** 0.5 m **27** 1.8 m **28** 1.7 m **29** 0.4 m **30** 0.3 m
31 1.2 m **32** 1.2 m **33** £0.80 **34** £0.60 **35** £1.90 **36** £1.70
37 £0.20 **38** £0.50 **39** £1.40 **40** £1.20

C

1 3.17 **2** 1.82 **3** 4.35 **4** 3.6 **5** 0.41 **6** 2.03
7 $\frac{9}{10}$ **8** 10 **9** 4 **10** $\frac{7}{10}$ **11** $\frac{9}{10}$ **12** 6
13 $\frac{9}{10}$ **14** 30 **15** $\frac{7}{10}$ **16** 7 **17** $\frac{3}{10}$ **18** $\frac{7}{100}$
19 $\frac{2}{10}$ **20** $\frac{4}{100}$ **21** 5 **22** 8 **23** $\frac{3}{100}$ **24** $\frac{5}{10}$
25 1.9 **26** 3.0 **27** 1.0 **28** 0.9 **29** 4.3 **30** 3.4
31 1.8 **32** 0.8 **33** 1.0 **34** 1.7 **35** 0.4 **36** 1.3
37 3.4 **38** 3.2 **39** 2.4 **40** 3.9

Page 48

A

1 92 **2** 94 **3** 117 **4** 126 **5** 114 **6** 120
7 153 **8** 132 **9** 123 **10** 183 **11** 161

B

1 272 **2** 480 **3** 432 **4** 593 **5** 784 **6** 536
7 543 **8** 711 **9** 889 **10** 794 **11** 349 **12** 383

C

1 821 **2** 915 **3** 1104 **4** 1204 **5** 1233 **6** 754
7 1480 **8** 1471 **9** 971 **10** 1211 **11** 1264 **12** 664

Page 49

A

1 23 **2** 18 **3** 36 **4** 38 **5** 26 **6** 19
7 27 **8** 28 **9** 47 **10** 39 **11** 56 years

B

1 72 **2** 185 **3** 275 **4** 86 **5** 513 **6** 203
7 351 **8** 529 **9** 83 **10** 225 **11** 87 **12** 74

C

1 1086 **2** 1176 **3** 485 **4** 345 **5** 140 **6** 514
7 1189 **8** 2285 **9** 176 **10** 1465 **11** 155 **12** 124

Page 50

A

1 12 **2** 15 **3** 30 **4** 40 **5** 14 **6** 48
7 20 **8** 27 **9** 10 **10** 28 **11** 18 **12** 60
13 2 **14** 3 **15** 5 **16** 9 **17** 6 **18** 4
19 7 **20** 8 **21** 9 **22** 2 **23** 8 **24** 4

B

1 5 **2** 9 **3** 2 **4** 7 **5** 9 **6** 3
7 24 **8** 10 **9** 24 **10** 70 **11** 54 **12** 8
13 160 **14** 420 **15** 450 **16** 120 **17** 90 **18** 1000
19 320 **20** 180 **21** 160 **22** 450 **23** 800 **24** 300
25 50 **26** 100 **27** 20 **28** 90 **29** 40 **30** 80
31 50 **32** 60 **33** 70 **34** 30 **35** 40 **36** 90

C

1 9 **2** 6 **3** 5 **4** 90 **5** 40 **6** 70
7 200 **8** 160 **9** 300 **10** 150 **11** 100 **12** 300
13 21 **14** 70 **15** 42 **16** 49 **17** 40 **18** 72
19 16 **20** 48 **21** 27 **22** 63 **23** 36 **24** 72
25 5 **26** 8 **27** 4 **28** 9 **29** 3 **30** 7
31 8 **32** 4 **33** 5 **34** 10 **35** 6 **36** 9

Page 51 (top half)

A

1 70 **2** 620 **3** 450 **4** 82 **5** 49 **6** 100
7 300 **8** 700 **9** 1000 **10** 5 **11** 4 **12** 10

B

1 290 **2** 5720 **3** 4000 **4** 1380 **5** 2800 **6** 6500
7 10 000 **8** 7900 **9** 90 **10** 358 **11** 240 **12** 761
13 20 **14** 13 **15** 5 **16** 38

C

1 14 700 **2** 82 600 **3** 439 × 100 **4** 160 × 10
5 387 × 100 **6** 7125 × 10 **7** 9460 **8** 20
9 5200 ÷ 100 **10** 35 100 ÷ 10 **11** 47 800 ÷ 100 **12** 6900 ÷ 10

Page 51 (bottom half)

A

1 60 **2** 80 **3** 200 **4** 150 **5** 120 **6** 100
7 100 **8** 90 **9** 160 **10** 60 **11** 250 **12** 120

B

1 150 **2** 240 **3** 90 × 4 **4** 70 × 5 **5** 3 × 30
6 5 × 20 **7** 40 **8** 70 **9** 180 ÷ 9 **10** 400 ÷ 5
11 240 ÷ 4 **12** 300 ÷ 6

C

1 3200 **2** 4500 **3** 700 × 6 **4** 200 × 8 **5** 900 × 6
6 300 × 7 **7** 600 **8** 400 **9** 2400 ÷ 3 **10** 6300 ÷ 7
11 5600 ÷ 8 **12** 3600 ÷ 6

Page 52

A

1 28 **2** 45 **3** 85 **4** 52 **5** 58 **6** 165
7 108 **8** 100 **9** 69 **10** 90 cm **11** £1.16 **12** 68 p

B

1 48 **2** 130 **3** 78 **4** 147 **5** 112 **6** 141
7 245 **8** 340 **9** 184 **10** 288 **11** 301 **12** 264
13 268 **14** 405 **15** 189 **16** 216 **17** 144 **18** £4.95
19 384

C

1 508 **2** 645 **3** 1498 **4** 1224 **5** 1344 **6** 1476
7 966 **8** 2056 **9** 184 **10** 2925 **11** 301 **12** 1503
13 1440 **14** 3752 **15** 1372 **16** 2565 **17** £596 **18** 3206
19 1 kg 960 g **20** 1 litre 50 ml

Page 53

A

1 13 **2** 12 **3** 16 **4** 15 **5** 14 **6** 13
7 17 **8** 16 **9** 18 **10** 19 **11** 15 **12** 19
13 13 **14** 19 **15** 17 **16** 18 **17** 13 r 1 **18** 16 r 1
19 16 r 3 **20** 16 r 3

B

1 18 **2** 19 **3** 16 **4** 14 **5** 23 **6** 12
7 34 **8** 14 **9** 24 **10** 18 **11** 34 **12** 17
13 28 **14** 17 **15** 29 **16** 22 **17** £17 **18** 21

C

1 19 **2** 21 **3** 22 **4** 18 **5** 21 **6** 15
7 18 r 5 **8** 25 **9** 27 **10** 23 **11** 29 **12** 22
13 24 **14** 31 **15** 23 r 7 **16** 34 **17** 28 **18** 35 litres
19 264

Page 54

A

1 11, 12 **2** 8, 9 **3** 19, 20 **4** 25, 26 **5** 4, 10 **6** 6, 14
7 13, 17 **8** 49, 51 **9** 2, 3 **10** 2, 7 **11** 4, 5 **12** 2, 10
13 There are 55 possible solutions.

B

1 3, 4, 5 **2** 8, 9, 10 **3** 12, 13, 14 **4** 29, 30, 31
5 Ramiz is correct.
1 + 2 + 3 = 6 2 + 3 + 4 = 9 3 + 4 + 5 = 12 etc.
6 3, 4 **7** 6, 7 **8** 9, 10 **9** 8, 9
10 32 **11** 91 **12** There are 45 possible solutions.

C

1 Lucie is not correct e. g. 1 + 2 + 3 + 4 = 10
2 11, 12 **3** 14, 15 **4** 17, 18 **5** 12, 13
6 19, 20 **7** 15, 16 **8** 22, 23 **9** 20, 21
10 24, 25 **11** 26, 27 **12** 30, 31 **13** 28, 29
14 4, 5, 6 **15** 8, 9, 10 **16** 14, 15, 16 **17** 19, 20, 21
18 32, 33, 34 **19** 110, 111, 112 **20** 41, 42, 43 **21** 100, 101, 102
22 86, 87, 88 **23** 36, 37, 38 **24** 149, 150, 151 **25** 78, 79, 80
26 There are 55 possible solutions.

Page 55

A

1 20 **2** 24 **3** 10 **4** 12 **5** 36 **6** 30
7 14 **8** 45 **9** 60 **10** 48 **11** 3 **12** 20
13 100 **14** 8 **15** 28 **16** 15 **17** 18 **18** 54
19 0 **20** 35 **21** 16 **22** 18 **23** 40 **24** 15
25 4 **26** 9 **27** 5 **28** 7 **29** 8 **30** 3
31 9 **32** 1 **33** 7 **34** 6 **35** 8 **36** 10
37 5 **38** 4 **39** 9 **40** 3 **41** 5 **42** 6
43 10 **44** 6 **45** 8 **46** 4 **47** 3 **48** 6

B

1 7 **2** 6 **3** 8 **4** 9 **5** 2 **6** 7
7 16 **8** 18 **9** 45 **10** 36 **11** 50 **12** 28
13 3 **14** 5 **15** 2 **16** 4 **17** 10 **18** 6
19 4 **20** 3 **21** 5 **22** 2 **23** 10 **24** 6

C

1 8 **2** 9 **3** 7 **4** 90 **5** 80 **6** 100
7 180 **8** 300 **9** 200 **10** 300 **11** 210 **12** 480
13 240 **14** £4.50 **15** £2.70 **16** 280 ml **17** 8

Page 56

A

1 16 **2** 7 **3** 20 **4** 9 **5** 40 **6** 6
7 12 **8** 9 **9** 35 **10** 8 **11** 18 **12** 6
13 28 **14** 8 **15** 30 p **16** 24

B

1 36 **2** 4 **3** 3 **4** 63 **5** 20 **6** 8
7 42 **8** 36 p **9** 5 **10** 5

C

1 240 **2** 7 hours **3** 6 **4** 720 **5** 5 **6** 420 g
7 4 litres **8** £540 **9** 6 **10** 2.8 km

Page 57

A

1 24 **2** 12 **3** 40 **4** 4 **5** 20 **6** 32
7 8 **8** 28 **9** 16 **10** 36 **11** 32 **12** 8
13 64 **14** 40 **15** 16 **16** 80 **17** 56 **18** 24
19 72 **20** 48
21

Twos	2	4	6	8	10	12	14	16	18	20
Fours	4	8	12	16	20	24	28	32	36	40
Eights	8	16	24	32	40	48	56	64	72	80

B

1 24	**2** 80	**3** 48	**4** 0	**5** 72	**6** 32
7 56	**8** 8	**9** 64	**10** 40	**11** 10	**12** 3
13 9	**14** 6	**15** 1	**16** 8	**17** 4	**18** 7
19 5	**20** 2	**21** 5	**22** 3	**23** 6	**24** 2
25 9	**26** 7	**27** 4	**28** 8	**29** 24	**30** 56
31 8	**32** 32	**33** 64	**34** 48	**35** 40	**36** 72

C

1 320	**2** 160	**3** 560	**4** 400	**5** 640	**6** 480
7 240	**8** 720	**9** 40	**10** 20	**11** 60	**12** 30
13 80	**14** 70	**15** 90	**16** 50	**17** 32	**18** 80
19 112	**20** 48	**21** 144	**22** 96	**23** 128	**24** 64
25 320	**26** 480	**27** 232 miles		**28** 288	

Page 58

A

1 4	**2** 6	**3** 16	**4** 10	**5** 14	**6** 18
7 8	**8** 12	**9** 80	**10** 120	**11** 180	**12** 20
13 160	**14** 60	**15** 140	**16** 100	**17** 30	**18** 34
19 24	**20** 36	**21** 26	**22** 32	**23** 28	**24** 38
25 8	**26** 6	**27** 9	**28** 7	**29** 30	**30** 50
31 40	**32** 20	**33** 15	**34** 35	**35** 25	**36** 45

B

1 46	**2** 62	**3** 44	**4** 70	**5** 88	**6** 58
7 50	**8** 76	**9** 54	**10** 90	**11** 72	**12** 98
13 48	**14** 74	**15** 56	**16** 92	**17** 11	**18** 23
19 42	**20** 34	**21** 21	**22** 13	**23** 32	**24** 44
25 17	**26** 29	**27** 36	**28** 18	**29** 47	**30** 26
31 38	**32** 48	**33** 128	**34** 112	**35** 156	**36** 186
37 134	**38** 118	**39** 81	**40** 67	**41** 79	**42** 89
43 58	**44** 87				

C

1 31	**2** 38	**3** 68	**4** 92	**5** 760	**6** 690
7 3900	**8** 580	**9** 184	**10** 152	**11** 118	**12** 108
13 1540	**14** 1960	**15** 14 600	**16** 17 200	**17** 286	**18** 312
19 334	**20** 348	**21** 276	**22** 358	**23** 370	**24** 394
25 122	**26** 169	**27** 128	**28** 177	**29** 196	**30** 148
31 159	**32** 188				

Page 59

A

1 A regular hexagon	B quadrilateral	C equilateral triangle
D irregular heptagon	E square	F right-angled triangle
G irregular hexagon	H quadrilateral	I rectangle
J triangle	K irregular pentagon	L square
M irregular hexagon	N regular octagon	O rectangle
P isosceles triangle	Q regular pentagon	R irregular octagon

B

1 D, M, R   **3** A, C, E, H, I, L, N, O, P, Q

Page 60

B

1 6	**2** 6	**3** 8	**4** 6	**5** 8	**6** 12
7 7	**8** 9	**9** 8	**10** 7	**11** 10	**12** 6
13 7	**14** 8	**15** 9			

C

1 3	**2** 6	**3** 8	**4** 10	**5** 4	**6** 4
7 9	**8** 11	**9** 24	**10** 17	**11** 2	**12** 6
13 13	**14** 4	**15** 9			

Page 61

A

1 square based pyramid	**2** cylinder
3 triangular based prism	**4** hemisphere
5 hexagonal based prism	**6** cuboid
7 sphere	**8** octagonal based prism
9 cone	**10** cube
11 triangular based pyramid	**12** pentagonal based prism

B

1 4 triangles	**2** 2 pentagons, 5 rectangles
3 6 squares	**4** 2 hexagons, 6 rectangles
5 cuboid	**6** square based pyramid
7 hexagonal based prism	**8** cylinder
9 octagonal based prism	**10** triangular based prism

C

1 cube, cuboid
2 (a) cone, cylinder, hemisphere
(b) triangular and square based pyramids, triangular based prism
3 triangular based pyramid
4 (a)8   (b) 9

Page 62

A

1 2 m	**2** 1m 50 cm	**3** 300 cm
4 550 cm	**5** 1 km	**6** 3 km 500 m
7 5000 m	**8** 4500 m	**9** 3 kg
10 1 kg 500 g	**11** 4 litres	**12** 2 litres 500 ml
13 metres	**14** grams	**15** kilometres
16 litres		

B

1 4 cm 7 mm	**2** 2 cm 4 mm	**3** 59 mm
4 11 mm	**5** 1 m 20 cm	**6** 0 m 34 cm
7 820 cm	**8** 670 cm	**9** 1kg 600g
10 3 litres 200 ml	**11** 1400g	**12** 2700 ml
13 millilitres	**14** centimetres	**15** millimetres
16 kilograms		

C

1 18 mm	**2** 43 mm	**3** 2.6 cm	**4** 3.2 cm
5 115 cm	**6** 60 cm	**7** 2.2 m	**8** 0.75 m
9 6.3 km	**10** 2.7 km	**11** 7250 m	**12** 5600 m
13 3 kg	**14** 2 litres	**15** 1 g	**16** 50 mm

Page 63

A

1 1 kg, 2 kg	**2** 150 g, 300 g	**3** 4 mm, 7 mm
4 2 cm, 8 cm	**5** 1 litre, 1.5 litres	**6** 100 ml, 300 ml
7 15 mm, 23 mm	**8** 42 cm, 52 cm	**9** 1 kg, 2.5 kg
10 50 g, 75 g		

B

1 1.5 kg, 3.5 kg	**2** 10 g, 50 g	**3** 4 mm, 18 mm
4 40 cm, 70 cm	**5** 0.25 litres, 0.75 litres	**6** 25 ml, 150 ml
7 33 cm, 42 cm	**8** 8 cm, 15 cm	**9** 0.25 kg, 1.5 kg
10 500 g, 750 g		

C

1 0.25 kg, 1.5 kg	**2** 125 g, 375 g	**3** 84 cm, 96 cm
4 28 cm, 34 cm	**5** 1.7 litres, 3.2 litres	**6** 25 ml, 150 ml
7 47 mm, 56 mm	**8** 88 mm, 97 mm	**9** 1.2 kg, 3.6 kg
10 375 g, 750 g		

Page 64

A

1

Drinks	Total
Blackcurrant	6
Cola	8
Lemonade	4
Orange	10

2

Instrument	Total
Cello	11
Guitar	4
Piano	8
Violin	5

Page 65

B

1

Pet	Total
cat	7
dog	15
hamster	2
rabbit	6

2 (a)

	walk	not walk
over 133 cm	B H M O Q R U X Y A_2 C_2	E G J S B_2
not over 133 cm	D F K L V	A C I N P T W Z D_2

(b) Hugh was right.

C

1

Height (cm)	121–125	126–130	131–135	136–140	141–145
Total	3	6	9	7	5

2 (a)

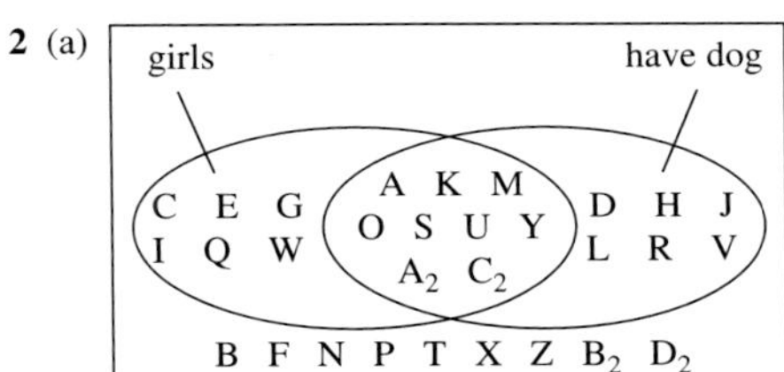

(b) Girls in class 4 were more likely than boys to have a dog.

3 (a)

	walk	not walk
have dog	D H K L M O R U V Y A2 C2	A J S
not have dog	B F Q X	C E G I N P T W Z B2 D2

(b) Children who had dogs were more likely to walk to school than those who did not have dogs.

Page 66

A

1 (a) 12 (b) 14 (c) Wednesday (d) Friday
(e) Friday (f) 4 (g) 6 (h) 60
(i) 12 (j) 30

2

Day	Apples sold
Monday	14
Tuesday	10
Wednesday	16
Thursday	12
Friday	8

Page 67

B

1 (a) 25 (b) pistachio (c) 20 (d) 25
(e) vanilla, chocolate (f) mint (g) 170

2

Flavour	Total sold
Chocolate	40
Coffee	25
Mint	15
Pistachio	30
Strawberry	20
Vanilla	40

C

1 (a) 250 (b) 125 (c) 25 (d) 175
(e) 9 pm performance, e.g. Few children in the audience.
(f) 1350
(g) weekend e.g. large afternoon audiences for a family film
(h) $8\frac{1}{2}$

2

Performance	Audience
1 pm	250
3 pm	275
5 pm	450
7 pm	250
9 pm	125

Page 68

A

1 (a) 0.5 cm (b) 2 cm (c) 3.5 cm (d) 4.5 cm (e) 6 cm
(f) 7.5 cm (g) 8.5 cm (h) 10 cm (i) 11.5 cm
2 13 cm **3** 8.5 cm **4** 4.5 cm **5** 14.5 cm **6** 6 cm
7 10.5 cm **8** 3.5 cm

B

1 (a) 0.3 cm (b) 1.7 cm (c) 3.4 cm (d) 4.9 cm (e) 6.6 cm
(f) 8.1 cm (g) 9.8 cm (h) 11.2 cm (i) 12.7 cm (j) 14.3 cm
2 12.2 cm **3** 9.8 cm **4** 15.1 cm **5** 5.7 cm **6** 9.4 cm
7 7.3 cm **8** 14.8 cm

C

1 allow +/– 0.1 cm
(a) 6.8 cm, 4.2 cm, 6.4 cm (b) 17.4 cm
(a) 8.2 cm, 3.3 cm, 7.7 cm, 3.6 cm (b) 22.8 cm
(a) 8.8 cm, 2.7 cm, 6.2 cm, 4.3 cm (b) 22.0 cm
(a) 6.7 cm, 3.6 cm, 5.7 cm (b) 16.0 cm

Page 70

A

1 14 cm **2** 14 cm **3** 18 cm **4** 16 cm **5** 12 cm
6 18 cm **7** 24 cm **8** 22 cm **9** 32 cm
10 sides of 5 cm

Page 71

B

Allow +/– 0.2 cm for (1) to (3).
1 16.0 cm **2** 12.8 cm **3** 14.2 cm
4 10 cm, 12 cm, 12 cm, 14 cm

C

1

Length	3	7	10	6	6	15	18	11	20	8
Width	4	3	8	5	2	9	12	5	4	7
Perimeter	14	20	36	22	16	48	60	32	48	30

2 32 cm **3** 34 cm **4** 80 cm **5** 52 cm **6** 15 cm **7** 22 cm
8 17.4 cm **9** 17.8 cm

Page 72

A

1 500 cm **2** 200 cm **3** 600 cm **4** 3 m **5** 1 m
6 4 m **7** 3000 m **8** 7000 m **9** 4000 m **10** 6 km
11 1 km **12** 10 km **13** 5 km **14** $\frac{1}{2}$ m **15** 40 cm
16 $\frac{1}{2}$ km

B

1 6 cm **2** 0.5 cm **3** 3 cm 5 mm **4** 20 mm
5 0.41 m **6** 1.93 m **7** 7 m 60 cm **8** 58 cm
9 0.5 km **10** 2.75 km **11** 250 m **12** 1 km 300 m
13 millimetres **14** kilometres **15** centimetres **16** millimetres

C

1 1 cm 8 mm **2** 9 mm **3** 0.4 cm **4** 5.2 cm
5 3 m 67 cm **6** 83 cm **7** 4.9 m **8** 0.09 m
9 738 m **10** 2 km 100 m **11** 0.96 km **12** 1.45 km
13 < **14** > **15** < **16** = **17** < **18** =
19 > **20** =

Page 73

A

1 79 **2** 123 **3** 124 **4** 131 **5** 170 **6** 44
7 26 **8** 17 **9** 27 **10** 51 **11** 34

B

1 302 **2** 622 **3** 774 **4** 919 **5** 555 **6** 704
7 74 **8** 139 **9** 262 **10** 537 **11** 154 **12** 231

C

1 2270 **2** 2540 **3** 5464 **4** 5437 **5** 7941 **6** 515
7 4278 **8** 4732 **9** 1553 **10** 1918 **11** 1153 **12** £574

Page 74

A

1 64 **2** 95 **3** 62 **4** 78 **5** 100 **6** 84
7 94 **8** 130 **9** 18 **10** 15 **11** 16 **12** 14
13 14 **14** 19 **15** 14 **16** 26 **17** 95p **18** 18
19 144 **20** 16

B

1 340 **2** 270 **3** 208 **4** 261 **5** 371 **6** 378
7 432 **8** 222 **9** 13 **10** 28 r 1 **11** 19 **12** 16 r 3
13 17 r 3 **14** 17 r 4 **15** 15 r 1 **16** 18 **17** 23 **18** 17

C

1 1309 **2** 1720 **3** 1176 **4** 1431 **5** 1722 **6** 1428
7 3366 **8** 1512 **9** 24 **10** 27 r 7 **11** 24 r 4 **12** 38
13 25 r 5 **14** 35 r 2 **15** 23 r 4 **16** 28 r 4 **17** £870 **18** 39
19 £2232 **20** 64 g

Page 75

A

1 71 cm **2** 28 **3** £14 **4** 72 **5** £57, £131

B

1 38 cm **2** £2.53 **3** 560 ml **4** 20 m **5** Sanjay 38 kg
Kumar 34 kg

C

1 53 cm **2** 1224 **3** 185 miles **4** £8.15 **5** 1.175 litres **6** £13.49

Page 76

A

1 greater **2** right ∠ **3** less **4** greater
5 right ∠ **6** less **7** 6 o'clock **8** 6 o'clock
9 6 o'clock **10** 3 o'clock **11** 3 o'clock **12** 9 o'clock
13 180° **14** 90° **15** 90° **16** 180°
17 360° **18** 180° **19** 180° **20** 90°

Page 77

B

1 4 o'clock **2** 5 o'clock **3** 4 o'clock **4** 11 o'clock
5 2 o'clock **6** 7 o'clock **7** 1 o'clock **8** 2 o'clock
9 90° **10** 180° **11** 90° **12** 360°
13 90° **14** 180° **15** 90°
16 90° **17** A C D B **18** 360°

C

1 8 o'clock **2** 6 o'clock **3** 7 o'clock **4** 1 o'clock
5 11 o'clock **6** 12 o'clock **7** 3 o'clock **8** 9 o'clock
9 90° **10** 45° **11** 180° **12** 45°
13 90° **14** 45° **15** 45° **16** 180°
17 A B C **18** D B C A **19** C A B **20** D C A B
21 180°

Page 78

A

1 ○ blue **2** □ green **3** □ green **4** ◇ yellow
5 ◇ red **6** ◇ green **7** □ red **8** □ yellow

B

1 Garbury **2** Charing **3** Ashdean **4** Farham
5 Emford **6** Garbury **7** Charing **8** Ashdean
9 S **10** NE **11** E **12** SE
13 SW **14** NW **15** N **16** SW

C

1 WORD **2** PAIN **3** MOVE **4** BURN
5 Start at D NE5 W2 S6 **6** Start at M NE2 NW2 NE1
7 Start at K N5 W5 SE5 **8** Start at H NW1 E3 N3
9 Start at L NW2 S3 SE2 **10** Start at G S2 SE2 NW3
11 Start at H NW1 W1 N3 SE2 **12** Start at Q NW2 SW2 W1 N3
13 Start at F SW4 NW2 N2 SE1 **14** Start at B NE3 W1 N2 S3 NW2
15 Start at S N1 NW1 E2 NW3 SE2
16 Start at S NW2 E1 NW2 S4 E6

Page 79

A

1 25 **2** 36 **3** 48 **4** 24 **5** 42 **6** 0
7 40 **8** 45 **9** 64 **10** 18 **11** 28 **12** 54
13 8 **14** 9 **15** 8 **16** 6 **17** 7 **18** 9
19 10 **20** 8 **21** 6 **22** 9 **23** 8 **24** 7

B

1 28 **2** 56 **3** 21 **4** 49 **5** 63 **6** 35
7 14 **8** 42 **9** 3 **10** 5 **11** 7 **12** 2
13 6 **14** 9 **15** 4 **16** 8 **17** 5 **18** 7
19 4 **20** 9 **21** 21 **22** 42 **23** 14 **24** 56
25 3 **26** 8 **27** 10 **28** 7 **29** 28 **30** 63
31 35 **32** 140

C

1 140 **2** 350 **3** 560 **4** 280 **5** 490 **6** 210
7 630 **8** 420 **9** 70 **10** 40 **11** 20 **12** 80
13 50 **14** 30 **15** 60 **16** 90 **17** 70 **18** 28

19 84 **20** 126 **21** 42 **22** 112 **23** 56 **24** 98

25 364 **26** 32 **27** 91 **28** 363

Page 80

A

4 5 meals for adults costing £25 and 3 meals for children costing £9

or

2 meals for adults costing £10 and 8 meals for children costing £24.

B

1 23

2 3 bags of apples, 9 bags of oranges 6 bags of apples, 1 bag of oranges

C

1 13 four min. and 3 five min. songs

8 four min. and 7 five min. songs

3 four min. and 11 five min. songs

2 (a) 75 (accept 111, 147, etc.)

(b) 12 bags of 4, 3 bags of 9, 3 bags of 4, 7 bags of 9

Page 81

A

1 $\frac{3}{3}$ **2** $\frac{10}{10}$ **3** $\frac{6}{6}$ **4** $\frac{8}{8}$

5 4 quarters **6** 2 halves **7** 5 fifths **8** 100 hundredths

9 $2, 2\frac{1}{2}, 3, 3\frac{1}{2}$ **10** $1\frac{2}{3}, 2, 2\frac{1}{3}, 2\frac{2}{3}$

11 $1, 1\frac{1}{5}, 1\frac{2}{5}, 1\frac{3}{5}$ **12** $\frac{5}{6}, 1, 1\frac{1}{6}, 1\frac{2}{6}$

B

1 $2\frac{3}{4}$ **2** $3\frac{1}{3}$ **3** $4\frac{5}{8}$ **4** $1\frac{5}{6}$ **5** $3\frac{1}{2}$ **6** $2\frac{1}{4}$

7 $1\frac{2}{5}$ **8** $4\frac{3}{8}$ **9** $1\frac{2}{3}$ **10** $1\frac{1}{2}$ **11** $1\frac{3}{10}$ **12** $2\frac{2}{6}$

13 $4\frac{4}{5}$ **14** $1\frac{5}{8}$ **15** $3\frac{1}{3}$ **16** $1\frac{1}{6}$

C

1 $3\frac{6}{10}$ **2** $5\frac{1}{2}$ **3** $1\frac{5}{7}$ **4** $4\frac{3}{4}$ **5** $1\frac{68}{100}$ **6** $7\frac{2}{3}$

7 $1\frac{5}{12}$ **8** $7\frac{3}{5}$ **9** 23 sevenths **10** 37 quarters

11 84 tenths **12** 31 sixths **13** 17 fifths

14 49 eighths **15** 23 thirds **16** 491 hundredths

17 $1\frac{4}{5}, 2\frac{1}{5}, 2\frac{3}{5}, 3$ **18** $3, 3\frac{2}{3}, 4\frac{1}{3}, 5$ **19** $1\frac{1}{8}, 1\frac{3}{8}, 1\frac{5}{8}, 1\frac{7}{8}$

20 $\frac{75}{100}, \frac{90}{100}, 1\frac{5}{100}, 1\frac{20}{100}$

Page 82

A

1 3 thirds **2** 10 tenths **3** 6 sixths **4** 8 eighths **5** $\frac{1}{3} + \frac{2}{3}$

6 $\frac{6}{10} + \frac{4}{10}$ **7** $\frac{3}{5} + \frac{2}{5}$ **8** $\frac{90}{100} + \frac{10}{100}$ **9** $\frac{1}{4}$ **10** $\frac{5}{6}$

11 $\frac{5}{9}$

B

1 $\frac{5}{8} + \frac{3}{8}$ **2** $\frac{9}{10} + \frac{1}{10}$ **3** $\frac{5}{7} + \frac{2}{7}$ **4** $\frac{2}{6} + \frac{4}{6}$ **5** $\frac{7}{12} + \frac{5}{12}$ **6** $\frac{4}{9} + \frac{5}{9}$

7 $\frac{83}{100} + \frac{17}{100}$ **8** $\frac{24}{50} + \frac{26}{50}$ **9** £7 **10** 5 **11** 24

C

1 $\frac{1}{5} + \frac{2}{5} + \frac{2}{5}$ **2** $\frac{1}{8} + \frac{2}{8} + \frac{5}{8}$ **3** $\frac{2}{6} + \frac{1}{6} + \frac{3}{6}$ **4** $\frac{5}{10} + \frac{3}{10} + \frac{2}{10}$

5 $\frac{4}{12} + \frac{3}{12} + \frac{5}{12}$ **6** $\frac{4}{9} + \frac{3}{9} + \frac{2}{9}$ **7** $\frac{25}{100} + \frac{40}{100} + \frac{35}{100}$ **8** $\frac{7}{20} + \frac{4}{20} + \frac{9}{20}$

9 $\frac{2}{10}$ **10** 30 **11** 300 g

Page 83

A

1 $\frac{2}{3} = \frac{4}{6}$ **2** $\frac{3}{4} = \frac{6}{8}$ **3** $\frac{1}{2} = \frac{5}{10}$ **4** $\frac{1}{3} = \frac{4}{12}$

5 $\frac{1}{2} = \frac{4}{8}$ **6** $\frac{4}{10} = \frac{2}{5}$ **7** $\frac{2}{3} = \frac{6}{9}$ **8** $\frac{4}{16} = \frac{1}{4}$

B

1 $\frac{2}{6} = \frac{4}{12}$ **2** $\frac{1}{2} = \frac{2}{4}$ **3** $\frac{2}{3} = \frac{4}{6}$ **4** $\frac{1}{4} = \frac{3}{12}$

5 $\frac{5}{6} = \frac{10}{12}$ **6** $\frac{1}{3} = \frac{4}{12}$ **7** $\frac{1}{2} = \frac{3}{6}$ **8** $\frac{2}{3} = \frac{8}{12}$

9 $\frac{1}{6} = \frac{2}{12}$ **10** $\frac{3}{4} = \frac{9}{12}$ **11** $\frac{1}{3} = \frac{2}{6}$ **12** $\frac{4}{6} = \frac{8}{12}$

13 $\frac{4}{8} = \frac{5}{10} = \frac{6}{12} = \frac{7}{14} = \frac{8}{16}$ **14** $\frac{8}{12} = \frac{10}{15} = \frac{12}{18} = \frac{14}{21} = \frac{16}{24}$

15 $\frac{4}{16} = \frac{5}{20} = \frac{6}{24} = \frac{7}{28} = \frac{8}{32}$ **16** $\frac{12}{20} = \frac{15}{25} = \frac{18}{30} = \frac{21}{35} = \frac{24}{40}$

C

1 $\frac{1}{2} = \frac{4}{8}$ **2** $\frac{3}{5} = \frac{6}{10}$ **3** $\frac{2}{10} = \frac{20}{100}$ **4** $\frac{1}{5} = \frac{4}{20}$

5 $\frac{3}{4} = \frac{6}{8}$ **6** $\frac{5}{10} = \frac{10}{20}$ **7** $\frac{2}{3} = \frac{6}{9}$ **8** $\frac{8}{25} = \frac{32}{100}$

9 $\frac{7}{8} = \frac{14}{16}$ **10** $\frac{3}{4} = \frac{15}{20}$ **11** $\frac{4}{9} = \frac{8}{18}$ **12** $\frac{7}{10} = \frac{35}{50}$

13 $\frac{8}{12}$ **14** $\frac{16}{20}$ **15** $\frac{4}{9}$ **16** $\frac{50}{100}$ **17** $\frac{15}{20}$ **18** $\frac{12}{18}$

19 = **20** > **21** = **22** < **23** > **24** <

25 > **26** =

Page 84

A

1 4 **2** 2 **3** 3 **4** 4 **5** 6 **6** 5

7 2 **8** 6 **9** 3 **10** 9 **11** 5 **12** 4

13 10 **14** 5 **15** 8 **16** 3 **17** 8 **18** 8

19 20

B

1 2 **2** 9 **3** 7 p **4** 10 p **5** 6 **6** 9

7 £10 **8** £7 **9** 5 **10** 9 **11** 4 cm **12** 8 cm

13 9 **14** 15 **15** 60 g **16** 100 g **17** (a) 2 (b) 6

18 (a) 4 (b) 8 **19** (a) 2 (b) 8 **20** (a) 3 (b) 15

21 (a) 4 (b) 8 **22** (a) 5 (b) 15

C

1 10 **2** 60 **3** 20 **4** 12 **5** 6 **6** 30

7 5 p **8** 15 cm **9** 14 p **10** 210 g **11** 16 m **12** 42 ml

13 4 **14** 20 **15** 28

Page 85

A

1 A $\frac{2}{10}$, 0.2 B $\frac{6}{10}$, 0.6 C $\frac{9}{10}$, 0.9

2 D $\frac{1}{4}$, 0.25 E $\frac{1}{2}$, 0.5 F $\frac{3}{4}$, 0.75

3 G $\frac{34}{100}$, 0.34 H $\frac{55}{100}$, 0.55 I $\frac{66}{100}$, 0.66

4 (a) $\frac{9}{10}$ (b) 0.9 **5** (a) $\frac{1}{4}$ (b) 0.25

6 (a) $\frac{1}{2}$ (b) 0.5 **7** (a) $\frac{1}{5}$ (b) 0.2

8 (a) $\frac{7}{10}$ (b) 0.7 **9** (a) $\frac{3}{4}$ (b) 0.75

B

1 $\frac{3}{10} + \frac{5}{100} = \frac{35}{100} = 0.35$ **2** $\frac{9}{10} + \frac{2}{100} = \frac{92}{100} = 0.92$

3 $\frac{1}{10} + \frac{2}{100} = \frac{12}{100} = 0.12$ **4** $\frac{4}{10} + \frac{7}{100} = \frac{47}{100} = 0.47$

5 $\frac{16}{100}$ **6** $\frac{1}{2}$ **7** $\frac{4}{100}$ **8** $\frac{87}{100}$ **9** $\frac{3}{10}$ **10** $\frac{5}{100}$

11 $\frac{3}{4}$ **12** $\frac{21}{100}$ **13** 0.51

14 0.02 **15** 0.8 **16** 0.32 **17** 0.15 **18** 0.25 **19** 0.99
20 0.09 **21** $\frac{1}{2}$ **22** 0.4 **23** $\frac{3}{4}$ **24** 0.9

C

1 $2\frac{16}{100}$ **2** $9\frac{7}{10}$ **3** $5\frac{3}{4}$ **4** $6\frac{1}{100}$ **5** $1\frac{84}{100}$ **6** $3\frac{3}{10}$
7 $4\frac{1}{2}$ **8** $8\frac{9}{100}$ **9** $3\frac{27}{100}$ **10** $2\frac{6}{10}$ **11** $7\frac{95}{100}$ **12** $5\frac{1}{4}$
13 3.1 **14** 1.39 **15** 6.5 **16** 0.04 **17** 2.03 **18** 8.75
19 7.62 **20** 4.25 **21** 1.07 **22** 9.8 **23** 3.11 **24** 5.05
25 0.64 **26** 0.95 **27** 0.45 **28** 0.74

Page 86

A

1 7 9 11 13 15 17
2 15 20 25 30 35 40
3 4 8 12 16 20 24
4 15 18 21 24 27 30
5 –10 –9 –8 –7 –6 –5
6 £0.10 £0.20 £0.30 £0.40 £0.50 £0.60
7 34 32 30 28 26 24
8 125 115 105 95 85 75
9 22 19 16 13 10 7
10 0 –1 –2 –3 –4 –5
11 36 30 24 18 12 6
12 £5.00 £4.50 £4.00 £3.50 £3.00 £2.50

B

1 ….48 54 **2** ….43 41 **3** ….87 90
4 ….100 120 **5** –1 0... **6** –5 –2…
7 ….1 3 **8** ….0 –2 **9** ….0.9 m 1.1 m
10 ….0.75 m 0.5 m **11** ….£1.00 £0.80 **12** ….£0.10 £0.12

C

1 65 67 69 add 2 **2** 110 106 102 subtract 4
3 74 81 88 add 7 **4** 29 20 11 subtract 9
5 0 –2 –4 subtract 2 **6** 0 5 10 add 5
7 2 6 10 add 4 **8** –2 –8 –14 subtract 6
9 1.0 1.2 1.4 add 0.2 **10** 1.0 0.9 0.8 subtract 0.1
11 1.0 1.01 1.02 add 0.01 **12** 1.0 0.95 0.9 subtract 0.05

Page 87 (top half)

A

1 40 **2** 80 **3** 60 **4** 30 **5** 10 **6** 70
7 45 **8** 15 **9** 85 **10** 55 **11** 5 **12** 75

B

1 27 **2** 61 **3** 36 **4** 9 **5** 52 **6** 73
7 150 **8** 650 **9** 950 **10** 350 **11** 250 **12** 850

C

1 490 **2** 240 **3** 610 **4** 860 **5** 180 **6** 540
7 420 **8** 390 **9** 750 **10** 70 **11** 230 **12** 550

Page 87 (bottom half)

A

1 87 **2** 83 **3** 42 **4** 61 **5** 54 **6** 79
7 55 **8** 31 **9** 45 **10** 76 **11** 45 **12** 35

B

1 73 **2** 84 **3** 48 **4** 32 **5** 61 **6** 95
7 27 **8** 23 **9** 82 **10** 102 **11** 39 **12** 35

C

1 28 **2** 54 **3** 133 **4** 122 **5** 49 **6** 37
7 184 **8** 151 **9** 32 **10** 41 **11** 145 **12** 122

Page 88

A

1 92 **2** 105 **3** 91 **4** 118 **5** 119 **6** 164
7 113 **8** 141 **9** 112 **10** 130 **11** 122 **12** 117
13 £104

B

1 235 **2** 485 **3** 318 **4** 736 **5** 385 **6** 231
7 649 **8** 226 **9** 738 **10** 935 **11** 609 **12** 421
13 £553

C

1 755 **2** 451 **3** 453 **4** 2457 **5** 2737 **6** 635
7 421 **8** 1944 **9** 2334 **10** 2365 **11** 1051 **12** £3277

Page 89

A

1 105 **2** 116 **3** 82 **4** 181 **5** 135 **6** 77
7 £1.12 **8** £2.21 **9** £1.33 **10** £1.05 **11** £1.27 **12** £1.29
13 73

B

1 83 **2** 179 **3** 282 **4** 49 **5** 382 **6** 283
7 £1.34 **8** £2.04 **9** £3.46 **10** £1.66 **11** £2.84 **12** £1.75
13 £5.89 **14** 176

C

1 1183 **2** 2253 **3** 4564 **4** 3073 **5** 5586 **6** 6057
7 £11.56 **8** £2.86 **9** £8.32 **10** £7.04 **11** £10.92 **12** £4.95
13 £773 **14** £3.68

Page 90

A

1 34 **2** 69 **3** 60 **4** 105 **5** 52 **6** 95
7 54 **8** 230 **9** 108 **10** 72kg **11** 70

B

1 134 **2** 104 **3** 192 **4** 287 **5** 195 **6** 177
7 166 **8** 140 **9** 112 **10** 148 **11** 184 **12** 365
13 200 **14** 171 **15** 174 **16** 204 **17** 182 **18** 232
19 270 **20** 144

C

1 1840 **2** 2516 **3** 548 **4** 1715 **5** 942 **6** 2925
7 1176 **8** 1794 **9** 3488 **10** 1422 **11** 1908 **12** 1456
13 2365 **14** 2303 **15** 2214 **16** 3176 **17** 2016 miles
18 900 g **19** 1920 **20** 944

Page 91

A

1 12 **2** 16 **3** 14 **4** 19 **5** 13 **6** 15
7 18 **8** 17 **9** 12 **10** 16 **11** 19 **12** 14
13 13 **14** 15 **15** 18 **16** 17 **17** 14 **18** 18
19 16 **20** 17

B

1 18 **2** 15 r 3 **3** 16 **4** 12 r 4 **5** 23 r 1 **6** 12 r 3
7 19 **8** 31 r 1 **9** 17 r 1 **10** 18 **11** 11 r 3 **12** 16 r 2
13 18 r 4 **14** 17 **15** 13 r 1 **16** 17 r 5 **17** 21 **18** 25
19 23 **20** 21

C

1 19 **2** 21 **3** 22 **4** 18 **5** 21 **6** 15
7 18 r 5 **8** 25 **9** 27 **10** 23 **11** 29 **12** 22

13 24 **14** 31 **15** 23 r 7 **16** 34 **17** 28 **18** 45 litres
19 56 **20** 16

Page 92

A

1 13 **2** 8 **3** 6 **4** 7 **5** 8 **6** 9
7 6

B

1 11 **2** 7 **3** 11 **4** 13 **5** 8 **6** 10
7 17

C

1 32 **2** 14 **3** 16 **4** 8 **5** 23 **6** 9

Page 93

A

1 Day 1 7 Day 2 5 Day 3 3
2 Day 1 2 Day 2 3 Day 3 4 Day 4 5 Day 5 6

B

1 Day 1 28 Day 2 26 Day 3 24 Day 4 22 Day 5 20
2 Day 1 34 Day 2 36 Day 3 38 Day 4 40 Day 5 42
Day 6 44 Day 7 46

C

1 Day 1 7 Day 2 9 Day 3 11 Day 4 13 Day 5 15
Day 6 17 Day 7 19 Day 8 21
2 Day 1 25 Day 2 35 Day 3 45 Day 4 55 Day 5 65
Day 6 75
3 65 p, 85 p

Page 94

A

1 £4.17 **2** 12 **3** 83 **4** 80 cm **5** £3.87

B

1 217 **2** £136 **3** 2.4 kg **4** 98 **5** 63 **6** £6.04

C

1 £15.07 **2** 257 **3** 10 **4** 48 **5** 15 minutes **6** 633

Page 95

B

1 36 **2** 72 **3** 9 **4** 90 **5** 0 **6** 54
7 81 **8** 45 **9** 63 **10** 27 **11** 5 **12** 9
13 6 **14** 2 **15** 4 **16** 7 **17** 10 **18** 8
19 3 **20** 1 **21** 6 **22** 4 **23** 9 **24** 10
25 3 **26** 8 **27** 5 **28** 7 **29** 36 **30** 90
31 72 **32** 27 **33** 63 **34** 9 **35** 54 **36** 81

C

1 270 **2** 450 **3** 630 **4** 180 **5** 360 **6** 720
7 540 **8** 810 **9** 30 **10** 50 **11** 20 **12** 90
13 40 **14** 60 **15** 80 **16** 70 **17** 54 **18** 108
19 36 **20** 90 **21** 144 **22** 72 **23** 162 **24** 126
25 76 **26** £756

Page 96

A

1 5×3, 3×5 **2** 2×6, 6×2 **3** 5×4, 4×5 **4** 7×3, 3×7
5 50 **6** 18 **7** 36 **8** 16 **9** No **10** Yes
11 No **12** Yes

B

1 5×7 array **2** 6×3 array **3** 2×7 array
4 $5 \times 7 = 35$ $2 \times 7 = 14$ $6 \times 3 = 18$
$7 \times 5 = 35$ $7 \times 2 = 14$ $3 \times 6 = 18$
$35 \div 5 = 7$ $14 \div 2 = 7$ $18 \div 3 = 6$
$35 \div 7 = 5$ $14 \div 7 = 2$ $18 \div 6 = 3$
5 42 **6** 48 **7** 56 **8** 60 **9** 1, 3, 5, 15
10 1, 2, 3, 6, 9, 18 **11** 1, 7, 49 **12** 1, 2, 3, 4, 6, 8, 12, 24
13 28, 56, etc. **14** 40, 80, etc. **15** 30, 60, etc. **16** 27, 54, etc.

C

1 60 **2** 360 **3** 4, 5, 8 **4** 3, 4, 9 **5** 3, 5, 9
6 3, 4, 8 **7** 20, 40, etc. **8** 21, 42, etc. **9** 36, 72, etc.
10 30, 60, etc. **11** 24, 26, 32, 34, 36, 42, 46, 52, 54, 56, 62, 64
12 25, 35, 45, 65 **13** 24, 32, 36, 52, 56, 64
14 24, 36, 42, 45, 54, 63

Page 97

A

1 14, 140, 1400 **2** 26, 260 **3** 3, 30, 300 **4** 9, 90
5 600 **6** 80 **7** 180 **8** 400 **9** 160 **10** 1000
11 28 **12** 320 **13** 38 **14** 240 **15** 340 **16** 30
17 400 **18** 35 **19** 100 **20** 15 **21** 500 **22** 200
23 7 **24** 60 **25** 9 **26** 45 **27** 6 **28** 90

B

1 54 **2** 170 **3** 84 **4** 136 **5** 142 **6** 68
7 192 **8** 106 **9** 7200 **10** 1040 **11** 1740 **12** 4800
13 1820 **14** 8600 **15** 5600 **16** 1500 **17** 42 **18** 93
19 67 **20** 46 **21** 79 **22** 38 **23** 71 **24** 87
25 70 **26** 800 **27** 3400 **28** 95 **29** 630 **30** 65
31 4800 **32** 910 **33** 1, 3, 7, 15, 31, 63, 127, 255
34 2, 4, 8, 16, 32, 64, 128 **35** The gaps double.

C

1 820 **2** 790 **3** 660 **4** 4900 **5** 2700 **6** 880
7 740 **8** 970 **9** 1720 **10** 7800 **11** 1960 **12** 13 000
13 1540 **14** 1680 **15** 13 800 **16** 1940
17 1, 2, 4, 8, 16, etc. The gaps double.
18 1, 2, 4, 8, 16, etc. The gaps in the gaps also double.

Page 98

A

1 14 **2** 15 **3** 13 **4** 14 **5** 15 **6** 17
7 13 **8** 18 **9** 7 **10** 8 **11** 7 **12** 9
13 5 **14** 9 **15** 8 **16** 7
17 $17 - 10 = 7$
$18 - 11 = 7$
$19 - 12 = 7$
$15 - 8 = 7$
$14 - 7 = 7$
$13 - 6 = 7$

B

1 150 **2** 120 **3** 120 **4** 110 **5** 160 **6** 120
7 120 **8** 180 **9** 120 **10** 70 **11** 80 **12** 90
13 60 **14** 90 **15** 60 **16** 90 **17** 1400 **18** 1300
19 1600 **20** 1600 **21** 1500 **22** 1400 **23** 1300 **24** 760
25 800 **26** 500 **27** 500 **28** 600 **29** 800 **30** 900
31 800 **32** 800

C

1 0.8 **2** 0.9 **3** 0.5 **4** 0.6 **5** 0.6 **6** 0.9
7 0.7 **8** 0.7 **9** 0.7 **10** 0.9 **11** 0.8 **12** 0.8
13 1.4 **14** 1.3 **15** 1.6 **16** 1.4

Page 99

A

1

+	8	9	6
9	17	18	15
7	15	16	13
8	16	17	14

2

–	8	7	9
19	11	12	10
16	8	9	7
18	10	11	9

3

+	24	32	53
15	39	47	68
43	67	75	96
34	58	66	87

4

–	43	26	55
78	35	52	23
63	20	37	8
99	56	73	44

5

+	9	21	29
62	71	83	91
35	44	56	64
57	66	78	86

6

–	11	19	21
48	37	29	27
24	13	5	3
76	65	57	55

7

+	34	75	93
200	234	275	293
800	834	875	893
500	534	575	593

–	7	9	6
104	97	95	98
503	496	494	497
605	598	596	599

B

1 1273 **2** 90 **3** 293 **4** 68 **5** 1300 **6** 471
7 117 **8** 7994 **9** 55 **10** 557 **11** 71 **12** 47
13 120 **14** 93 **15** 396 **16** 8 **17** 99 **18** 72
19 96 **20** 105 **21** 357 **22** 287 **23** 24 **24** 72
25 47 **26** 27 **27** 45 **28** 19 **29** 43 + 57
30 92 + 8 **31** 14 + 86

C

1 450 + 280 **2** 720 – 290 **3** 4005 – 1012 **4** 8.3 – 6.5
5 360 + 190 **6** 985 – 565 **7** 1361 – 800 **8** 6.2 + 3.8
9 5002 – 103 **10** 567 + 33 **11** 740 – 460 **12** 4.2 + 0.8
13 350 + 160 **14** 1231 – 531 **15** 329 + 71

Page 100

A

1 2.4 kg **2** 260 ml **3** 19 **4** 8 **5** 75 p

B

1 12 **2** 1.5 litres **3** 10 cm **4** 101 **5** 176 **6** £8.50
7 285

C

1 1.3 kg **2** 667 **3** 25 cm **4** 541 **5** 50 **6** £117

Page 101

C

4 (not including rotations/reflections) (a) 8 (b) 4 (c) 0

Page 102

A

1 24 **3** 12 × 1 or 6 × 2 **4** 24 × 1, 12 × 2, 8 × 3, 6 × 4

B

1 60
2 e.g. 60 × 1 × 1 30 × 2 × 1 20 × 3 × 1 15 × 4 × 1
15 × 2 × 2 12 × 5 × 1 10 × 6 × 1 10 × 3 × 2
6 × 5 × 2 5 × 4 × 3

C

1 72 **2** 72 × 1 × 1 12 × 3 × 2
36 × 2 × 1 9 × 8 × 1
24 × 3 × 1 9 × 4 × 2
18 × 4 × 1 8 × 3 × 3
18 × 2 × 2 6 × 6 × 2
12 × 6 × 1 6 × 4 × 3

Page 103

A

1 10 kg, 25 kg **2** 50 g, 75 g **3** 1 cm, 9 cm
4 2 cm, 7 cm **5** 2 litres, 3.5 litres **6** 50 ml, 300 ml
7 16 cm, 22 cm **8** 42 cm, 53 cm **9** 3 kg, 4.5 kg
10 150 g, 350 g

B

1 5 kg, 15 kg **2** 25 g, 125 g **3** 4 cm, 10 cm
4 40 cm, 70 cm **5** 0.5 litres, 0.75 litres **6** 50 ml, 175 ml
7 18 cm, 26 cm **8** 47 cm, 58 cm **9** 5 mm, 35 mm
10 1.5 cm, 2.5 cm

C

1 5 mm, 35 mm **2** 1.5 cm, 2.5 cm **3** 24 cm, 32 cm
4 15 cm, 35 cm **5** 0.7 litres, 3.2 litres **6** 140 ml, 260 ml
7 12 mm, 28 mm **8** 6.2 cm, 7.4 cm **9** 5 mm, 30 mm
10 17 mm, 28 mm

Page 104

A

1

Time	9:00–9:05	11:00–11:05	1:00–1:05	3:00–3:05
Total	29	14	9	33

2

Colour	Black	Grey	Red	White
Total	11	9	5	7

Page 105

B

1

Feature	Goalpost	Gate	Tree	Playground	Classroom
Difference	18 m	10 m	22 m	13 m	19 m

2

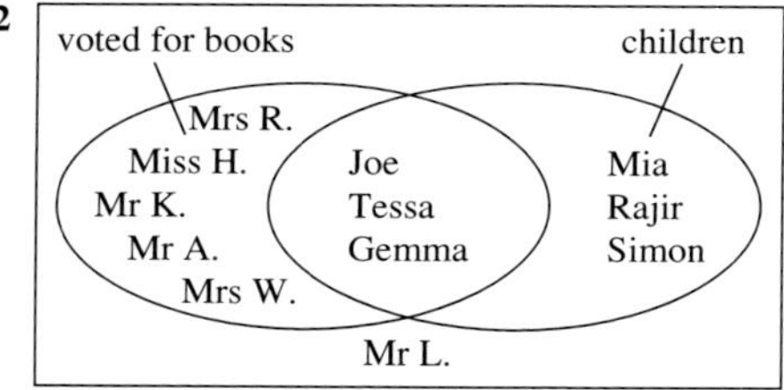

C

1

Passengers	Total
0	19
1	15
2	8
3	6
4	2

2 (a)

	under 10	not under 10
over 150 cm	Bob Mia Ian	Joe Pam Dee
not over 150 cm	Tom Ron Fay	Ann Sam Eve

(b)

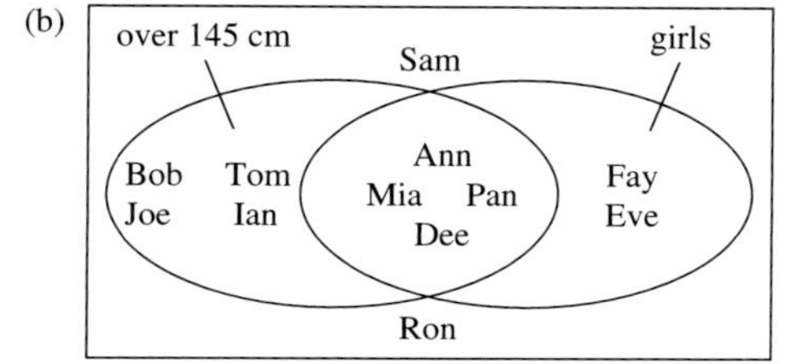

Page 106

A

1 lolly 2 pizza 3 4 4 Belle 5 Nigel
6 Rosy, Dina, Mick 7 (a) Tuesday (b) Thursday
8 (a) 30 mins. (b) 75 mins. 9 6 hours

Page 107

B

1 42 2 12:00–12:10 3 48 4 102

5

Equipment	Board Games	Hoops	Netballs	Ropes	Skittles
Votes	25	45	30	35	15

C

1 Metres
2 Difference between estimate and measure is calculated by subtracting measure from estimate. If the measured distance is greater than the estimated distance it will give a negative number of metres.
3 classroom 77
tree –9
gate 35
pond 81

Page 108

A

1 300 cm 2 500 cm 3 2 m 4 4 m 5 1 km
6 6 km 7 9000 m 8 3000 m 9 2 litres 10 5000 ml
11 4 kg 12 7000 g 13 kilometres 14 millilitres 15 metres
16 centimetres

B

1 2.5 cm 2 4 cm 3 15 mm 4 30 mm
5 280 cm 6 140 cm 7 5.2 m 8 1.1 m
9 4.3 kg 10 7.5 litres 11 2600 g 12 1900 ml
13 millimetres 14 grams 15 millimetres 16 litres

C

1 7.2 cm 2 10.9 cm 3 54 mm 4 7 mm
5 2.64 m 6 0.95 m 7 477 cm 8 120 cm
9 8900 m 10 6370 g 11 500 ml 12 3110 g
13 400 ml 14 200 cm 15 500 g

Page 109

A

1 1000 ml 2 2000 ml 3 1 litre 4 1.5 litres
5 500 ml 6 2500 ml 7 3 litres 8 3.5 litres
9 A 0.5 litres B 0.2 litres C 0.5 litres
10 D 100ml E 50 ml F 160 ml 11 1 ml 12 5 litres 13 2 litres

B

1 1.3 litres 2 0.75 litres 3 800 ml 4 1250 ml
5 4.75 litres 6 3.6 litres 7 250 ml 8 400 ml
9 G 0.2 litres H 0.6 litres I 0.8 litres
10 J 100 ml K 20 ml L 160 ml
11 litres 12 millilitres 13 millilitres 14 litres
15 millilitres

C

1 1950 ml 2 470 ml 3 3.08 litres 4 0.06 litres
5 3290 ml 6 10400 ml 7 0.01 litres 8 2.05 litres
9 M 0.5litres N 0.15 litres O 0.7 litres
10 P 80 ml Q 120 ml R 160 ml
11 115 ml, 1050 ml, 1.5 litres 12 200 ml, 0.23 litres, 2.3 litres
13 0.04 litres, 47 ml, 0.07 litres 14 6.6 litres, 6.69 litres, 6900 ml
15 508 ml, 0.58 litres, 0.8 litres 16 227 ml, 0.27 litres, 272 ml

Page 110

A

1 12.8 cm 2 7.9 cm 3 11.6 cm 4 5.2 cm
5 14.4 cm 6 10.3 cm

Page 111

A

1 50 mins. 2 40 mins. 3 50 mins. 4 45 mins.
5 30 mins. 6 55 mins. 7 9:25

B

1 11:25 2 2:20 3 5:55 4 8:30
5 4:35 6 25 mins.

C

1 1 h. 50 mins. 2 10:15 3 8:50 4 2:10
5 1 h 35 mins. 6 4:25

Page 112

A

1 6:30 2 6:50 3 7:05 4 20 mins.
5 10 mins. 6 30 mins. 7 25 mins. 8 15 mins.

B

1 12:05 2 7:50 3 10:35 4 7:15
5 11:55 6 10:05 7 30 mins. 8 10 mins.
9 20 mins. 10 40 mins. 11 (a) Bus 1 (b) Bus 4

C

1 Bus 1 45 mins. Bus 2 1 h. 20 mins.
Bus 3 1 h. 10 mins. Bus 4 1 h.
Bus 5 55 mins.
2 Bus 2 3 Bus 4 4 Bus 3 5 Bus 1
6 10:20 7 11:30 8 6:35 9 7:50

Page 113

A

1 48 m 2 £3.50 3 200 g 4 160 litres
5 6 g 6 70 cm

B

1 800 g 2 60 p 3 2.4 metres 4 100 ml
5 4 cm 6 45 p

C

1 3.75 kg 2 6 km 3 £6.15 4 1.8 litres
5 72 cm 6 £8

Page 114

A

1 less 2 right ∠ 3 greater 4 right ∠
5 less 6 greater 7 right ∠ 8 less
10 less 11 90° 12 greater 13 90°
14 less 15 less

B

1 less 2 greater 3 less 4 greater
5 less 6 less 8 (c) 30°–60° 9 (e) over 60°
10 (b) 30° 11 (d) 60° 12 (d) 60° 13 (c) 30°–60°
14 (a) below 30° 15 (b) 30°

C

1 135° **2** 90° **3** 270° **4** 225° **5** 45° **6** 180°
7 135° **8** 315° **10** (a) C is 30° (b) B is 60°
11 90° **12** 180° **13** 30° **14** 150° **15** 240° **16** 330°
17 60° **18** 210°

Page 116

A

1 8 cm^2 **2** 5 cm^2 **3** 7 cm^2 **4** 10 cm^2
5 (a) 10 cm^2 (b) 14 cm **6** (a) 6 cm^2 (b) 12 cm
7 (a) 9 cm^2 (b) 10 cm **8** (a) 7 cm^2 (b) 16 cm

Page 117

B

1 (a) 7 cm^2 (b) 16 cm **2** (a) 7 cm^2 (b) 16 cm
3 (a) 10 cm^2 (b) 22 cm **7** N 16 squares O 14 squares

C

1 12 cm **2** 12 cm **3** 12.5 cm

4

Length	7	9	20	14	11	25	8	30
Width	6	3	2	5	7	4	5	1
Perimeter	26	24	44	38	36	58	26	62
Area	42	27	40	70	77	100	40	30

5 10 000 **6** £180 **7** 6

Page 118

A

1 less **2** greater **3** greater **4** less
5 greater **6** greater **7** less **8** less
9 equal **10** greater **11** less **12** equal
13 equal **14** less **15** equal **16** greater

B

1 $\frac{8}{10}$ **2** $\frac{2}{10}$ **3** $\frac{1}{4}$ **4** $\frac{5}{6}$
5 $\frac{4}{12}$ **6** $\frac{2}{6}$ **7** $\frac{5}{6}$ **8** $\frac{9}{10}$
9 $2\frac{1}{2}, 3, 3\frac{1}{2}, 4, 4\frac{1}{2}$ **10** $1\frac{1}{4}, 1\frac{1}{2}, 1\frac{3}{4}, 2, 2\frac{1}{4}$
11 $5\frac{3}{10}, 5\frac{2}{10}, 5\frac{1}{10}, 5, 4\frac{9}{10}$ **12** $1\frac{2}{3}, 1\frac{1}{3}, 1, \frac{2}{3}, \frac{1}{3}$
13 $1\frac{1}{2}, 1\frac{3}{4}, 2\frac{1}{5}, 3\frac{1}{10}$ **14** $2\frac{2}{10}, 2\frac{2}{5}, 3\frac{1}{8}, 4\frac{1}{3}$
15 $1\frac{1}{2}, 1\frac{2}{3}, 2\frac{3}{7}, 2\frac{1}{2}$ **16** $4\frac{3}{10}, 4\frac{1}{2}, 5\frac{1}{2}, 5\frac{5}{8}$

C

1 $\frac{2}{6}, \frac{1}{2}, \frac{2}{3}$ **2** $\frac{3}{10}, \frac{2}{5}, \frac{1}{2}$ **3** $\frac{1}{2}, \frac{5}{8}, \frac{3}{4}$ **4** $\frac{1}{3}, \frac{4}{9}, \frac{1}{2}$
5 $\frac{25}{100}, \frac{1}{2}, \frac{6}{10}$ **6** $\frac{4}{9}, \frac{1}{2}, \frac{4}{7}$ **7** $2\frac{1}{4}, 2\frac{3}{4}, 3\frac{1}{4}$ **8** $3\frac{1}{3}, 4, 4\frac{2}{3}$
9 $1\frac{1}{9}, 1\frac{3}{9}, 1\frac{5}{9}$ **10** $6\frac{1}{4}, 7\frac{1}{2}, 8\frac{3}{4}$
11 B **12** G **13** D **14** A **15** E **16** F
17 H **18** C

Page 119

A

1 $\frac{3}{5} = \frac{6}{10}$ **2** $\frac{4}{8} = \frac{1}{2}$ **3** $\frac{2}{3} = \frac{4}{6}$ **4** $\frac{3}{12} = \frac{1}{4}$
5 $\frac{6}{8} = \frac{3}{4}$ **6** $\frac{1}{2} = \frac{5}{10}$ **7** $\frac{4}{12} = \frac{2}{6}$ **8** $\frac{2}{3} = \frac{6}{9}$

B

1 A $\frac{1}{4} = \frac{2}{8}$ B $\frac{2}{4} = \frac{4}{8}$ C $\frac{3}{4} = \frac{6}{8}$ **2** D $\frac{1}{5} = \frac{2}{10}$
E $\frac{3}{5} = \frac{6}{10}$ F $\frac{4}{5} = \frac{8}{10}$ **3** G $\frac{1}{3} = \frac{2}{6}$ H $\frac{2}{3} = \frac{4}{6}$
4 I $\frac{1}{4} = \frac{5}{20}$ J $\frac{2}{4} = \frac{10}{20}$ K $\frac{3}{4} = \frac{15}{20}$

C

1 > **2** = **3** < **4** > **5** = **6** >
7 = **8** < **9** > **10** = **11** < **12** >
13 $\frac{4}{12}$ **14** $\frac{10}{30}$ **15** $\frac{8}{12}$ **16** $\frac{20}{50}, \frac{12}{20}$
17 $\frac{20}{24} = \frac{25}{30} = \frac{30}{36} = \frac{35}{42} = \frac{40}{48}$

Page 120

1 A $\frac{1}{4}$, 0.25 B $\frac{1}{2}$, 0.5 C $\frac{3}{4}$, 0.75
2 D $\frac{2}{10}$, 0.2 E $\frac{4}{10}$, 0.7 F $\frac{7}{10}$, 0.7
3 G $\frac{63}{100}$, 0.63 H $\frac{67}{100}$, 0.67 I $\frac{76}{100}$, 0.76
4 (a) $\frac{8}{10}$ (b) 0.8 **5** (a) $\frac{3}{4}$ (b) 0.75
6 (a) $\frac{1}{2}$ (b) 0.5 **7** (a) $\frac{3}{10}$ (b) 0.3
8 (a) $\frac{7}{10}$ (b) 0.7 **9** (a) $\frac{1}{4}$ (b) 0.25

B

1 A $\frac{1}{4}$, 0.25 B $\frac{1}{2}$, 0.5 C $1\frac{1}{4}$, 1.25 D $1\frac{3}{4}$, 1.75
2 E $1\frac{3}{10}$, 1.3 F $1\frac{8}{10}$, 1.8 G $2\frac{4}{10}$, 2.4 H $\frac{7}{10}$, 0.7
3 (a) $\frac{56}{100}$ (b) 0.56 **4** (a) $\frac{23}{100}$ (b) 0.23
5 (a) $\frac{87}{100}$ (b) 0.87 **6** (a) $\frac{9}{100}$ (b) 0.09
7 (a) $\frac{62}{100}$ (b) 0.62 **8** (a) $\frac{34}{100}$ (b) 0.34

C

1 $2\frac{82}{100}$ **2** $9\frac{7}{100}$ **3** $5\frac{61}{100}$ **4** $4\frac{1}{4}$
5 $1\frac{3}{10}$ **6** $7\frac{8}{100}$ **7** $4\frac{1}{2}$ **8** $3\frac{94}{100}$
9 $2\frac{1}{100}$ **10** $6\frac{42}{100}$ **11** $8\frac{3}{4}$ **12** $5\frac{19}{100}$
13 1.6 **14** 3.48 **15** 4.5 **16** 6.05 **17** 2.67 **18** 9.75
19 4.02 **20** 1.87 **21** 8.4 **22** 5.14 **23** 4.25 **24** 7.03
25 0.65 **26** 1.9 **27** 2.31 **28** 3.3

Page 121

A

1 6 **2** 12 **3** 9 **4** 50 **5** 8 p **6** 30 p
7 14 cm **8** 25 cm **9** 3 **10** 4 **11** 9 **12** 5
13 8 p **14** 2 p **15** 10 cm **16** 6 cm **17** 4 **18** 20
19 6 **20** 5 **21** 10 p **22** 7 p **23** 2 cm **24** 9 cm
25 9

B

1 8 **2** 16 **3** 6 **4** 18 **5** 5 **6** 10
7 7 **8** 35 **9** 24 **10** 21 **11** 25 **12** 18
13 18 **14** 14 **15** 20 **16** 56 **17** $\frac{1}{10}$ **18** $\frac{1}{2}$
19 $\frac{1}{5}$ **20** $\frac{1}{4}$ **21** $\frac{1}{100}$ **22** $\frac{1}{4}$ **23** $\frac{1}{10}$ **24** $\frac{1}{2}$
25 (a) 16 (b) 8 **26** (a) 20 (b) 15 (c) 25

C

1 £1.20 **2** £1.20 **3** £2.25 **4** £8.75 **5** 90 cm **6** 32 cm
7 3 m **8** 1.02 m **9** $\frac{1}{20}$ **10** $\frac{1}{4}$ **11** $\frac{1}{10}$ **12** $\frac{1}{8}$
13 $\frac{1}{4}$ **14** $\frac{1}{10}$ **15** $\frac{1}{8}$ **16** $\frac{1}{5}$ **17** 8 **18** 24

Page 122

A

1 30 **2** 230 **3** 84 **4** 68 **5** 177 **6** 140
7 156 **8** 122 **9** 126 **10** £1.04 **11** 185

B

1 270 **2** 801 **3** 454 **4** 600 **5** 567 **6** 688
7 108 **8** 665 **9** 752 **10** 492 **11** 511 **12** 423
13 424 **14** 588 **15** 468 **16** 216 **17** £1.75 **18** 576
19 £2.94 **20** 333

C

1 865 **2** 2214 **3** 864 **4** 2009 **5** 1341 **6** 1800
7 1050 **8** 1992 **9** 2149 **10** 2403 **11** 594 **12** 1680
13 3008 **14** 2100 **15** 3283 **16** 1242 **17** 816 **18** 2.6 kg
19 £4833 **20** 1092

Page 123

A

1 13 **2** 13 **3** 12 **4** 15 **5** 17 **6** 15 **7** 18
8 16 **9** 17 **10** 14 **11** 17 **12** 15 **13** 18 **14** 13
15 11 **16** 13 **17** 16 **18** 18 **19** 19 **20** 15

B

1 18 **2** 12 **3** 16 **4** 14 **5** 19 r 2 **6** 13
7 13 r 2 **8** 14 **9** 13 r 6 **10** 19 **11** 18 r 4 **12** 16
13 16 r 4 **14** 37 r 2 **15** 18 r 6 **16** 15 r 3 **17** 15 p **18** 14
19 18

C

1 18 r 3 **2** 21 r 5 **3** 36 r 2 **4** 19 **5** 27 **6** 38 r 4
7 34 **8** 23 r 2 **9** 24 r 1 **10** 38 **11** 18 r 6 **12** 26 r 6
13 37 **14** 48 **15** 27 r 2 **16** 36 r 4 **17** 24 g **18** 39
19 161 **20** 38 miles

Page 124

A

1

Tickets	5	10	15	20	25	30	35	40	45	50
Prizes	1	2	3	4	5	6	7	8	9	10

2

Tickets	4	8	12	16	20	24	28	32	36	40
Prizes	1	2	3	4	5	6	7	8	9	10

3 (a) 9 (b) 28

4

Red beads	2	4	6	8	10	12	14	16	18	20
Beads	5	10	15	20	25	30	35	40	45	50

5

Blue beads	1	2	3	4	5	6	7	8	9	10
Beads	3	6	9	12	15	18	21	24	27	30

6 (a) 6 (b) 24 (c) 36

Page 125

B

1 (a) 4 (b) 3 **2** (a) 2 (b) 3 **3** (a) 2 (b) 5
7 (a) $\frac{2}{3}$ (b) $\frac{1}{3}$ **8** 5 **9** (a) $\frac{1}{4}$ (b) $\frac{3}{4}$
10 (a) $\frac{2}{5}$ (b) $\frac{3}{5}$

C

1 $\frac{1}{2}$ **2** $\frac{1}{6}$ **3** $\frac{2}{6}$ or $\frac{1}{3}$ **4** 15 **5** 10 **6** 28
7 6 **8** 10 **9** 49, 21 **10** 6, 24 **11** 28 **12** 15
13 20 **14** 42

Page 126

A

1 28 **2** 12 **3** 56 **4** 27 **5** 60 **6** 32
7 27 **8** 21 **9** 64 **10** 42 **11** 20 **12** 81
13 5 **14** 4 **15** 9 **16** 6 **17** 7 **18** 5
19 7 **20** 9 **21** 8 **22** 3 **23** 5 **24** 6

B

1 8 **2** 3 **3** 6 **4** 7 **5** 9 **6** 10
7 1000 **8** 320 **9** 96 **10** 98 **11** 288 **12** 486
13 240 **14** 490 **15** 240 **16** 720 **17** 160 **18** 630
19 360 **20** 450 **21** 320 **22** 350 **23** 320 **24** 360
25 60 **26** 100 **27** 80 **28** 30 **29** 30 **30** 20
31 70 **32** 40 **33** 100 **34** 9 **35** 70 **36** 100

C

1 240 **2** 360 **3** 270 **4** 140 **5** 560 **6** 480
7 50 **8** 70 **9** 90 **10** 8 **11** 5 **12** 9
13 2400 **14** 7200 **15** 1800 **16** 1600 **17** 2800 **18** 4500
19 3500 **20** 2400 **21** 8000 **22** 2400 **23** 5400 **24** 1400
25 700 **26** 400 **27** 500 **28** 800 **29** 900 **30** 700
31 500 **32** 800 **33** 600 **34** 900 **35** 700 **36** 200

Page 127

A

[1] 6	[2] 9	■	[3] 2	[4] 7
[5] 3	5	■	[6] 3	0
■	[7] 1	[8] 7	0	■
[9] 6	■	5	■	[10] 1
[11] 1	7	■	[12] 3	8

B

[1] 1	[2] 4	■	[3] 6	[4] 8
[5] 2	8	■	[6] 1	9
6	■	[7] 8	5	■
■	[8] 2	1	■	[9] 2
[10] 1	5	■	[11] 9	4

C

[1] 4	[2] 9	3	■	[3] 6
[4] 8	7	■	[5] 9	0
■	■	[6] 7	2	■
[7] 6	[8] 9	■	[9] 5	[10] 4
[11] 3	2	0	■	9

Page 128

A

1 three hundred and eight
2 one thousand two hundred and ninety-seven
3 four thousand three hundred and sixty-two
4 one thousand five hundred
5 two thousand six hundred and five
6 three thousand and eighty-nine
7 five thousand two hundred and forty
8 eight thousand and sixty
9 600 **10** 70 **11** 8 **12** 5000 **13** 80 **14** 6000
15 4 **16** 500 **17** 287 **18** 420 **19** 606 **20** 535

21 2231 **22** 3369 **23** 5224 **24** 4492 **25** 2235 **26** 4810
27 1497 **28** 5063 **29** 1480 **30** 530 **31** 2170 **32** 5700
33 250 **34** 7810 **35** 6900 **36** 4360 **37** 200 **38** 324
39 39 **40** 470 **41** 861 **42** 500 **43** 180 **44** 652
45 7198, 7981, 8197, 8719 **46** 1782, 1827, 2178, 2187
47 3469, 3496, 3649, 3694 **48** 1375, 1537, 1573, 1735
49 3, 6 **50** 6, 18 **51** 5, 35 **52** 80, 40 **53** 70 **54** 150
55 330 **56** 290 **57** 600 **58** 1000 **59** 300 **60** 800
61 A –7 B –2 C 4 D 7
62 (a) 5, 23, 47, 91 (b) 38, 54, 270, 316
63 10, 20, 30, 40, 50, 60 **64** 6, 12, 18, 24, 30, 36
65 4, 8, 12, 16, 20, 24 **66** 9, 18 27, 36, 45, 54
67 14, 18, 20, 60 **68** 15, 18, 21, 60
69 15, 20, 35, 60 **70** 14, 21, 35, 49

Page 129

1 $1\frac{1}{6}$ **2** $2\frac{2}{3}$ **3** $3\frac{5}{8}$ **4** $4\frac{2}{6}$ **5** $\frac{3}{10}$ **6** $\frac{3}{4}$
7 $\frac{4}{5}$ **8** $\frac{5}{9}$ **9** $\frac{1}{2}=\frac{4}{8}$ **10** $\frac{1}{4}=\frac{4}{16}$ **11** $\frac{1}{3}=\frac{2}{6}$ **12** $\frac{3}{5}=\frac{6}{10}$
13 $\frac{1}{4}=\frac{2}{8}$ **14** $\frac{1}{2}=\frac{3}{6}$ **15** $1=\frac{3}{3}$ **16** $\frac{1}{2}=\frac{5}{10}$ **17** $1=\frac{10}{10}$ **18** $\frac{2}{3}=\frac{4}{6}$
19 $\frac{2}{5}=\frac{4}{10}$ **20** $1=\frac{8}{8}$ **21** 15 **22** 6 **23** 8 **24** 5
25 8p **26** 6 m **27** £4 **28** 500 g **29** $\frac{1}{2}$ **30** $\frac{1}{5}$
31 $\frac{1}{100}$ **32** $\frac{1}{4}$ **33** $\frac{2}{10}$ **34** $\frac{4}{100}$ **35** $\frac{5}{10}$ **36** 9
37 $\frac{5}{100}$ **38** 10 **39** $\frac{4}{10}$ **40** $\frac{9}{100}$ **41** $\frac{1}{10}$ **42** $\frac{1}{4}$
43 $\frac{67}{100}$ **44** $\frac{3}{100}$ **45** $\frac{1}{2}$ **46** $\frac{82}{100}$ **47** $\frac{5}{100}$ or $\frac{1}{20}$
48 $\frac{3}{4}$ **49** 0.5 **50** 0.2 **51** 1.0 **52** 0.43 **53** 0.75
54 0.09 **55** 0.7 **56** 0.25 **57** A 0.2 B 0.6 C 1.4 D 1.8
58 0.7 **59** 0.9 **60** 1.8 **61** 1.7 **62** 0.3 **63** 0.5
64 1.1 **65** 1.6 **66** 1.5, 2.4, 4.2, 5.1 **67** 3.3, 3.8, 8.3, 8.8
68 4.5, 5.4, 45, 54 **69** $2\frac{1}{4}, 2\frac{1}{2}, 3\frac{2}{5}, 3\frac{2}{3}$ **70** $1\frac{3}{8}, 1\frac{1}{2}, 2\frac{1}{2}, 2\frac{3}{5}$

Page 130

1 174 **2** 75 **3** 600 + 700 **4** 156 + 44 **5** 111 + 40
6 43 + 76 **7** 44 **8** 436 **9** 204 – 7 **10** 1000 – 750
11 258 – 90 **12** 177 – 32 **13** 229 **14** 293 **15** 649
16 374 **17** 136 **18** 336 **19** 562 **20** 505
21 312 **22** 202 **23** £4.86 **24** £4.26 **25** 71
26 334 **27** £2.73 **28** £2.28 **29** £105 **30** 56 years
31 92 **32** 132 **33** 8 × 4 **34** 6 × 0 **35** 29 × 2
36 5 × 7 **37** 8 **38** 40 **39** 16 ÷ 1 **40** 27 ÷ 9
41 6000 ÷ 10 **42** 1920 ÷ 2 **43** 150 **44** 504 **45** 306
46 364 **47** 17 **48** 15 **49** 18 **50** 14
51 7 r 1 **52** 16 r 5 **53** 8 r 2 **54** 6 r 3 **55** £21.50
56 £6.70 **57** £8.25 **58** £2.20 **59** 120 **60** 23
61 161 **62** £16.50

Page 131

1 1 m **2** 50 cm **3** 10 cm **4** $\frac{1}{4}$ m
5 1000 m **6** 100 m **7** $\frac{1}{2}$ km **8** 1 mm
9 1 cm **10** 5 cm **11** 1000 g **12** 2 kg
13 $\frac{1}{10}$ kg **14** 500 g **15** $\frac{1}{2}$ litre **16** 4000 ml
17 1 litre **18** 100 ml **19** A 20 cm, B 85 cm
20 C $1\frac{1}{2}$ kg, D 3 kg **21** E $1\frac{1}{4}$ litres, F $\frac{1}{2}$ litre
22 G 180 ml, H 40 ml **23** 1 m 35 cm
24 3 cm **25** 500g **26** 800 ml **27** 8 cm²
28 12 cm **31** 35 days **32** 3 mins. **33** $2\frac{1}{2}$ years
34 240 mins. **35** 48 hours **36** 80 yrs. **37** 156 weeks
38 $1\frac{1}{2}$ hours **39** 30 **40** 31 **41** 30
42 31 **43** (a) 20 past 3 (b) 3:20 pm
44 (a) 22 mins. to 3 (b) 2:38 am
45 (a) 9 mins. to 9 (b) 8:51 am
46 (a) 14 mins. past 6 (b) 6:14 pm
47 10:45 **48** 12:15

Page 132

1 equilateral triangle **2** quadrilateral
3 regular hexagon **4** isosceles triangle
5 square **6** right-angled triangle
7 irregular pentagon **8** regular octagon
9 regular pentagon **10** irregular heptagon
11 1, 3, 5, 8, 9 **12** 3, 0, 6, 1, 4, 0, 0, 8, 5, 1
15 (a) 2 (b) 3 **16** cone
17 triangular based pyramid (tetrahedron)
18 cuboid **19** cylinder
20 hemisphere **21** hexagonal based prism
22 7 **23** 9 **25** yellow △ **26** blue □ **27** red ◇
28 red ○ **29** D3 **30** C5 **31** B2 **32** D6
33 180° **34** 90° **35** 45° **36** 180° **37** 45°
38 3 o'clock **39** 7 o'clock **40** 5 o'clock **41** 8 o'clock
42 10 o'clock

Page 133

1

	even	not even
2-digits	58 92 74	15 81 63
not 2-digits	4 150 126 300	7 219

2

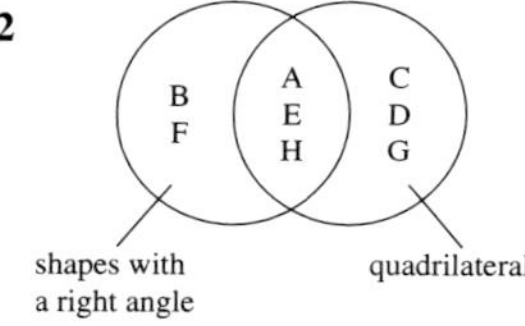

3

Method	Total
Walk	14
Bus	6
Car	8
Train	2

4 (a) 10 (b) violin (c) recorder (d) 5 (e) 80

5

Meal	Total
Eggs	4
Meat	14
Fish	10
Salad	8

6 (a) red (b) green (c) green (d) 25 (e) 25 (f) 145

Page 134 (Test 1)

1 1238 **2** 500 **3** 175 **4** 2 **5** 45 **6** 200
7 28 **8** 180 **9** 58 p **10** 6 **11** 4 **12** $\frac{3}{10}$
13 600 ml **14** 3:55 pm **15** £18 **16** 8 **17** 1.7
18 2 kg **19** 180 **20** 8, 16, 24, 32, 40

Page 134 (Test 2)

1 60 **2** 5 **3** –2°C **4** 0.5
5 28 **6** 27 **7** 2076 **8** 316
9 £28 **10** 45° **11** 5 **12** 2 m 40 cm
13 56 **14** £24 **15** 2 kg **16** 6
17 560 **18** 500 ml **19** 11:35 **20** 20

Page 135 (Test 3)

1 28	**2** 0.8	**3** 120	**4** 25p
5 30	**6** 1250 m	**7** 4756	**8** 180°
9 8	**10** 1309	**11** 21	**12** £2
13 250 ml	**14** 20 cm	**15** 800	**16** 1.9
17 2 kg	**18** 3	**19** 175	**20** 335 or 336

Page 135 (Test 4)

1 45	**2** 3°C	**3** 95	**4** 75 p
5 2500 ml	**6** $\frac{7}{10}$	**7** 4	**8** £4
9 4	**10** 1 m 40 cm	**11** 32	**12** £1.65
13 5007	**14** 35 mins.	**15** 673	**16** 10 o'clock
17 1994	**18** 1 kg 300 g	**19** 0.25	**20** 7

ISBN 978-1-902214-96-2

D2 WRITTEN METHOD (+/−)

I can add and subtract three-digit numbers using a written method.

Examples

249 + 173 rounds to 200 + 200
rounds to about 400

```
  249      249      249
 +173     +173     +173
 ----     ----     ----
  300       12      422
  110      110       11
   12      300
 ----     ----
  422      422
 ----     ----
```

427 − 185 rounds to 400 − 200
rounds to about 200

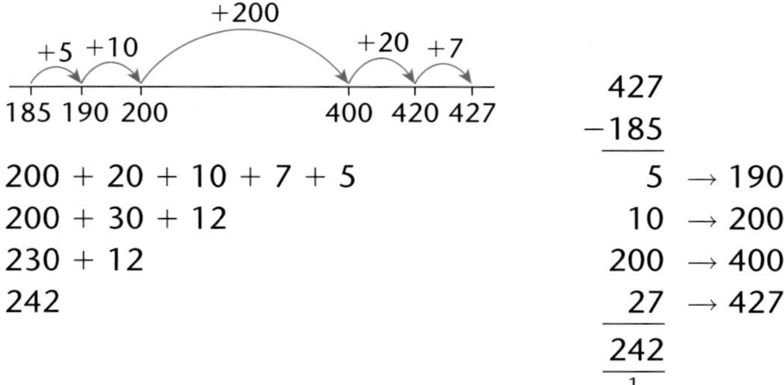

200 + 20 + 10 + 7 + 5
200 + 30 + 12
230 + 12
242

```
  427
 −185
 ----
    5  → 190
   10  → 200
  200  → 400
   27  → 427
 ----
  242
    1
```

A

Work out

1	56 + 23	**6**	68 − 24
2	78 + 45	**7**	93 − 67
3	85 + 39	**8**	52 − 35
4	67 + 64	**9**	86 − 59
5	94 + 76	**10**	74 − 23

11 Alison knits 61 rows. Joanne knits 27 rows. How many more rows does Alison knit than Joanne?

B

Work out

1	147 + 155	**6**	851 − 147
2	389 + 233	**7**	324 − 250
3	476 + 298	**8**	575 − 436
4	535 + 384	**9**	630 − 368
5	298 + 257	**10**	716 − 179

11 In November a shop sold 163 TVs. In December 317 were sold. How many more TVs were sold in December?

12 There are 472 pupils in a school. 241 are boys. How many are girls?

C

Work out

1	1782 + 488	**6**	1340 − 825
2	2175 + 365	**7**	5653 − 1375
3	4297 + 1167	**8**	8217 − 3485
4	3969 + 1468	**9**	2462 − 909
5	5756 + 2185	**10**	4021 − 2103

11 The population of a village was 2358. Ten years later it was 3511. What was the increase in population?

12 In one month Cindy earned £2517. She spent £1943. How much did she save?

D2 WRITTEN METHOD (×/÷)

I can multiply and divide a two-digit number by one-digit number.

Examples

27×6,
27×6 rounds to 30×6
27×6 is less than 180

×	6
20	120
7	42
	162

$$\begin{array}{r} 20 + 7 \\ \times \quad 6 \\ \hline 120 \\ 42 \\ \hline 162 \end{array}$$

a) $86 \div 5$

Estimate
$5 \times 10 = 50$
$5 \times 20 = 100$
$50 < 86 < 100$
$10 < \text{Answer} < 20$

$$\begin{array}{rl} 86 & \\ -\underline{50} & (5 \times 10) \\ 36 & \\ -\underline{35} & (5 \times 7) \\ 1 & \end{array}$$

Answer 17R1

b) $186 \div 5$

$$\begin{array}{rl} 186 & \\ -\underline{150} & (5 \times 30) \\ 36 & \\ -\underline{35} & (5 \times 7) \\ 1 & \end{array}$$

Answer 37R1

A

Work out

1. 16×4
2. 19×5
3. 31×2
4. 13×6
5. 25×4
6. 28×3
7. 47×2
8. 26×5
9. $36 \div 2$
10. $45 \div 3$
11. $96 \div 6$
12. $56 \div 4$
13. $70 \div 5$
14. $57 \div 3$
15. $84 \div 6$
16. $52 \div 2$
17. One pencil costs 19p. How much do 5 cost?
18. There are 54 children in Year 4. One third have brown eyes. How many children have brown eyes?
19. How many chairs are needed to make six rows of 24?
20. Eighty books are sorted into 5 equal piles. How many books are there in each pile?

B

Work out

1. 68×5
2. 45×6
3. 26×8
4. 87×3
5. 53×7
6. 42×9
7. 54×8
8. 37×6
9. $91 \div 7$
10. $57 \div 2$
11. $114 \div 6$
12. $147 \div 9$
13. $71 \div 4$
14. $140 \div 8$
15. $106 \div 7$
16. $162 \div 9$
17. There are three darts in each packet. How many packets can be made from 70 darts?

18. A school buys some tennis rackets for £153. Each racket costs £9. How many rackets does the school buy?

C

Work out

1. 187×7
2. 215×8
3. 196×6
4. 159×9
5. 246×7
6. 238×6
7. 374×9
8. 189×8
9. $144 \div 6$
10. $250 \div 9$
11. $172 \div 7$
12. $304 \div 8$
13. $230 \div 9$
14. $212 \div 6$
15. $188 \div 8$
16. $200 \div 7$
17. One plane ticket costs £145. How much will six tickets cost?
18. There are 3 darts in each packet. How many packets can be made from 117 darts?
19. Nine people share a prize. They each receive £248. How much was the prize?
20. Five packets of sweets weigh 320 g. How much does each packet weigh?

I can solve one and two-step word problems.

Example

In a sale Marsha buys three dresses for the price of two. She pays £58. How much would the three dresses cost if they were not sold in a sale?

£58 ÷ 2 = £29
£58 + £29 = £87
The three dresses would cost £87 if they were not sold in a sale.

A

1. A snail crawls 45 cm. it crawls a further 26 cm. How far has the snail crawled altogether?
2. There are 65 people on a coach. 37 are adults. How many are children?
3. One train ticket costs £3·50. How much do four tickets cost?
4. There are twice as many apple trees as pear trees in an orchard. There are 48 apple trees. How many trees are there altogether?
5. Marsha and Davina go shopping together. Marsha spends £94. Davina spends £37. How much more does Marsha spend? How much do they spend altogether?

B

1. Axel is 1·38 m tall. His father is 1·76 m tall. How much taller is father than son?
2. How much change would you receive if you buy three sandwiches at £2·49 each and pay with a £10 note?

3. Libby mixes 375 ml of white paint with 185 ml of red paint. How much pink paint does she make?
4. Robyn swims four 35 m lengths. Shaun swims eight 15 m widths. How much further does Robyn swim?
5. Sanjay and Kumar have a combined weight of 72 kg. Sanjay weighs 4 kg more than Kumar. How much does each boy weigh?

C

1. At eight o'clock in the morning a shadow was 1·4 m long. At midday it was 87 cm shorter. How long was the shadow at midday?
2. A multi storey car park has 9 levels. There are 136 parking spaces on each level. How many cars can park in the car park?
3. Janet drives the same route to work every day. After three days she has driven 111 miles. How far does she drive in five days?
4. Tony buys three sandwiches at £1·85 each and four drinks at 65p each. How much does he pay?
5. A 2 litre bottle of milk has 825 ml left. How much has been used?
6. You buy two cards at £1·35 each and a computer game. You pay with a £20 note and receive £3·81 change. How much does the game cost?

D2 ANGLES

I can order a set of angles and follow directions which involve half turns or turns through 90° or 360°.

Angles are measured in degrees (°).

A whole turn is 360°.

A half turn is 180°.

A quarter turn is a right angle. It is 90°.

Examples

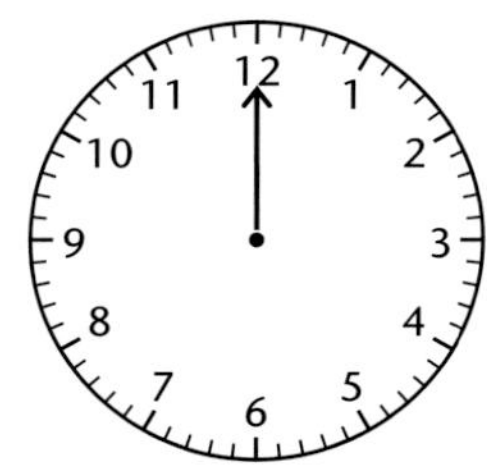

The minute hand of a clock turns:

360° in one hour

180° in 30 minutes

90° in 15 minutes.

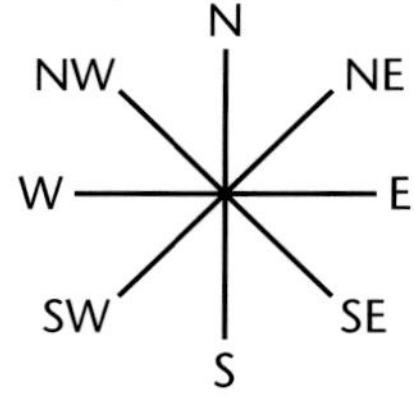

Turning in a clockwise direction from:

N to S is a half turn or 180°

N to E is a right angle or 90°

N to NE is 45°.

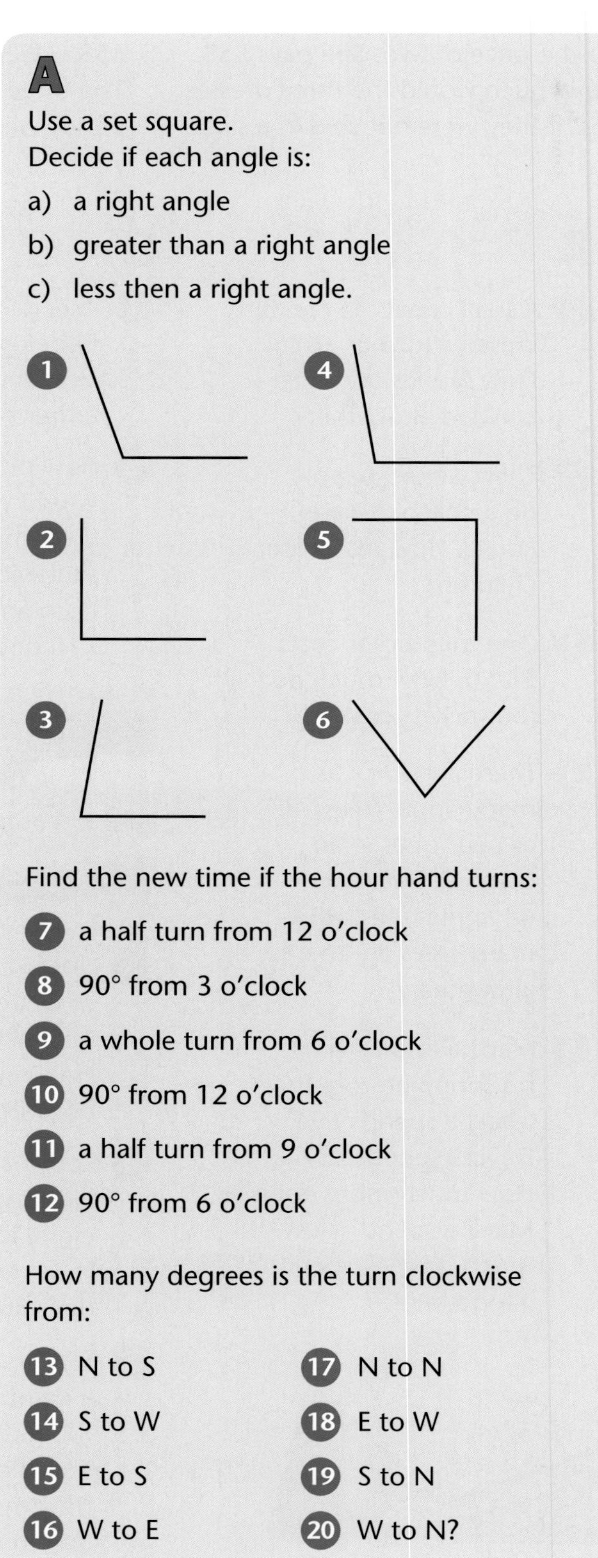

A

Use a set square.

Decide if each angle is:

a) a right angle

b) greater than a right angle

c) less then a right angle.

1 **2** **3** **4** **5** **6**

Find the new time if the hour hand turns:

7 a half turn from 12 o'clock

8 90° from 3 o'clock

9 a whole turn from 6 o'clock

10 90° from 12 o'clock

11 a half turn from 9 o'clock

12 90° from 6 o'clock

How many degrees is the turn clockwise from:

13 N to S

14 S to W

15 E to S

16 W to E

17 N to N

18 E to W

19 S to N

20 W to N?

Find the new time if the hour hand turns:

1. 90° from 1 o'clock
2. 360° from 5 o'clock
3. 180° from 10 o'clock
4. 90° from 8 o'clock
5. 360° from 2 o'clock
6. 90° from 4 o'clock
7. 180° from 7 o'clock
8. 90° from 11 o'clock

How many degrees is the turn:

9. clockwise from N to E
10. clockwise from SE to NW
11. clockwise from NW to NE
12. clockwise from S to S
13. anti-clockwise from E to N
14. anti-clockwise from SW to NE
15. anti-clockwise from W to S
16. anti-clockwise from NW to SW?
17. Place the angles in order of size, smallest first.

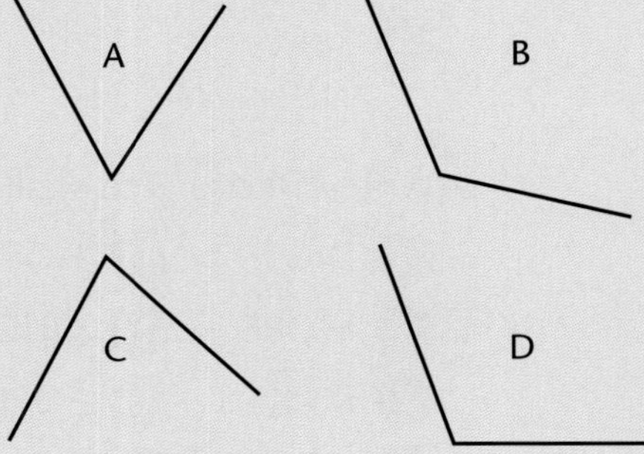

18. What is the sum of the angles of a square?

C

Find the new time if the hour hand turns:

1. 90° from 5 o'clock
2. 30° from 5 o'clock
3. 60° from 5 o'clock
4. 90° from 10 o'clock
5. 30° from 10 o'clock
6. 60° from 10 o'clock
7. 30° from 2 o'clock
8. 60° from 7 o'clock

How many degrees is the turn:

9. clockwise from SW to NW
10. clockwise from NE to E
11. clockwise from SW to NE
12. clockwise from S to SW
13. anti-clockwise from SE to NE
14. anti-clockwise from NW to W
15. anti-clockwise from S to SE
16. anti-clockwise from NE to SW?

Place the angles in each shape in order of size, smallest first.

17.

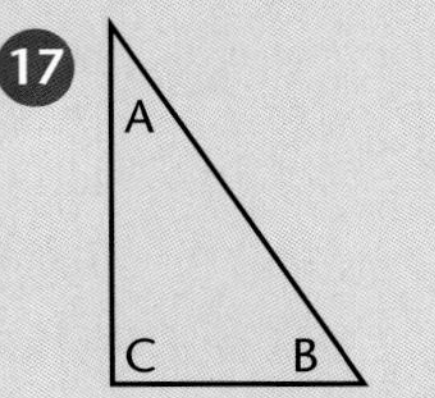

19.

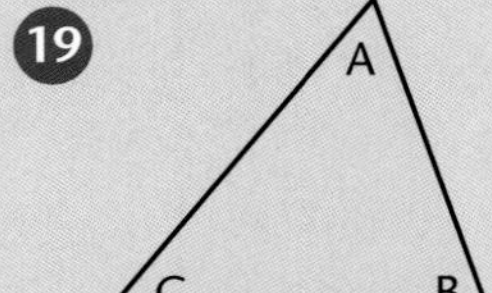

18.

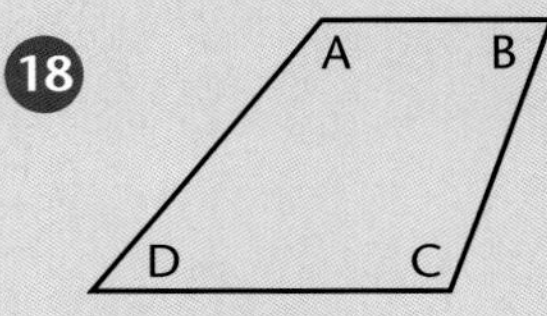

20.

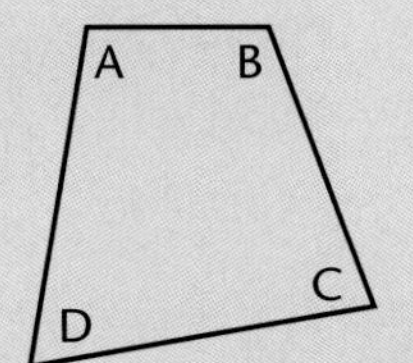

21. What is the sum of the angles of a set square?

I can use the eight points to give and follow directions.

Example
Start at B3
North 2 squares
South East 3 squares
West 4 squares
Arrive at A2

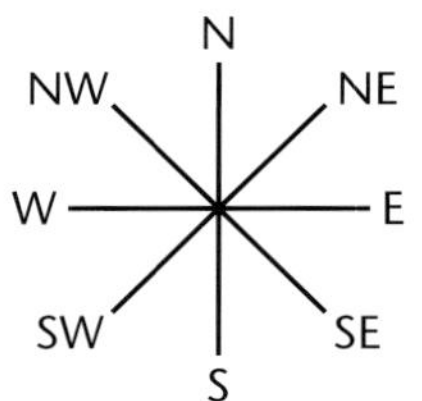

A

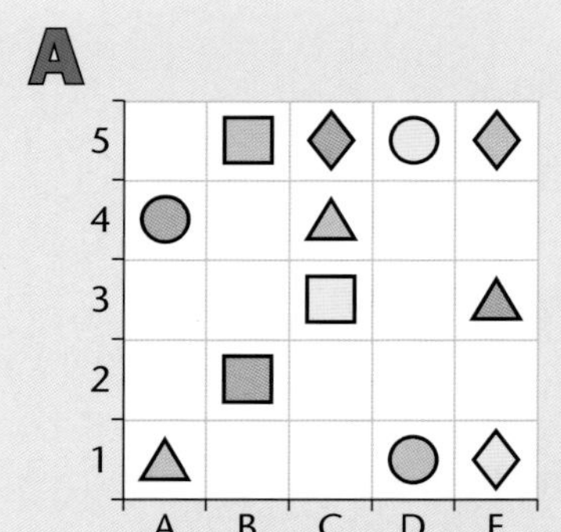

Start at the square given.
Follow the directions.
Draw the symbol you find at the end.

1. B3
   North 2
   East 2
   South 4
2. C3
   East 2
   North 2
   West 3
3. E3
   South 2
   West 3
   North 4
4. D5
   West 2
   South 4
   East 3
5. D4
   SW3
   North 4
   East 2
6. A1
   East 2
   NW1
   NE 3
7. C3
   SE2
   North 4
   SW3
8. D5
   South 4
   West 3
   NE2

B

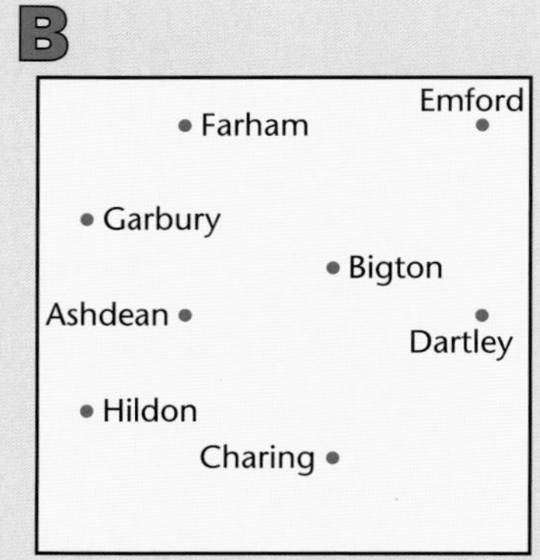

Which town would you come to if you travel:

1. North from Hildon
2. SE from Ashdean
3. West from Dartley
4. NW from Bigton
5. East from Farham
6. SW from Farham
7. South from Bigton
8. NE from Hildon?

In which direction would you travel going from:

9. Farham to Ashdean
10. Charing to Dartley
11. Ashdean to Dartley
12. Garbury to Ashdean
13. Emford to Bigton
14. Bigton to Farham
15. Hildon to Garbury
16. Ashdean to Hildon

C

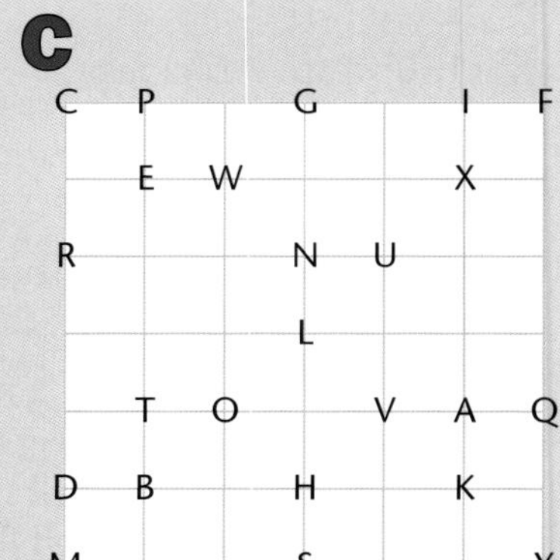

Example FLY
Start at F, SW3, SE3.
Follow the directions to find the word.

1. Start at W
   S3 NW2 S3
2. Start at P
   SE4 N4 SW2
3. Start at M
   NE2 E2 NW3
4. Start at B
   NE3 W4 E3

Write directions to spell:

5. DIGS
6. MORE
7. KICK
8. HOAX
9. LETS
10. GNAW
11. HOTEL
12. QUOTE
13. FORCE
14. BUNGLE
15. SHOVEL
16. STORMY
17. Find other words and write their directions.

E2 MULTIPLICATION FACTS FOR 7

I know the 7 times-table.

A

What is

1. 5×5
2. 9×4
3. 6×8
4. 8×3
5. 7×6
6. 0×2
7. 4×10
8. 9×5
9. 8×8
10. 6×3
11. 7×4
12. 9×6
13. $16 \div 2$
14. $45 \div 5$
15. $32 \div 4$
16. $36 \div 6$
17. $56 \div 8$
18. $27 \div 3$
19. $100 \div 10$
20. $48 \div 6$
21. $24 \div 4$
22. $72 \div 8$
23. $40 \div 5$
24. $21 \div 3$

B

Write the answers only.

1. 4×7
2. 8×7
3. 3×7
4. 7×7
5. 9×7
6. 5×7
7. 2×7
8. 6×7
9. $21 \div 7$
10. $35 \div 7$
11. $49 \div 7$
12. $14 \div 7$
13. $42 \div 7$
14. $63 \div 7$
15. $28 \div 7$
16. $56 \div 7$

Copy and complete.

17. $\square \times 7 = 35$
18. $\square \times 7 = 49$
19. $\square \times 7 = 28$
20. $\square \times 7 = 63$
21. $\square \div 7 = 3$
22. $\square \div 7 = 6$
23. $\square \div 7 = 2$
24. $\square \div 7 = 8$

How many weeks make:

25. 21 days
26. 56 days
27. 70 days
28. 49 days?

How many days make:

29. 4 weeks
30. 9 weeks
31. 5 weeks
32. 20 weeks?

C

Write the answers only.

1. 20×7
2. 50×7
3. 80×7
4. 40×7
5. 70×7
6. 30×7
7. 90×7
8. 60×7
9. $490 \div 7$
10. $280 \div 7$
11. $140 \div 7$
12. $560 \div 7$
13. $350 \div 7$
14. $210 \div 7$
15. $420 \div 7$
16. $630 \div 7$

Work out by multiplying by 7 and doubling.

17. 5×14
18. 2×14
19. 6×14
20. 9×14
21. 3×14
22. 8×14
23. 4×14
24. 7×14
25. How many days make 52 weeks?
26. How many weeks are there in 224 days?
27. Each minibus can carry 13 passengers. How many passengers can be carried in 7 minibuses?

28. What number is seven times greater than seven times seven?

E2 MULTIPLES PROBLEMS

I can use my knowledge of multiples to solve problems.

Example

Anton has less than 30 books. He sorts them into piles of 4 and he has 1 left over. He sorts them into piles of 5 and he has 2 left over. How many books does he have?

Write out the multiples of 4 plus 1 to 30 and the multiples of 5 plus 2 to 30.

FOURS + 1	5	9	13	17	21	25	29
FIVES + 2	7	12	17	22	27		

17 appears in both lists.

Answer: *Anton has 17 books.*

A

Meals for adults cost £5. Meals for children cost £3. The bill for the Davis family comes to £34. How many adults and how many children had meals?

1. Write out multiples of 3 to 34.
2. Write out the multiples of 5 to 34.
3. Look for a pair of numbers, one from each list, that add up to 34.
4. Copy and complete this sentence. The Davis family bought ☐ meals for adults costing £☐ and ☐ meals for children costing £☐.
5. There are two possible solutions. Look at your lists of multiples. Find another pair of numbers that add up to 34. Copy and complete the above sentence for this solution as well.

B

1. Jo has between 20 and 30 cans of cat food. She sorts them into piles of 3 and she has 2 left over. She sorts them into piles of 4 and she has 3 left over. How many cans does she have?

2. Apples are sold in bags of eight. Oranges are sold in bags of three. Linda buys 51 apples and oranges altogether. How many of each fruit does she buy?
Find all the possible solutions.

C

1. The songs on a CD last for either 4 or 5 minutes. The CD lasts for 67 minutes. How many songs are 4 minutes long and how many last for 5 minutes?
Find all the possible solutions.

2. A greengrocer has over 50 apples. He sorts them into bags of 4 and he has 3 left over. He sorts them into bags of 9 and he has 3 left over again.
   a) How many apples does the greengrocer have?
   b) How could he sort them into bags of 4 *and* bags of 9 and not have any left over?
   Find both possible solutions.

I can write fractions bigger than one whole as mixed numbers.

Examples

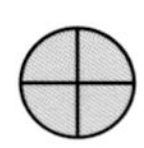

$\frac{4}{4} = 1$ $\frac{5}{4} = 1\frac{1}{4}$ $\frac{6}{4} = 1\frac{2}{4}$

Counting using improper fractions $0, \frac{1}{4}, \frac{2}{4}, \frac{3}{4}, \frac{4}{4}, \frac{5}{4}, \frac{6}{4}, \frac{7}{4}, \frac{8}{4}\ldots$

Counting using mixed numbers $0, \frac{1}{4}, \frac{2}{4}, \frac{3}{4}, 1, 1\frac{1}{4}, 1\frac{2}{4}, 1\frac{3}{4}, 2\ldots$

A

Use the diagram to help complete the fraction.

1. $1 = \frac{\square}{3}$ 
2. $1 = \frac{\square}{10}$ 
3. $1 = \frac{\square}{\square}$ 
4. $1 = \frac{\square}{\square}$ 

Copy and complete.

5. 1 = ☐ quarters
6. 1 = ☐ halves
7. 1 = ☐ fifths
8. 1 = ☐ hundredths

Write the next four terms in each sequence as mixed numbers.

9. $0, \frac{1}{2}, 1, 1\frac{1}{2}$
10. $0, \frac{1}{3}, \frac{2}{3}, 1, 1\frac{1}{3}$
11. $0, \frac{1}{5}, \frac{2}{5}, \frac{3}{5}, \frac{4}{5}$
12. $0, \frac{1}{6}, \frac{2}{6}, \frac{3}{6}, \frac{4}{6}$

B

Write the shaded area as a mixed number

1.
2.
3.
4.
5.
6.
7.
8.

Copy and complete.

9. 5 thirds = 1☐
10. 3 halves = ☐$\frac{1}{2}$
11. 13 tenths = 1☐
12. 14 sixths = ☐$\frac{2}{6}$
13. 24 fifths = ☐
14. 13 eighths = ☐
15. 10 thirds = ☐
16. 7 sixths = ☐

C

Change to mixed numbers.

1. $\frac{36}{10}$
2. $\frac{11}{2}$
3. $\frac{12}{7}$
4. $\frac{19}{4}$
5. $\frac{168}{100}$
6. $\frac{23}{3}$
7. $\frac{17}{12}$
8. $\frac{38}{5}$

Copy and complete.

9. $3\frac{2}{7}$ = ☐ sevenths
10. $9\frac{1}{4}$ = ☐ quarters
11. $8\frac{4}{10}$ = ☐ tenths
12. $5\frac{1}{6}$ = ☐ sixths
13. $3\frac{2}{5}$ = ☐ fifths
14. $6\frac{1}{8}$ = ☐ eighths
15. $7\frac{2}{3}$ = ☐ thirds
16. $4\frac{91}{100}$ = ☐ hundredths

Write the next four terms in each sequence using mixed numbers.

17. $\frac{1}{5}, \frac{3}{5}, 1, 1\frac{2}{5}$
18. $\frac{1}{3}, 1, 1\frac{2}{3}, 2\frac{1}{3}$
19. $\frac{1}{8}, \frac{3}{8}, \frac{5}{8}, \frac{7}{8}$
20. $\frac{15}{100}, \frac{30}{100}, \frac{45}{100}, \frac{60}{100}$

E2 FRACTIONS THAT TOTAL 1

I can find pairs of fractions that total 1 and use this to solve problems.

Examples

What number when added to $\frac{3}{10}$, makes one whole?

Answer $\frac{7}{10}$, because $\frac{10}{10} = 1$

There are 30 apples. One fifth are rotten. How many can be eaten?

$\frac{1}{5}$ of 30 = 6 (6 rotten apples)

30 − 6 = 24 (good apples)

Answer *24 apples can be eaten.*

A

Copy and complete.

1. 1 = ☐ thirds
2. 1 = ☐ tenths
3. 1 = ☐ sixths
4. 1 = ☐ eighths

Copy and complete.

5. $1 = \frac{1}{3} + \frac{\square}{3}$
6. $1 = \frac{6}{10} + \frac{\square}{10}$
7. $1 = \frac{3}{5} + \frac{\square}{5}$
8. $1 = \frac{90}{100} + \frac{\square}{100}$
9. Three quarters of the potatoes in the shop have been sold. What fraction have not been sold?
10. One sixth of the children chose mint ice cream. What fraction chose other flavours?
11. A carpenter cuts off four ninths of a plank. What fraction of the plank is left?

B

Write the missing fraction.

1. $1 = \frac{5}{8} + \square$
2. $1 = \frac{9}{10} + \square$
3. $1 = \frac{5}{7} + \square$
4. $1 = \frac{2}{6} + \square$
5. $1 = \frac{7}{12} + \square$
6. $1 = \frac{4}{9} + \square$
7. $1 = \frac{83}{100} + \square$
8. $1 = \frac{24}{50} + \square$
9. Josie has £35. She spends four fifths of her money. How much does she have left?
10. There are 15 children at a party. Two thirds are girls. How many boys are there?

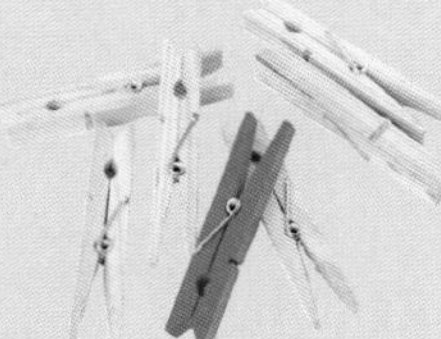

11. There are 28 pegs in a bag. One seventh are red and the rest are white. How many white pegs are there?

C

Copy and complete.

1. $1 = \frac{1}{5} + \frac{2}{5} + \square$
2. $1 = \frac{1}{8} + \square + \frac{5}{8}$
3. $1 = \frac{2}{6} + \frac{1}{6} + \square$
4. $1 = \square + \frac{3}{10} + \frac{2}{10}$
5. $1 = \frac{4}{12} + \square + \frac{5}{12}$
6. $1 = \square + \frac{3}{9} + \frac{2}{9}$
7. $1 = \frac{25}{100} + \frac{40}{100} + \square$
8. $1 = \frac{7}{20} + \square + \frac{9}{20}$
9. A football team played 50 matches in one season. They won $\frac{5}{10}$ of their matches and lost $\frac{3}{10}$. How many were drawn?
10. There were 240 passengers on a plane. Three eighths were women and four eighths were men. How many children were on the plane?
11. A cake weighs 1 kg. Two fifths is eaten. A further three tenths is eaten. How much is left?

E2 EQUIVALENT FRACTIONS

I can find other fractions that are equivalent to a given fraction.

Examples

Equivalent fractions are fractions that look different but are the same.

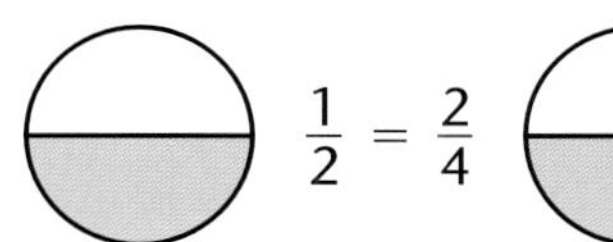

$\frac{1}{2} = \frac{2}{4}$

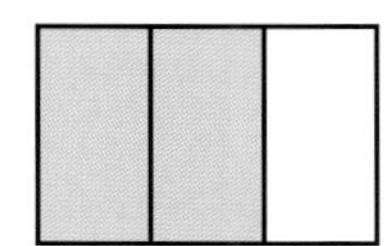

$\frac{2}{3} = \frac{4}{6}$

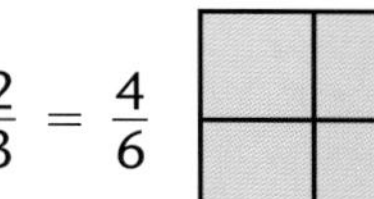

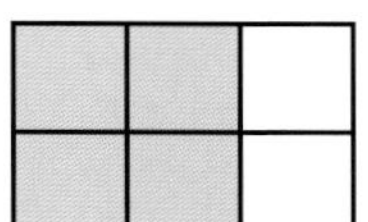

A

Write the equivalent fractions shown in each pair of diagrams.

1 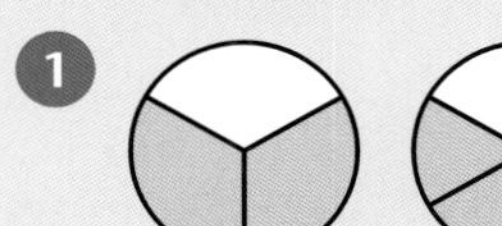

2 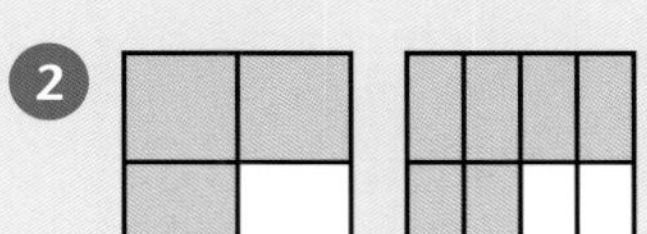

3 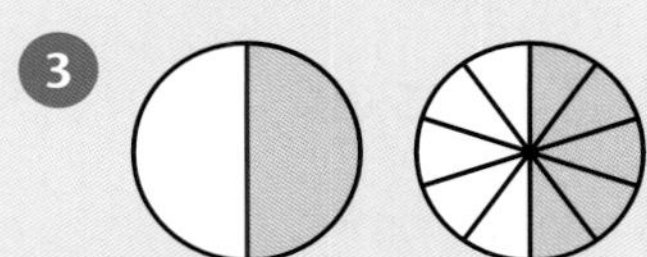

4 

5 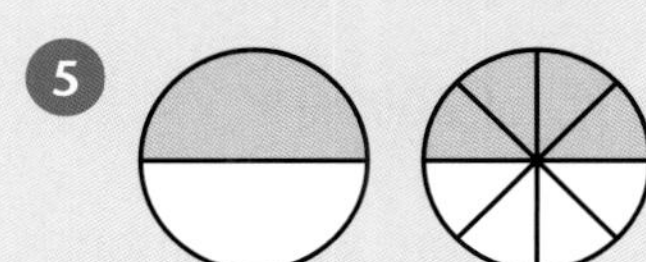

6 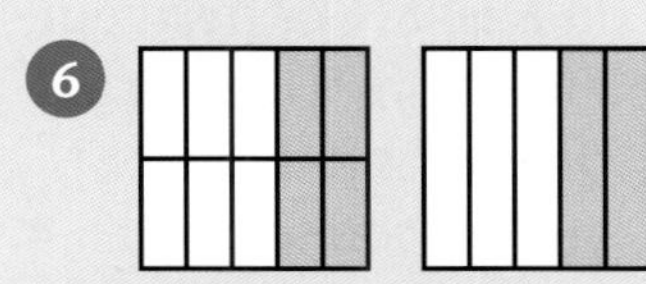

7 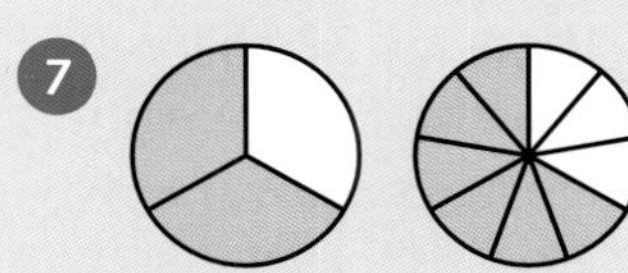

8 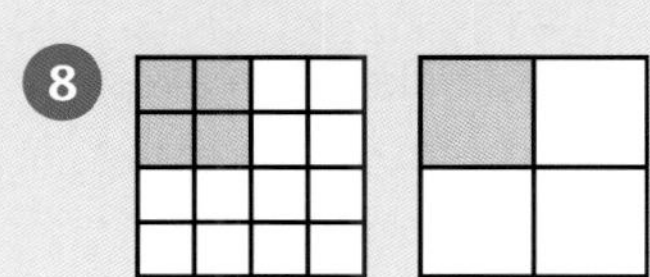

B

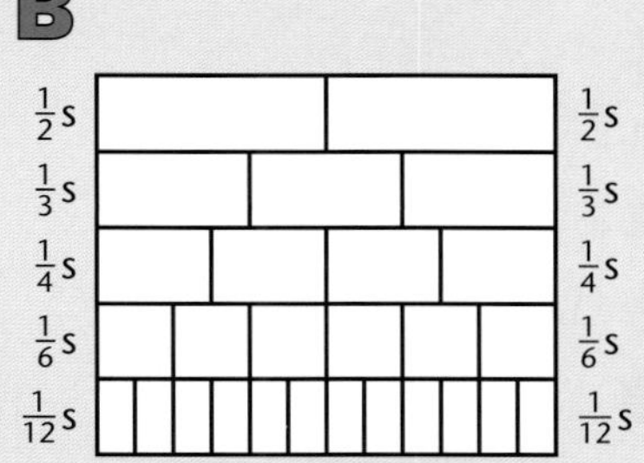

Use the fraction chart. Copy and complete.

1. $\frac{2}{6} = \frac{\square}{12}$
2. $\frac{1}{2} = \frac{\square}{4}$
3. $\frac{2}{3} = \frac{\square}{6}$
4. $\frac{1}{4} = \frac{\square}{12}$
5. $\frac{5}{6} = \frac{\square}{12}$
6. $\frac{1}{3} = \frac{\square}{12}$
7. $\frac{1}{2} = \frac{\square}{6}$
8. $\frac{2}{3} = \frac{\square}{12}$
9. $\frac{1}{6} = \frac{\square}{12}$
10. $\frac{3}{4} = \frac{\square}{12}$
11. $\frac{1}{3} = \frac{\square}{6}$
12. $\frac{4}{6} = \frac{\square}{12}$

Write the next five fractions in these chains.

13. $\frac{1}{2} = \frac{2}{4} = \frac{3}{6}$
14. $\frac{2}{3} = \frac{4}{6} = \frac{6}{9}$
15. $\frac{1}{4} = \frac{2}{8} = \frac{3}{12}$
16. $\frac{3}{5} = \frac{6}{10} = \frac{9}{15}$

C

Copy and complete.

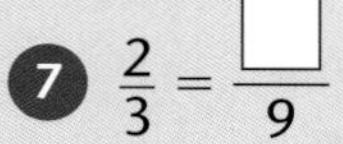

1. $\frac{1}{2} = \frac{\square}{8}$
2. $\frac{3}{5} = \frac{\square}{10}$
3. $\frac{2}{10} = \frac{\square}{100}$
4. $\frac{1}{5} = \frac{\square}{20}$
5. $\frac{3}{4} = \frac{\square}{8}$
6. $\frac{5}{10} = \frac{\square}{20}$
7. $\frac{2}{3} = \frac{\square}{9}$
8. $\frac{8}{25} = \frac{\square}{100}$
9. $\frac{7}{8} = \frac{\square}{16}$
10. $\frac{3}{4} = \frac{\square}{20}$
11. $\frac{4}{9} = \frac{\square}{18}$
12. $\frac{7}{10} = \frac{\square}{50}$

Which is the odd one out in each set of fractions?

13. $\frac{4}{8}$ $\frac{6}{12}$ $\frac{5}{10}$ $\frac{8}{12}$
14. $\frac{3}{4}$ $\frac{9}{12}$ $\frac{16}{20}$ $\frac{6}{8}$
15. $\frac{4}{9}$ $\frac{2}{6}$ $\frac{10}{30}$ $\frac{4}{12}$
16. $\frac{12}{20}$ $\frac{50}{100}$ $\frac{6}{10}$ $\frac{30}{50}$
17. $\frac{15}{20}$ $\frac{7}{10}$ $\frac{35}{50}$ $\frac{70}{100}$
18. $\frac{10}{12}$ $\frac{25}{30}$ $\frac{15}{18}$ $\frac{12}{18}$

Write >, < or = in each box.

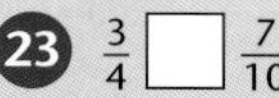

19. $\frac{2}{3} \square \frac{4}{6}$
20. $\frac{3}{5} \square \frac{5}{10}$
21. $\frac{1}{2} \square \frac{4}{8}$
22. $\frac{5}{6} \square \frac{11}{12}$
23. $\frac{3}{4} \square \frac{7}{10}$
24. $\frac{5}{8} \square \frac{11}{16}$
25. $\frac{1}{2} \square \frac{9}{20}$
26. $\frac{1}{3} \square \frac{4}{12}$

E2 FRACTIONS OF QUANTITIES

I can find a fraction of a number or a quantity.

Examples

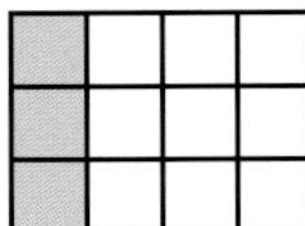

$\frac{1}{4}$ of 12 = 3

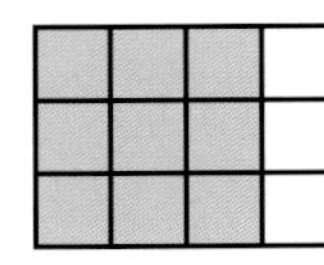

$\frac{3}{4}$ of 12 = 9

$\frac{1}{5}$ of 30 = 30 ÷ 5
= 6

$\frac{4}{5}$ of 30 = (30 ÷ 5) × 4
= 6 × 4
= 24

A

Use the array to help you find:

1. $\frac{1}{2}$ of 8
2. $\frac{1}{4}$ of 8
3. $\frac{1}{4}$ of 12
4. $\frac{1}{3}$ of 12
5. $\frac{1}{2}$ of 12
6. $\frac{1}{2}$ of 10
7. $\frac{1}{5}$ of 10
8. $\frac{1}{3}$ of 18
9. $\frac{1}{6}$ of 18
10. $\frac{1}{2}$ of 18

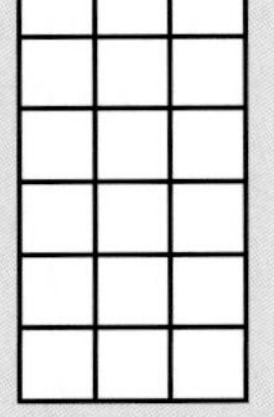

11. $\frac{1}{4}$ of 20
12. $\frac{1}{5}$ of 20
13. $\frac{1}{2}$ of 20

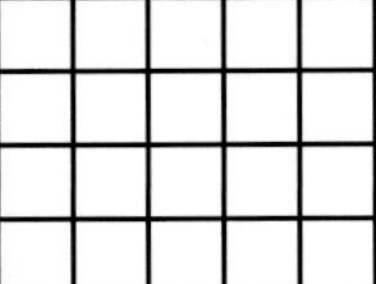

Find

14. $\frac{1}{5}$ of 25
15. $\frac{1}{2}$ of 16
16. $\frac{1}{10}$ of 30
17. $\frac{1}{5}$ of 40
18. $\frac{1}{10}$ of 80
19. $\frac{1}{2}$ of 40

B

Find $\frac{1}{3}$ of:

1. 6
2. 27
3. 21p
4. 30p

Find $\frac{1}{4}$ of:

5. 24
6. 36
7. £40
8. £28

Find $\frac{1}{6}$ of:

9. 30
10. 54
11. 24 cm
12. 48 cm

Find $\frac{1}{10}$ of:

13. 90
14. 150
15. 600 g
16. 1000 g

Look at the arrays in Section A. Work out:

17. a) $\frac{1}{4}$ of 8
    b) $\frac{3}{4}$ of 8
18. a) $\frac{1}{3}$ of 12
    b) $\frac{2}{3}$ of 12
19. a) $\frac{1}{5}$ of 10
    b) $\frac{4}{5}$ of 10
20. a) $\frac{1}{6}$ of 18
    b) $\frac{5}{6}$ of 18
21. a) $\frac{1}{5}$ of 20
    b) $\frac{2}{5}$ of 20
22. a) $\frac{1}{4}$ of 20
    b) $\frac{3}{4}$ of 20

C

Find:

1. $\frac{2}{3}$ of 15
2. $\frac{3}{4}$ of 80
3. $\frac{4}{5}$ of 25
4. $\frac{3}{10}$ of 40
5. $\frac{2}{7}$ of 21
6. $\frac{5}{6}$ of 36
7. $\frac{1}{100}$ of £5.00
8. $\frac{3}{8}$ of 40 cm
9. $\frac{2}{5}$ of 35p
10. $\frac{7}{10}$ of 300 g
11. $\frac{4}{9}$ of 36 m
12. $\frac{21}{100}$ of 200 ml
13. There are 20 questions in a quiz. Ivor gets four fifths right. How many questions did he not answer correctly?
14. There are 32 children in a class. Three eighths are boys. How many are girls?
15. Moiz bakes 36 cakes. Two ninths are eaten. How many are left?

I can recognise equivalent fractions and decimals.

Examples

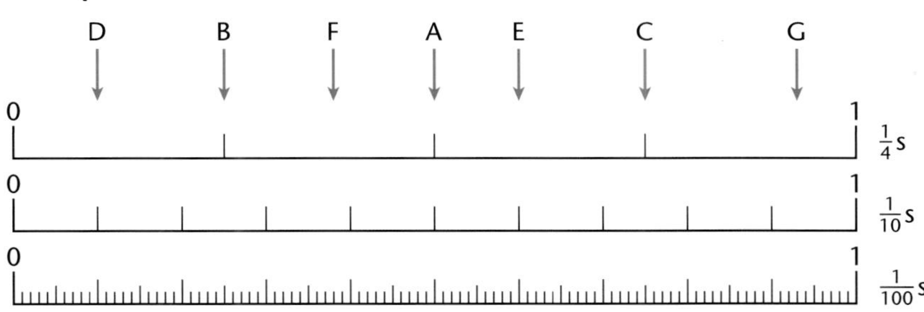

$A = \frac{1}{2} = \frac{5}{10} = 0{\cdot}5$

$B = \frac{1}{4} = \frac{25}{100} = 0{\cdot}25$

$C = \frac{3}{4} = \frac{75}{100} = 0{\cdot}75$

$D = \frac{1}{10} = \frac{10}{100} = 0{\cdot}1$

$E = \frac{60}{100} = \frac{6}{10} = 0{\cdot}6$

$F = \frac{38}{100} = 0{\cdot}38$

$G = \frac{93}{100} = 0{\cdot}93$

A

Write each of the letters as
a) a fraction
b) a decimal.

1
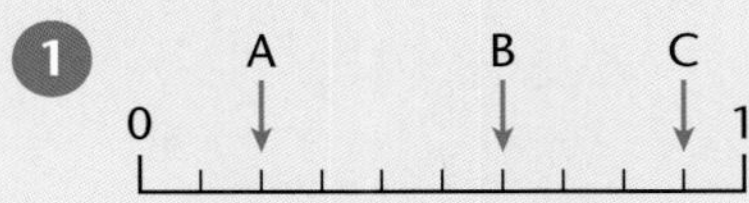

2
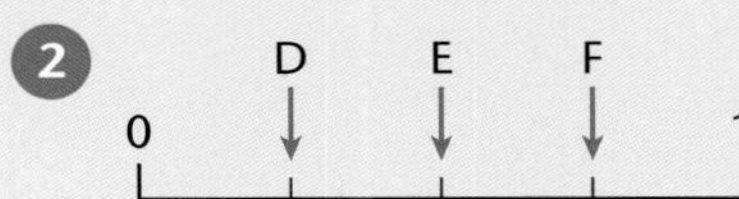

3 G H I — 0·3 0·4 0·5 0·6 0·7

Write the shaded part of each shape as:
a) a fraction
b) a decimal.

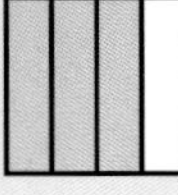

B

Copy and complete.

1 $\frac{3}{10} + \frac{5}{100} = \frac{\square}{100} = 0{\cdot}35$

2 $\frac{9}{10} + \frac{2}{100} = \frac{\square}{100} = \square$

3 $\frac{\square}{10} + \frac{\square}{100} = \frac{12}{100} = \square$

4 $\frac{\square}{10} + \frac{\square}{100} = \frac{47}{100} = \square$

Write as fractions.

5 0·16
6 0·5
7 0·04
8 0·87
9 0·3
10 0·05
11 0·75
12 0·21

Write as decimals.

13 $\frac{51}{100}$
14 $\frac{2}{100}$
15 $\frac{8}{10}$
16 $\frac{32}{100}$
17 $\frac{15}{100}$
18 $\frac{1}{4}$
19 $\frac{99}{100}$
20 $\frac{9}{100}$

Which is larger?

21 $\frac{1}{2}$ or 0·22
22 $\frac{1}{4}$ or 0·4
23 $\frac{3}{4}$ or 0·37
24 $\frac{19}{100}$ or 0·9

C

Write as mixed numbers.

1 2·16
2 9·7
3 5·75
4 6·01
5 1·84
6 3·3
7 4·5
8 8·09
9 3·27
10 2·6
11 7·95
12 5·25

Write as decimals.

13 $3\frac{1}{10}$
14 $1\frac{39}{100}$
15 $6\frac{1}{2}$
16 $\frac{4}{100}$
17 $2\frac{3}{100}$
18 $8\frac{3}{4}$
19 $7\frac{62}{100}$
20 $4\frac{1}{4}$
21 $1\frac{7}{100}$
22 $9\frac{8}{10}$
23 $3\frac{11}{100}$
24 $5\frac{5}{100}$

Give the answer as a decimal.

25 $\frac{1}{2} + 0{\cdot}14$

26 $0{\cdot}7 + \frac{1}{4}$

27 $\frac{3}{4} - 0{\cdot}3$

28 $0{\cdot}8 - \frac{6}{100}$

I can count on and back and develop number sequences.

Examples

To find the rule that links the numbers study the gaps.

a) −8 −6 −4 −2 The rule is *add 2*.

b) £3·00 £2·50 £2·00 £1·50 The rule is *subtract 50p*.

A

Write the first six numbers in each sequence.

	Start at	Rule		Start at	Rule
1	7	Add 2	7	34	Subtract 2
2	15	Add 5	8	125	Subtract 10
3	4	Add 4	9	22	Subtract 3
4	15	Add 3	10	0	Subtract 1
5	−10	Add 1	11	36	Subtract 6
6	£0.10	Add 10p	12	£5.00	Subtract 50p

B

Copy and complete by filling in the boxes.

1. 24 30 36 42 ☐ ☐
2. 51 49 47 45 ☐ ☐
3. 75 78 81 84 ☐ ☐
4. 20 40 60 80 ☐ ☐
5. ☐ ☐ −1 −2 −3 −4
6. ☐ ☐ 1 4 7 10
7. −7 −5 −3 −1 ☐ ☐
8. 8 6 4 2 ☐ ☐
9. 0·1 m 0·3 m 0·5 m 0·7 m ☐ ☐
10. 1·75 m 1·5 m 1·25 m 1·0 m ☐ ☐
11. £1·80 £1·60 £1·40 £1·20 ☐ ☐
12. £0·02 £0·04 £0·06 £0·08 ☐ ☐

C

Copy the sequences and write the next three numbers. What is the rule for each sequence?

1. 57 59 61 63
2. 126 122 118 114
3. 46 53 60 67
4. 65 56 47 38
5. 8 6 4 2
6. −20 −15 −10 −5
7. −14 −10 −6 −2
8. 22 16 10 4
9. 0·2 0·4 0·6 0·8
10. 1·4 1·3 1·2 1·1
11. 0·96 0·97 0·98 0·99
12. 1·2 1·15 1·1 1·05

I can find pairs of numbers that sum to 100.

A

Copy and complete.

1. 60 + ☐ = 100
2. 20 + ☐ = 100
3. 40 + ☐ = 100
4. 70 + ☐ = 100
5. 90 + ☐ = 100
6. 30 + ☐ = 100
7. 55 + ☐ = 100
8. 85 + ☐ = 100
9. 15 + ☐ = 100
10. 45 + ☐ = 100
11. 95 + ☐ = 100
12. 25 + ☐ = 100

B

Copy and complete.

1. 73 + ☐ = 100
2. 39 + ☐ = 100
3. 64 + ☐ = 100
4. 91 + ☐ = 100
5. 48 + ☐ = 100
6. 27 + ☐ = 100
7. 850 + ☐ = 1000
8. 350 + ☐ = 1000
9. 50 + ☐ = 1000
10. 650 + ☐ = 1000
11. 750 + ☐ = 1000
12. 150 + ☐ = 1000

C

Copy and complete.

1. 510 + ☐ = 1000
2. 760 + ☐ = 1000
3. 390 + ☐ = 1000
4. 140 + ☐ = 1000
5. 820 + ☐ = 1000
6. 460 + ☐ = 1000
7. 580 + ☐ = 1000
8. 610 + ☐ = 1000
9. 250 + ☐ = 1000
10. 930 + ☐ = 1000
11. 770 + ☐ = 1000
12. 450 + ☐ = 1000

I can add or subtract two-digit numbers mentally.

A

Work out

1. 53 + 34
2. 41 + 42
3. 76 − 34
4. 82 − 21
5. 35 + 19
6. 54 + 25
7. 98 − 43
8. 57 − 26
9. 22 + 23
10. 45 + 31
11. 64 − 19
12. 88 − 53

B

Work out

1. 36 + 37
2. 58 + 26
3. 86 − 38
4. 61 − 29
5. 26 + 35
6. 48 + 47
7. 55 − 28
8. 92 − 69
9. 53 + 29
10. 65 + 37
11. 74 − 35
12. 83 − 48

C

Copy and complete.

1. ☐ + 65 = 93
2. ☐ + 28 = 82
3. ☐ − 84 = 49
4. ☐ − 67 = 55
5. ☐ + 37 = 86
6. ☐ + 54 = 91
7. ☐ − 95 = 89
8. ☐ − 58 = 93
9. ☐ + 49 = 81
10. ☐ + 26 = 67
11. ☐ − 79 = 66
12. ☐ − 46 = 76

I can use a written method for addition calculations.

Examples

```
 384 = 300 +  80 +  4        384      384      384      384
+129 = 100 +  20 +  9       +129     +129     + 79     + 79
       400 + 100 + 13 = 513  400       13       13      463
                             100      100      150       11
                              13      400      300
                             513      513      463
```

A

Copy and complete.

1. 74 + 18
2. 58 + 47
3. 62 + 29
4. 87 + 31
5. 64 + 55
6. 96 + 68
7. 78 + 35
8. 89 + 52
9. 65 + 47
10. 92 + 38
11. Jamie has read 75 pages of his book. He has 47 more pages to read. How many pages does the book have?
12. Mia drives 63 miles on Saturday and 54 miles on Sunday. How many miles does she drive altogether?
13. Jenny buys a dress for £79 and a skirt for £25. How much has she spent altogether?

B

Copy and complete.

1. 163 + 72
2. 347 + 138
3. 236 + 82
4. 491 + 245
5. 258 + 127
6. 145 + 86
7. 365 + 284
8. 149 + 77
9. 573 + 165
10. 752 + 183
11. There are 482 cars and 127 lorries stuck in a traffic jam. How many vehicles are held up altogether?
12. 285 men and 136 women work in a factory. How many people work there altogether?
13. Rachel buys a television for £378 and a video recorder for £175. How much does she spend altogether?

C

Set out as in the example and add by carrying.

1. 487 + 268
2. 357 + 94
3. 268 + 185
4. 1695 + 762
5. 2259 + 478
6. 366 + 269
7. 297 + 124
8. 1569 + 375
9. 1408 + 926
10. 1872 + 493
11. In one day 657 adults and 394 children visit a zoo. How many people visit the zoo altogether?

12. Peter has £2794 in a savings account. He pays in £483. How much is now in the account?

I can find the difference between numbers with different numbers of digits and also between amounts of money.

Examples

325 − 78

Line up the units

```
  325
−  78
   22 → 100
  225 → 325
  247
```

£6.52 − £3.74

Change pounds to pence

```
  652
− 374
   26 → 400
  252 → 652
  278 → £2·78
```

Change answer to pounds.

or

```
  £6·52
− £3·74
  £0·26 → £4·00
  £2·52 → £6·52
  £2·78
```

A

Copy and complete.

1. 134 − 29
2. 163 − 47
3. 138 − 56
4. 253 − 72
5. 219 − 84
6. 142 − 65
7. £1·36 − £0·24
8. £3·58 − £1·37
9. £2·75 − £1·42
10. £4·30 − £3·25
11. £2·61 − £1·34
12. £3·87 − £2·58
13. There are 126 palm trees on an island. 53 are blown down in a hurricane. How many trees are left standing?

B

Set out as in the examples and find the differences.

1. 156 − 73
2. 248 − 69
3. 377 − 95
4. 136 − 87
5. 456 − 74
6. 319 − 36
7. £2·72 − £1·38
8. £4·61 − £2·57
9. £5·80 − £2·34
10. £3·35 − £1·69
11. £6·27 − £3·43
12. £5·53 − £3·78
13. Liam has £7·29 in his piggy bank. He takes out £1·40. How much money is left in the piggy bank?
14. A survey of visitors to a museum finds that 228 people came by car and 52 fewer people came by coach. How many people came by coach?

C

Set out as in the examples and find the differences.

1. 1306 and 123
2. 198 and 2451
3. 4623 and 59
4. 437 and 3510
5. 5732 and 146
6. 88 and 6145
7. £13·35 and £1·79
8. £2·84 and £5·70
9. £4·21 and £12·53
10. £6·13 and £13·17
11. £18·42 and £7·50
12. £7.97 and £12.92
13. An ice cream seller has takings of £1321 on Saturday and £548 on Sunday. What is the difference in the takings?
14. Olivia has £7·17 in her purse. She spends £3·49. How much money is left in the purse?

I can multiply two-digit numbers by one-digit numbers.

Example 27×6

Approximate first
27 rounds to 30
$30 \times 6 = 180$
27×6 is less than 180

×	6
20	120
7	42
	162

	20 + 7
×	6
	120
	42
	162

	20 + 7	
×	6	
	120	20 × 6
	42	7 × 6
	162	

A

Work out

1. 17×2
2. 23×3
3. 15×4
4. 21×5
5. 26×2
6. 19×5
7. 18×3
8. 46×5
9. There are 27 children in each class. There are four classes. How many children are there in the school?
10. Jennifer weighs 36 kg. Her father is twice as heavy. What does her father weigh?
11. There are 14 strawberries on each plate. How many are there on five plates?

B

Work out

1. 67×2
2. 26×4
3. 32×6
4. 41×7
5. 39×5
6. 59×3
7. 83×2
8. 28×5
9. 14×8
10. 37×4
11. 46×4
12. 73×5
13. 25×8
14. 19×9
15. 58×3
16. 34×6
17. Hari works out that it is 26 weeks until his birthday. How many days is 26 weeks?
18. There are four tennis balls in each can. How many balls are there in the 58 cans bought by a tennis club?
19. A necklace is made with 45 beads. How many beads are needed for six necklaces?
20. There are eight flowers in each bunch. How many flowers are there in 18 bunches?

C

Work out

1. 368×5
2. 629×4
3. 137×4
4. 245×7
5. 157×6
6. 325×9
7. 168×7
8. 598×3
9. 436×8
10. 158×9
11. 318×6
12. 182×8
13. 473×5
14. 329×7
15. 246×9
16. 397×8
17. A bus travels 36 miles eight times each day. How many miles does it travel in a week?
18. One can of fish weighs 225 g. What is the weight of four cans?
19. There are 6 eggs in each box. There are 64 boxes in each crate. How many eggs are there in five crates?
20. A Junior School has 118 pupils. A local Secondary School has eight times as many children. How many children go to the Secondary School?

I can divide a two-digit number by a one-digit number.

Examples

$86 \div 5$

Estimate

$5 \times 10 = 50$

$5 \times 20 = 100$

$10 < 86 \div 5 < 20$

$$\begin{aligned} 86 \div 5 &= (50 \div 5) + (36 \div 5) \\ &= 10 + 7R1 \\ &= 17R1 \end{aligned}$$

$$\begin{array}{rl} & 86 \\ - & \underline{50} \; (5 \times 10) \\ & 36 \\ - & \underline{35} \; (5 \times 7) \\ & 1 \end{array}$$

Answer 17R1

$186 \div 5$

$$\begin{array}{rl} & 186 \\ - & \underline{150} \; (5 \times 30) \\ & 36 \\ & \underline{35} \; (5 \times 7) \\ & 1 \end{array}$$

Answer 37R1

A

Work out

1. $24 \div 2$
2. $32 \div 2$
3. $28 \div 2$
4. $38 \div 2$
5. $39 \div 3$
6. $45 \div 3$
7. $54 \div 3$
8. $51 \div 3$
9. $48 \div 4$
10. $64 \div 4$
11. $76 \div 4$
12. $56 \div 4$
13. $65 \div 5$
14. $75 \div 5$
15. $90 \div 5$
16. $85 \div 5$
17. How many 3s are there in 42?
18. What is 72 divided by 4?
19. Share 80 by 5.
20. Divide 34 by 2.

B

Work out

1. $36 \div 2$
2. $78 \div 5$
3. $96 \div 6$
4. $88 \div 7$
5. $70 \div 3$
6. $99 \div 8$
7. $76 \div 4$
8. $94 \div 3$
9. $120 \div 7$
10. $108 \div 6$
11. $102 \div 9$
12. $130 \div 8$
13. $112 \div 6$
14. $153 \div 9$
15. $105 \div 8$
16. $124 \div 7$
17. Cakes are sold in packets of 8. How many packets are made up from 168 cakes?
18. 150 children are divided equally into 6 classes. How many children are there in each class?
19. Craig saves £9 every week. How many weeks will it take him to save £200?
20. How many complete weeks are there in 150 days?

C

Work out

1. $114 \div 6$
2. $147 \div 7$
3. $176 \div 8$
4. $162 \div 9$
5. $126 \div 6$
6. $105 \div 7$
7. $149 \div 8$
8. $225 \div 9$
9. $162 \div 6$
10. $161 \div 7$
11. $232 \div 8$
12. $198 \div 9$
13. $144 \div 6$
14. $217 \div 7$
15. $191 \div 8$
16. $306 \div 9$
17. A packet of sweets weighs 224 g. Each sweet weighs 8 g. How many sweets are there in the packet?
18. Seven oil drums contain 315 litres. How much oil is there in each drum?
19. Each container holds nine litres of petrol. How many containers are needed for 500 litres?
20. How many complete years are there in 200 months?

I can decide whether to round up or down after division.

Examples

- How many £6 tickets can I buy with £47?
  47 ÷ 6 = 7 remainder 5.
  Answer: *7 tickets can be bought.*

- An egg box holds 6 eggs.
  How many boxes do I need to hold 47 eggs?
  47 ÷ 6 = 7 remainder 5.
  Answer: *8 boxes are needed.*

A

1. How many pairs of socks can be made from 27 socks?
2. 4 children can sit at a table.
   How many tables are needed to seat the 30 children in a class?
3. Peppers are sold in packs of three.
   How many packs can be made from 20 peppers?

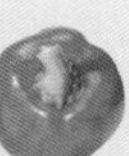

4. T-shirts cost £5 each.
   How many can be bought for £38?
5. 4 oranges can be packed into a bag.
   How many bags can be filled with 35 oranges?
6. A car can carry 5 passengers. How many cars are needed to carry 42 passengers?
7. Rubbers are sold in packets of 6.
   How many packets are needed for 32 children?

B

1. Tickets for a film show cost £3.
   How many tickets can be bought for £35?
2. A van can carry 8 large boxes.
   How many vans are needed to carry 50 boxes?
3. How many 5-a-side football teams can be made up from 59 players?
4. Six children can sleep in a large tent.
   How many tents are needed for 75 children?
5. Chocko chocolate bars are sold in packs of 6.
   How many packs can be made from 52 bars?
6. Ten videos can be stored on a shelf.
   How many shelves are needed to store 95 videos?
7. Tennis balls are sold in tubes of 4.
   How many tubes can be filled from 70 balls?

C

1. Cans of drink are sold in packs of 6. How many packs can be made from 194 cans?
2. Each tray holds nine flowers. How many trays are needed for 120 flowers?
3. A school hall can fit 20 chairs into one row.
   How many rows are needed to seat 312 parents for the school concert?
4. 80 cm of material is needed to make a costume.
   How many costumes can be made from 7 metres of material?
5. A baker puts his cakes onto trays which hold 8 cakes.
   How many trays are needed for 180 cakes?
6. Albert saved £600 every month. How many months did it take him to save £5000 for his new motor cycle?

A3 NUMBER PROBLEMS

I can solve mathematical problems.

Example

Each week Jacob saved £2 more than the week before.
After 5 weeks he had saved £100.
How much did he save each week?

£100 ÷ 5 = £20
This calculation gives the middle number in the sequence.

Answer
Week 1 – £16
Week 2 – £18
Week 3 – £20
Week 4 – £22
Week 5 – £24
Total £100

A

1. There are 15 chocolates in a box. Nikki eats 2 fewer each day. She finishes the box in three days. How many chocolates does she eat each day?

2. A gardener finds snails are eating his cabbages. Each day he removes one more snail than the day before. After five days he has removed 20 snails. How many has he removed each day?

B

1. A pizza parlour delivers 2 fewer pizzas each day than the day before. After 5 days 120 pizzas have been delivered. How many are delivered each day?

2. Bridget swims two lengths further each day than the day before. After seven days she has swum 280 lengths. How many lengths has she swum each day?

C

1. The camel train travels two miles further each day than the day before. After eight days it has travelled 112 miles. How far has it travelled each day?

2. Tania's book has 300 pages. Each day she reads 10 more pages than the day before. She finishes her book in 6 days. How many pages does she read each day?

3. Carlo buys two ice creams for £1·50. One ice cream costs 20p more than the other. How much does each ice cream cost?

A3 WORD PROBLEMS 94

I can solve one and two-step word problems.

Example

Rudi buys a pair of football boots and two footballs for £54·00.
The footballs cost £9·50 each.
How much do the boots cost?

£9·50 × 2 = £19·00
£54·00 − £19·00 = £35·00
Answer
The boots cost £35.

A

1. Rhys bought a book for £3·49. He had £0·68 left. How much money did he have before he bought the book?
2. There are 36 sweets in 3 packets. How many sweets are there in one packet?
3. Claire has 46 books on her top shelf and 9 less on her bottom shelf. How many books does she have altogether?
4. Alan has four lengths of railway track, each 20 cm long. How long is the track when he puts them together?
5. Hazel has £4·20 in her piggy bank. She puts in 12p. She takes out 45p. How much is left?

B

1. There were 176 adults, 9 girls and 32 boys on a plane. How many people were on the plane altogether?
2. A bicycle costs £195. The price is reduced by £59. What is the new price?

3. A can of beans weighs 400 g. How much do six cans weigh in kilograms?
4. Emma has 35 fish in her pond. James has 28 more fish than Emma. How many fish do they have altogether?
5. Salim had 84 conkers. He gave one quarter of them to his brother. How many did Salim have left?
6. Omar buys four books for £3·49 each. How much change would he have from a £20 note?

C

1. Priya spent £8·73 in the grocers, 96p in the newsagents and £5·38 in the chemists. How much did she spend altogether?
2. A builder orders 535 bricks. He uses 278 of them. How many bricks are left?
3. How many 150 ml glasses can be filled from one and a half litres?
4. Steven's book has 146 pages. He needs to read 25 more pages to reach half way. What page is he on?
5. Every day Sharon records her favourite programme, *Countdown*, which lasts for 45 minutes. After 5 days how much recording time is left on a 4 hour video tape?
6. A film was watched by 238 people in the afternoon. In the evening the audience increased by 157. What was the total audience for the two performances?

I know the 9 times-table.

A

1. Copy and complete the table by taking the ones from the tens to make the nines.

TIMES TABLES		
TENS	ONES	NINES
10	1	9
20	2	18
30	3	
40		
50		
60		
70		
80		
90		
100		

2. Copy and complete the table by adding the threes and sixes to make the nines.

TIMES TABLES		
THREES	SIXES	NINES
3	6	9
6	12	
9		
12		
15		
18		
21		
24		
27		
30		

B

Write the answers only.

1. 4×9
2. 8×9
3. 1×9
4. 10×9
5. 0×9
6. 6×9
7. 9×9
8. 5×9
9. 7×9
10. 3×9
11. $45 \div 9$
12. $81 \div 9$
13. $54 \div 9$
14. $18 \div 9$
15. $36 \div 9$
16. $63 \div 9$
17. $90 \div 9$
18. $72 \div 9$
19. $27 \div 9$
20. $9 \div 9$
21. $\square \times 9 = 54$
22. $\square \times 9 = 36$
23. $\square \times 9 = 81$
24. $\square \times 9 = 90$
25. $\square \times 9 = 27$
26. $\square \times 9 = 72$
27. $\square \times 9 = 45$
28. $\square \times 9 = 63$
29. $\square \div 9 = 4$
30. $\square \div 9 = 10$
31. $\square \div 9 = 8$
32. $\square \div 9 = 3$
33. $\square \div 9 = 7$
34. $\square \div 9 = 1$
35. $\square \div 9 = 6$
36. $\square \div 9 = 9$

C

Write the answers only.

1. 30×9
2. 50×9
3. 70×9
4. 20×9
5. 40×9
6. 80×9
7. 60×9
8. 90×9
9. $270 \div 9$
10. $450 \div 9$
11. $180 \div 9$
12. $810 \div 9$
13. $360 \div 9$
14. $540 \div 9$
15. $720 \div 9$
16. $630 \div 9$

Work out by multiplying by 9 and doubling.

17. 3×18
18. 6×18
19. 2×18
20. 5×18
21. 8×18
22. 4×18
23. 9×18
24. 7×18

25. 

There were 684 weddings at a church in one year. One ninth of the weddings were in June. How many weddings were in June?

26. One computer game costs £9. A shop sells 84. How much money is taken?

B3 MULTIPLICATION AND ARRAYS

I can use a range of vocabulary associated with multiplication and division and use arrays to identify factors of a number.

Example

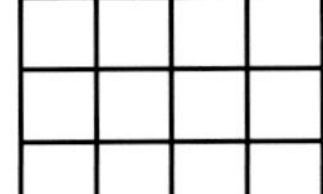

$4 \times 3 = 12$
$3 \times 4 = 12$
$12 \div 4 = 3$
$12 \div 3 = 4$

The product of 4 and 3 is 12.
12 is a multiple of both 3 and 4.
3 and 4 are factors of 12.

A

Write two multiplication facts for each of these arrays.

1. 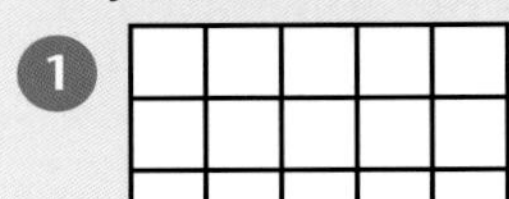
2. 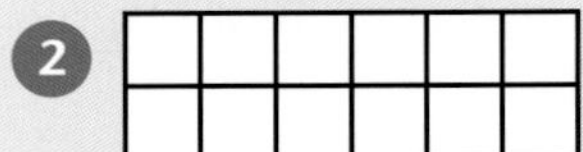
3. 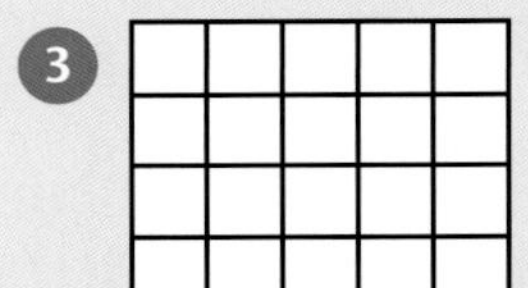
4. 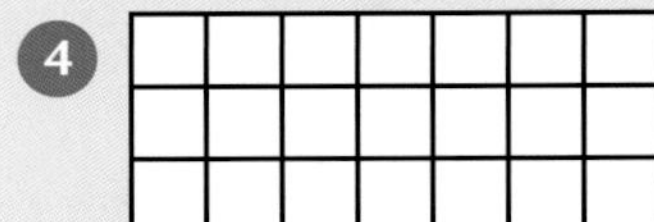

What is the product of:

5. 5 and 10
6. 3 and 6
7. 9 and 4
8. 2 and 8?

Write Yes or No.

9. Is 31 a multiple of 3?
10. Is 28 a multiple of 4?
11. Is 54 a multiple of 5?
12. Is 24 a multiple of 2?

B

Use squared paper.
Draw an array to show each of the statements below.

1. The product of 5 and 7 is 35.
2. 18 is a multiple of 3.
3. 2 and 7 are factors of 14.
4. For each of the three arrays you have drawn write down 2 multiplication facts and 2 division facts.

What is the product of:

5. 7 and 6
6. 4 and 12
7. 8 and 7
8. 3 and 20?

Write down:

9. the 4 factors of 15
10. the 6 factors of 18
11. the 3 factors of 49
12. the 8 factors of 24

Find a number that is a multiple of both:

13. 4 and 7
14. 5 and 8
15. 6 and 10
16. 3 and 9

C

Use these digits.

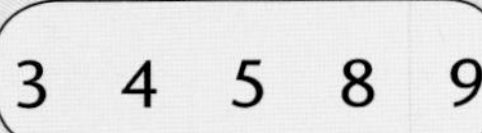

What is the product of:

1. the three smallest numbers?
2. the three largest numbers?

Which of the numbers in the box are factors of:

3. 40
4. 36
5. 45
6. 24?

Find two numbers that are multiples of both:

7. 4 and 10
8. 3 and 7
9. 4 and 9
10. 5 and 6

Use these digits:

Make as many 2-digit numbers as you can that are multiples of:

11. 2
12. 5
13. 4
14. 3.

I can work out doubles of two-digit numbers and of multiples of 10 and 100 and the corresponding halves.

Examples

Double 36
$30 + 6$
$\downarrow \quad \downarrow \times 2$
$60 + 12 = 72$

$36 \times 2 = 72$
$360 \times 2 = 720$
$3600 \times 2 = 7200$

Half of 94
$90 + 4$
$\downarrow \quad \downarrow \div 2$
$45 + 2 = 47$

or

Half of 94
$80 + 14$
$\downarrow \quad \downarrow \div 2$
$40 + 7 = 47$

$94 \div 2 = 47$
$940 \div 2 = 470$
$9400 \div 2 = 4700$

A

Copy and complete.

1. $7 \times 2 = \square$
   $70 \times 2 = \square$
   $700 \times 2 = \square$
2. $13 \times 2 = \square$
   $130 \times 2 = \square$
3. $6 \div 2 = \square$
   $60 \div 2 = \square$
   $600 \div 2 = \square$
4. $18 \div 2 = \square$
   $180 \div 2 = \square$

Double each number

5. 300
6. 40
7. 90
8. 200
9. 80
10. 500
11. 14
12. 160
13. 19
14. 120
15. 170
16. 15

Halve each number

17. 800
18. 70
19. 200
20. 30
21. 1000
22. 400
23. 14
24. 120
25. 18
26. 90
27. 12
28. 180

B

Double

1. 27
2. 85
3. 42
4. 68
5. 71
6. 34
7. 96
8. 53
9. 3600
10. 520
11. 870
12. 2400
13. 910
14. 4300
15. 2800
16. 750

Halve

17. 84
18. 186
19. 134
20. 92
21. 158
22. 76
23. 142
24. 174
25. 140
26. 1600
27. 6800
28. 190
29. 1260
30. 130
31. 9600
32. 1820

Investigate the number sequence made by this rule.
Start at 1. Double the last number and add 1.

33. What are the first 8 numbers?
34. What are the gaps between the numbers?
35. Is there a pattern to the numbers in the gaps?

C

Copy and complete.

1. $\square \times 2 = 1640$
2. $\square \times 2 = 1580$
3. $\square \times 2 = 1320$
4. $\square \times 2 = 9800$
5. $\square \times 2 = 5400$
6. $\square \times 2 = 1760$
7. $\square \times 2 = 1480$
8. $\square \times 2 = 1940$
9. $\square \div 2 = 860$
10. $\square \div 2 = 3900$
11. $\square \div 2 = 980$
12. $\square \div 2 = 6500$
13. $\square \div 2 = 770$
14. $\square \div 2 = 840$
15. $\square \div 2 = 6900$
16. $\square \div 2 = 970$

Investigate the number sequence made by this rule.
Start at 2. Double the last number and subtract 1.

17. Is there a pattern to the gaps?
18. Explore the gaps in the gaps.
19. Investigate other sequences made by doubling or halving.

I can use addition and subtraction facts to add and subtract multiples of 10, 100 and 1000.

A

Write the answers only.

1. 6 + 8
2. 8 + 7
3. 4 + 9
4. 7 + 7
5. 6 + 9
6. 9 + 8
7. 5 + 8
8. 9 + 9
9. 16 − 9
10. 15 − 7
11. 13 − 6
12. 17 − 8
13. 14 − 9
14. 15 − 6
15. 16 − 8
16. 14 − 7
17. Use the first fact to work out the other facts.

16 − 9 = 7
17 − □ = 7
18 − □ = 7
19 − □ = 7
□ − 8 = 7
□ − 7 = 7
□ − 6 = 7

B

Write the answers only.

1. 70 + 80
2. 30 + 90
3. 80 + 40
4. 50 + 60
5. 90 + 70
6. 70 + 50
7. 60 + 60
8. 90 + 90
9. 180 − 60
10. 150 − 80
11. 130 − 50
12. 160 − 70
13. 140 − 80
14. 180 − 90
15. 130 − 70
16. 170 − 80
17. 900 + 500
18. 600 + 700
19. 700 + 900
20. 800 + 800
21. 900 + 600
22. 600 + 800
23. 800 + 500
24. 700 + 60
25. 1400 − 600
26. 1700 − 1200
27. 1300 − 800
28. 1500 − 900
29. 1500 − 700
30. 1800 − 900
31. 1600 − 800
32. 1700 − 900

15 − 6 = 9

Use the above fact to make other related facts with an answer of:

33. 9
34. 90
35. 900
36. Find five pairs of two-digit numbers that total 100. You cannot use 0.

C

Copy and complete.

1. 0·9 + □ = 1·7
2. 0·6 + □ = 1·5
3. 0·8 + □ = 1·3
4. 0·7 + □ = 1·3
5. □ + 0·9 = 1·5
6. □ + 0·8 = 1·7
7. □ + 0·7 = 1·4
8. □ + 0·9 = 1·6
9. 1·3 − □ = 0·6
10. 1·8 − □ = 0·9
11. 1·6 − □ = 0·8
12. 1·5 − □ = 0·7
13. □ − 0·9 = 0·5
14. □ − 0·5 = 0·8
15. □ − 0·7 = 0·9
16. □ − 0·8 = 0·6

8 − 3 = 5

Use the above fact to make other related facts with an answer of:

17. 0·5
18. 1·5
19. 0·05
20. Find five pairs of three-digit decimal numbers that total 10. You cannot use 0.

I can use a variety of strategies to add or subtract pairs of numbers mentally.

A

Copy and complete the squares.

1

+	8	9	6
9	17		
7			
8			

2

−	8	7	9
19	11		
16			
18			9

3

+	24	32	53
15			
43			96
34			

4

−	43	26	55
78		52	
63			
99			

5

+	9	21	29
62			
35			
57			

6

−	11	19	21
48			
24			
76			

7

+	34	75	93
200			
800			
500			

8

−	7	9	6
104			
503			
605			

B

Write the answers only.

1. 1268 + 5
2. 150 − 60
3. 300 − 7
4. 76 − 8
5. 800 + 500
6. 463 + 8
7. 80 + 37
8. 8000 − 6
9. 85 − 30
10. 300 + 257
11. 48 + 23
12. 74 − 27
13. 70 + 50
14. 53 + 40
15. 405 − 9
16. 5001 − 4993

Add 49 to:

17. 50
18. 23
19. 47.

Add 57 to:

20. 48
21. 300
22. 230.

Take 71 from:

23. 95
24. 143
25. 118.

Take 36 from:

26. 63
27. 81
28. 55.

Make 100.

29. 43 + □
30. 92 + □
31. 14 + □

C

Copy and complete by writing the missing number in the box.

1. 450 + □ = 730
2. 720 − □ = 430
3. 4005 − □ = 2993
4. 8·3 − □ = 1·8
5. □ + 190 = 550
6. 985 − □ = 420
7. □ − 800 = 561
8. 6·2 + □ = 10·0
9. 5002 − □ = 4899
10. 567 + □ = 600
11. 740 − □ = 280
12. 4·2 + □ = 5
13. 350 + □ = 510
14. 1231 − □ = 700
15. 329 + □ = 400

I can solve one and two-step word problems.

Example

In one week Ryan practises playing his guitar for three 80 minute sessions and four 90 minute sessions. How many hours does he practise in the week?

3×80 mins. $= 240$ mins.
4×90 mins. $= 360$ mins.
$240 + 360 = 600$ mins.
$600 \div 60 = 10$ hours
Answer *Ryan practises for 10 hours.*

A

1. A can of beans weighs 400 g. How much do six cans weigh in kilograms?
2. A glass of orange squash is made with 30 ml of orange and 230 ml of water. How much orange squash is there?
3. There are 34 passengers on a bus. 15 get off. How many passengers are there now on the bus?
4. A class of 30 children were asked what was their favourite colour. Half the children chose red. 7 children chose blue. How many children chose a different colour?
5. One banana costs 15p. How much will a bunch of five bananas cost?

B

Write the answers only.

1. 48 children sit in 4 equal rows. How many children are there in each row?
2. An ice cream tub holds two litres. 500 ml is used. How much ice cream is left in the tub?
3. There are 20 magazines in a pile. Each magazine is 5 mm thick. How high is the pile in centimetres?
4. There are 86 people in a swimming pool. 28 get out. 43 go in. How many are there in the pool now?
5. There are twenty stacks of 6 chairs and fourteen stacks of 4 chairs. How many chairs are there altogether?
6. Four train tickets cost £34. How much does one ticket cost?
7. How many minutes are there in four and three quarter hours?

C

Copy and complete

1. To make four loaves a baker uses half a kilogram of wholemeal flour and 800 g of plain flour. How much flour does he use altogether?
2. 843 people live in Greater Wallop. 176 fewer people live in Little Wallop. How many people live in the smaller village?
3. 2 m of ribbon is cut into eight equal lengths. How long is each piece of ribbon?
4. England scored 314 runs in the first innings and 87 runs less in their second innings. How many runs did they score altogether?
5. A sweet shop had 100 ice lollies. One quarter were sold on Monday. One third of those left were sold on Tuesday. How many lollies were left?
6. Serena gets £2·25 pocket money each week. How much does she receive in one year?

I can draw polygons and describe their features.

POLYGONS
3 sides – triangles
4 sides – quadrilaterals
5 sides – pentagons
6 sides – hexagons
7 sides – heptagons
8 sides – octagons

Polygons can be:
regular – all sides and all angles equal
irregular – sides and angles not all equal
convex – no angle greater than 180°
concave – 1 angle greater than 180°.

Use triangular paper.

1. Copy these shapes

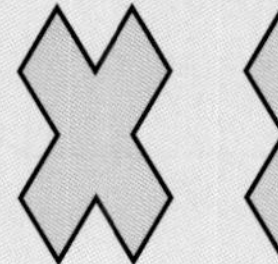

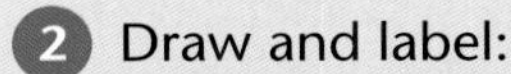

2. Draw and label:
   a) an equilateral triangle
   b) a regular hexagon.
3. Draw a quadrilateral with:
   a) one pair of equal sides
   b) 2 pairs of equal sides
   c) 4 equal sides.

   Draw on any lines of symmetry.
4. Use squared paper. Draw different quadrilaterals on grids of 4 squares.

Examples

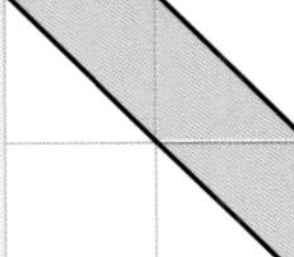
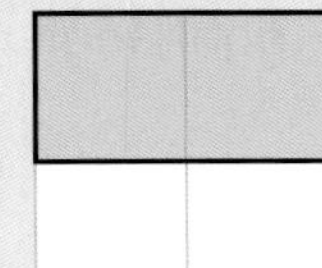

5. Label each shape square, rectangle or quadrilateral.
6. Draw on any lines of symmetry.

Use triangular paper.

1. Draw and label:
   a) a symmetrical pentagon
   b) a pentagon which is not symmetrical
   c) a concave pentagon.
2. Investigate the different hexagons you can draw. Describe the features of each shape and draw on any lines of symmetry.
3. Use squared paper. Draw different pentagons using the intersections of grids of 4 squares.

Examples

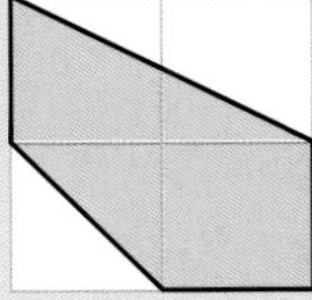
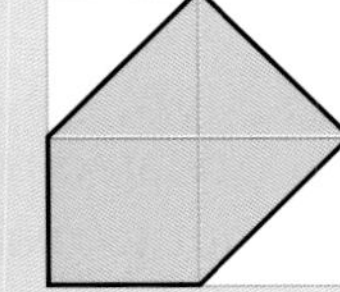

For each pentagon:
a) draw on any lines of symmetry
b) describe its features (concave or convex, number of equal sides or right angles, etc.)

C

Use triangular paper.

1. Draw different hexagons which are:
   a) symmetrical and concave
   b) symmetrical and convex
   c) not symmetrical and concave

   Draw on the lines of symmetry.
2. Investigate the different heptagons and octagons you can draw.
3. Use squared paper. Draw hexagons on a grid of 4 squares. Draw on any lines of symmetry.
4. Using a grid of 4 squares:
   a) how many different convex hexagons is it possible to draw?
   b) how many heptagons is it possible to draw?
   c) how many octagons is it possible to draw?

I can make different cuboids from a given number of cubes and construct nets of 3-D shapes.

A

1. How many cubes are needed to build this cuboid?

2. Use cubes to build the cuboid. Were you right?

3. Use the same number of cubes. Build a different cuboid which also has a height of 2 cubes. Write down the length and width of the cuboid.

4. Use the same number of cubes. Find 4 different cuboids with a height of 1 cm. Write down the length and width of each cuboid.

5. Copy these nets onto squared paper. Cut them out and fold them to make open cubes.

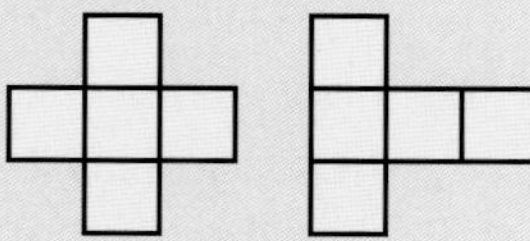

6. Find different nets that make open cubes.

B

1. How many cubes would be needed to build this cuboid? (lengths in cubes)

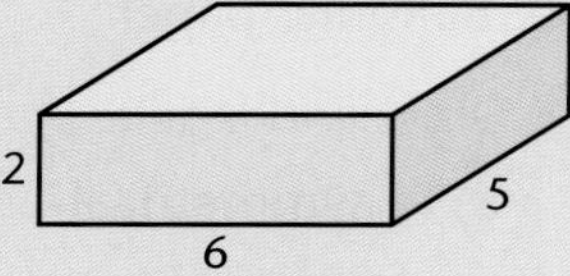

2. Find other cuboids you could build using this number of cubes. Write down the length, width and height of each cuboid.

3. Copy this net onto squared paper. Cut it out and fold it to make a closed cube.

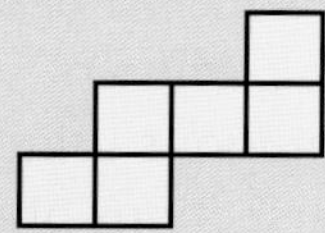

4. Find different nets that make closed cubes.

5. Copy this net onto squared paper. Cut it out to make a square based pyramid.

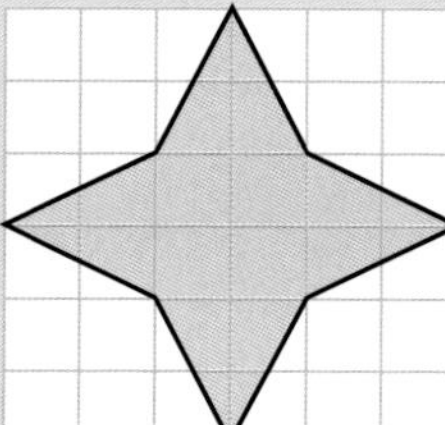

C

1. How many cubes would be needed to build this cuboid? (lengths in cubes)

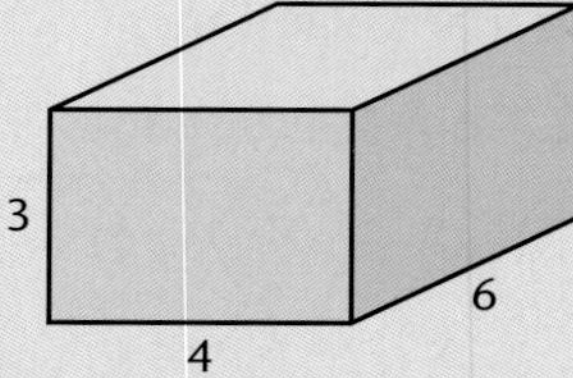

2. Work systematically to find all the different cuboids you could make using the same number of cubes.

Draw a net of these shapes.

3. a closed cube with edges of 3 cm

4. a square based pyramid with base sides 4·5 cm long and a height of 5 cm

5. the cuboid in question 1

6. Use 1 cm squared paper. Draw a net for this triangular prism. (The marked angle is a right angle.)

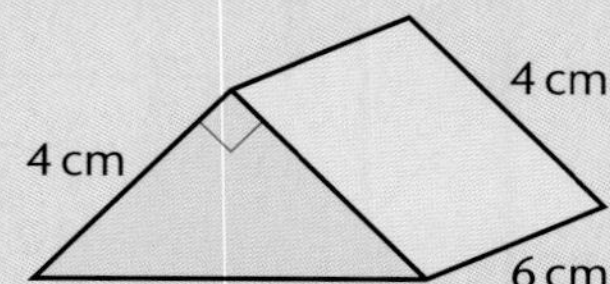

7. Use triangular paper. Draw a net for a triangular based pyramid.

I can read a scale accurately.

For each of the scales work out the measurement shown by each arrow.

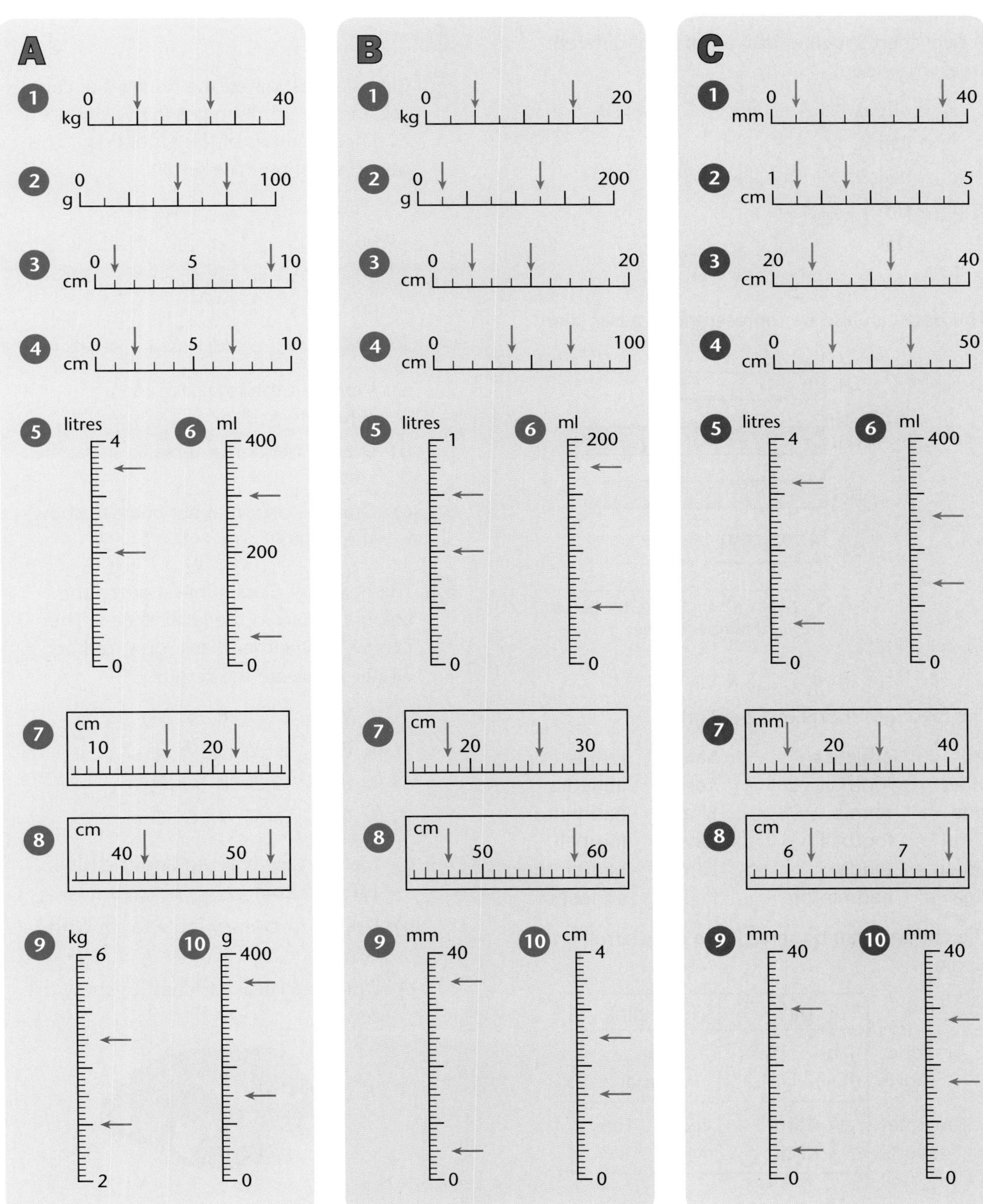

I can organise data using tables and tallies and present results in different ways including bar charts.

Examples

A tally chart showing the numbers of different trees in a wood.

Trees	Tally	Total
Ash	卌 卌 |	11
Beech	卌 卌 卌 ||	17
Elm	卌 卌 卌	15
Oak	卌 ||	7

The data can also be represented in a bar chart.

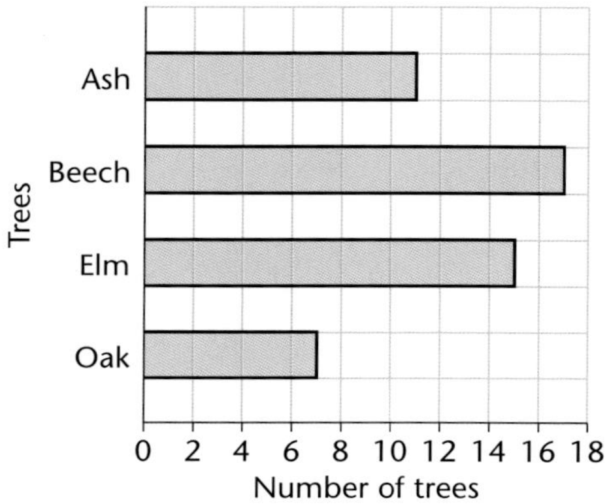

The favourite sports of 12 children.

Jed	athletics	Sara	tennis
Miles	football	Tony	athletics
Jane	tennis	Elsa	badminton
Carol	football	Ravi	football
Omar	tennis	Larry	badminton
Puja	badminton	Kacie	athletics

The children can be sorted into this Carroll diagram.

	girls	not girls
racquet sports	Jane Sara Puja Elsa	Larry Omar
not racquet sports	Carol Kacie	Jed Tony Miles Ravi

A

1 Class 4 investigated the number of cars passing the school gates in five minutes at different times of the school day. This tally chart shows the results.

Time	Tally
9:00– 9:05	卌 卌 卌 卌 卌 ||||
11:00–11:05	卌 卌 ||||
1:00– 1:05	卌 ||||
3:00– 3:05	卌 卌 卌 卌 卌 卌 |||

a) Work out the totals for each 5 minute period.

b) Draw a frequency table to show the results.

c) Draw a horizontal bar chart to show the results.

2 The next day Class 4 investigated the colours of cars in the local streets. The cars were all either black, grey, red or white. These are the results.

B W G B G R B W
G B R B W G W B
R B G W R B G B
W G B R G W B G

a) Make a tally chart to find the total for each colour.

b) Draw a frequency table to show the results.

c) Draw a vertical bar chart to show the results.

B

1 Lydia stood on the school field and estimated the distances to five features. Then she measured the actual distances. These are her results.

Feature	Estimated distance	Actual distance	Difference
Goalpost	36 m	54 m	18 m
Gate	44 m	34 m	
Tree	70 m	48 m	
Playground	51 m	64 m	
Classroom	78 m	59 m	

a) Work out the difference between Lydia's estimate and the actual distance for each of the other four features.

b) Draw a horizontal bar chart showing the differences.

2 The 12 members of the School Council voted to decide how to spend a £500 prize. The choices were a new printer for the Computer Room, fiction books for the Library or topic books for each class.

Printer	Fiction Books	Topic Books
Mr Lee	Miss Haines	Mr Adams
Mia	Joe	Gemma
Rajir	Mr Khan	Mrs Rogers
Simon	Tessa	Mrs West

Copy the Venn diagram. Sort the votes by writing the names in the right places.

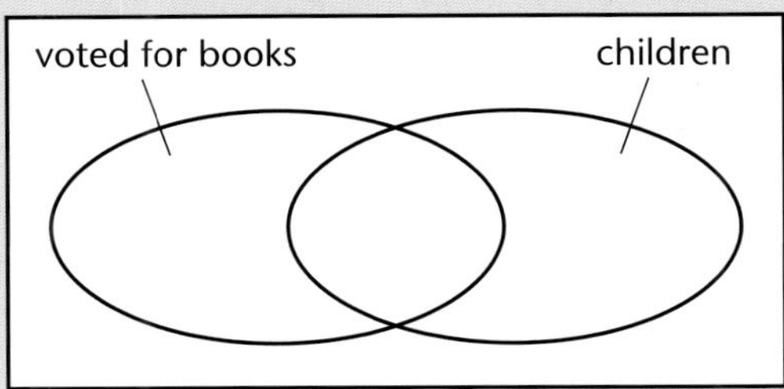

C

1 Louis wanted to know how many people were in each car passing the school. He counted the number of passengers other than the driver. These are the results.

0	2	1	0	4	0	1	3	1	0
0	1	3	0	1	2	0	1	2	0
2	0	1	2	1	0	3	1	0	3
1	0	4	1	3	0	0	2	1	0
3	1	0	2	0	1	2	0	0	1

a) Make a tally chart to find the total for each number of passengers.

b) Draw a frequency table to show the results.

c) Present the results in a bar chart.

2 Twelve children recorded their age and the distance they achieved in the standing long jump.

Name	Age	Jump
Ann	10	1·48 m
Bob	8	1·54 m
Joe	11	1·73 m
Mia	9	1·52 m
Sam	10	1·38 m
Tom	9	1·46 m
Pam	10	1·64 m
Ron	7	1·25 m
Ian	9	1·62 m
Dee	11	1·79 m
Fay	8	1·23 m
Eve	10	1·41 m

a) Use a Carroll diagram to sort the children into those under 10 and those not under 10, and those who jumped over 150 cm and those who did not.

b) Use a Venn diagram to sort the children. Label one ring *jumped over 145 cm* and the other *girls*.

I can interpret data shown in tables and charts and explain the effect of changing the scale of bar charts.

Examples

Time	Number of cars in car park
9:00	28
10:00	14
11:00	20
12:00	18

What information is shown? Look at the table headings. *The numbers of cars in a car park at different times.*

How many cars were parked at 11:00? *20*

When were there 14 cars in the car park? *10:00*

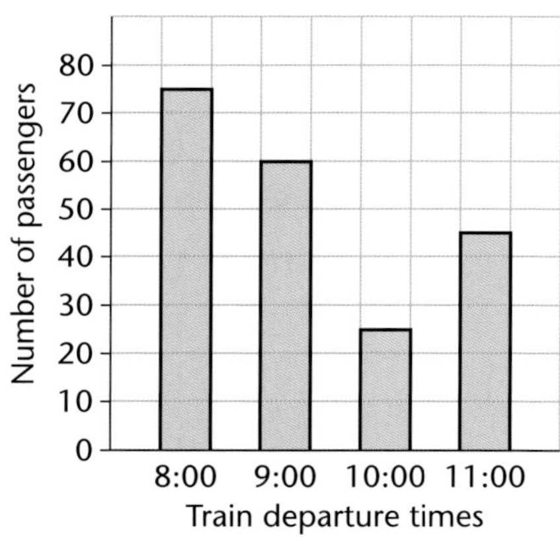

What information is shown? Look at the axis tables. *The number of passengers on trains leaving a station at different times.*

How many people were on the 9:00 train? *60*

Which train had 45 passengers? *11:00*

The meals chosen by six children at a party.

Name	Main course		Dessert	
	Pizza	Burger	Lolly	Peach
Rosy	✓		✓	
Nigel		✓	✓	
Belle	✓			✓
Dina	✓		✓	
Samed		✓		✓
Mick	✓		✓	

1. What was Nigel's dessert?
2. What was Dina's main course?
3. How many children chose a lolly?
4. Who chose pizza and a peach?
5. Who chose a burger and a lolly?
6. Which children chose a pizza and a lolly?

This bar chart shows the amount of time Helen watched television on 5 school days.

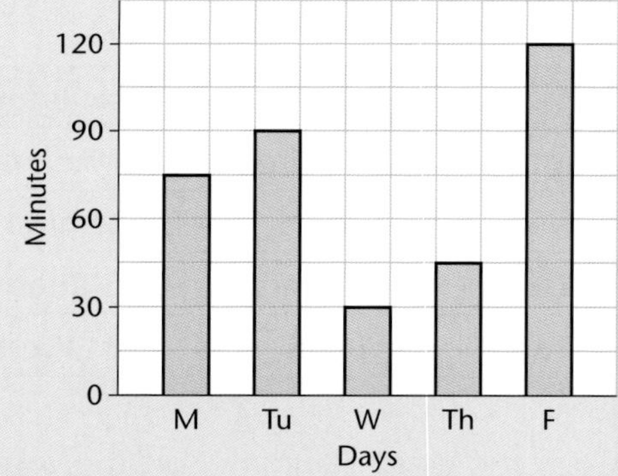

7. On which day did Helen watch television
   a) for one and a half hours
   b) for 45 minutes?
8. For how long did she watch television on:
   a) Wednesday **b)** Monday?
9. Altogether how many hours and minutes did Helen watch television during the 5 days?

B

Class 4 investigated the numbers of cars passing the school gates at different times. Here are the results.

Time	Cars going East	Cars going West
9:00– 9:10	74	26
10:00–10:10	42	21
11:00–11:10	59	43
12:00–12:10	35	59

1. How many cars went east between 10:00 and 10:10?
2. Between which times did 59 cars go west?
3. How many more cars went east than west between 9:00 and 9:10?
4. How many cars passed the school gates between 11:00 and 11:10?

The children in a school voted for the equipment they would like to be able to use at playtime.

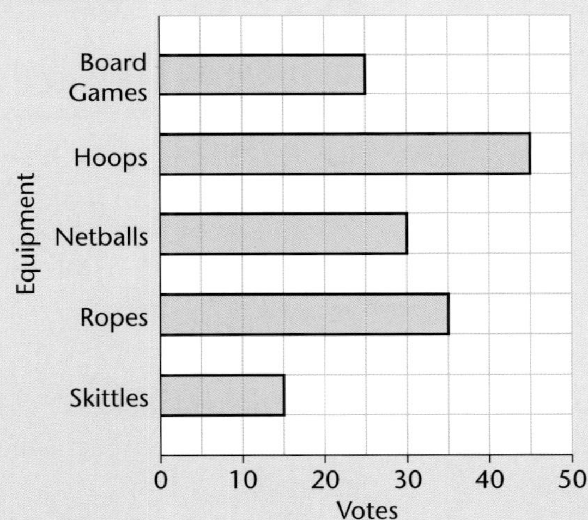

5. Draw a table to show the same data as in the bar chart.
6. Which way of presenting the information is better? Give a reason for your answer.
7. Show the same data in another horizontal bar chart but change the scale.
8. Which bar chart is better? Explain why.

C

Simon stood on the school football pitch and estimated the distance to 6 features. He then measured the distances. These are the results.

	Estimate (E) (u)	Measure (M) (u)	E–M (u)
goalpost	35	43	−8
playground	45	36	9
classroom	90		13
tree	65	74	
gate		52	−17
pond	75		−6

1. What are the missing units of measurement (u)?
2. Why is the difference between the estimated distance and the measured distance sometimes shown as a negative number?
3. What are the four missing numbers?
4. This table shows the number of diners each day at a restaurant.

Day	Diners
Monday	50
Tuesday	40
Wednesday	30
Thursday	60
Friday	90
Saturday	110

a) Show the data in a vertical bar chart. Use a scale of 1 square for 10 diners.

b) Show the same data in another vertical bar chart. Use a scale of 1 square for 20 diners.

c) Compare the bar charts. What is the effect of changing the scale?

I can choose and use metric units to measure lengths, weights or capacities.

Examples

LENGTH	10 mm = 1 cm	57 mm = 5 cm 7 mm	= 5·7 cm
	100 cm = 1 m	130 cm = 1 m 30 cm	= 1·3 m
	1000 m = 1 km	2300 m = 2 km 300 m	= 2·3 km
WEIGHT	1000 g = 1 kg	1600 g = 1 kg 600 g	= 1·6 kg
CAPACITY	1000 ml = 1 litre	2500 ml = 2 litres 500 ml	= 2·5 litres

A

Copy and complete.

1. 3 m = ☐ cm
2. 5 m = ☐ cm
3. 200 cm = ☐ m
4. 400 cm = ☐ m
5. 1000 m = ☐ km
6. 6000 m = ☐ km
7. 9 km = ☐ m
8. 3 km = ☐ m
9. 2000 ml = ☐ litres
10. 5 litres = ☐ ml
11. 4000 g = ☐ kg
12. 7 kg = ☐ g

Which metric unit would you use to measure:

13. the width of the North Sea
14. the capacity of a water bottle
15. the height of a garage
16. the width of a television?

B

Copy and complete.

1. 25 mm = ☐ cm
2. 40 mm = ☐ cm
3. 1·5 cm = ☐ mm
4. 3 cm = ☐ mm
5. 2·8 m = ☐ cm
6. 1·4 m = ☐ cm
7. 520 cm = ☐ m
8. 110 cm = ☐ m
9. 4300 g = ☐ kg
10. 7500 ml = ☐ litres
11. 2·6 kg = ☐ g
12. 1·9 litres = ☐ ml

Which metric unit would you use to measure:

13. the thickness of a newspaper
14. the weight of a cushion
15. the length of a stamp
16. the capacity of a bucket?

C

Copy and complete.

1. 72 mm = ☐ cm
2. 109 mm = ☐ cm
3. 5·4 cm = ☐ mm
4. 0·7 cm = ☐ mm
5. 264 cm = ☐ m
6. 95 cm = ☐ m
7. 4·77 m = ☐ cm
8. 1·2 m = ☐ cm
9. 8·9 km = ☐ m
10. 6·37 kg = ☐ g
11. 0·5 litres = ☐ ml
12. 3·11 kg = ☐ g

Copy the sentence choosing the most sensible estimate.

13. A bottle of shampoo holds (4 ml, 40 ml, 400 ml).
14. A fence is (20 cm, 200 cm, 2000 cm) tall.
15. A box of six eggs weighs (5 g, 50 g, 500 g).

D3 CAPACITY

I can use the relationship between litres and millilitres and read scales to the nearest division.

Remember
milli = $\frac{1}{1000}$
1 ml = $\frac{1}{1000}$ litre

1000 ml = 1 litre
2000 ml = 2 litres
3000 ml = 3 litres
and so on

100 ml = 0·1 litres
200 ml = 0·2 litres
300 ml = 0·3 litres
and so on

3250 ml = 3·25 ℓ
4500 ml = 4·5 ℓ
2750 ml = 2·75 ℓ

A

Copy and complete.

1. 1 litre = ☐ ml
2. 2 litres = ☐ ml
3. 1000 ml = ☐ litre
4. 1500 ml = ☐ litres
5. 0·5 litres = ☐ ml
6. 2·5 litres = ☐ ml
7. 3000 ml = ☐ litres
8. 3500 ml = ☐ litres

Give the capacity shown by each arrow.

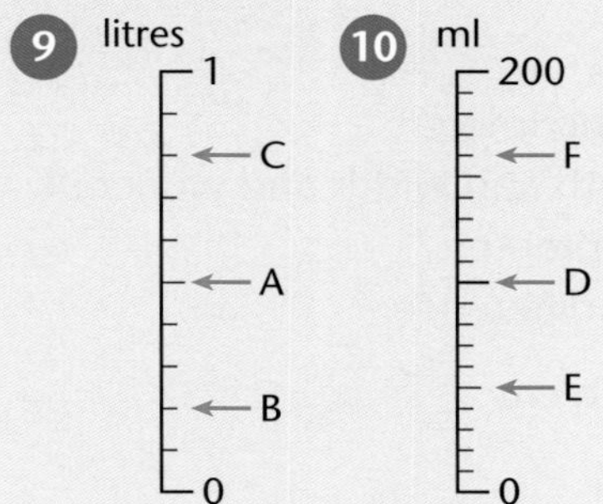

Choose the more sensible estimate.

11. a raindrop
 1 ml or 100 ml
12. a bucket
 500 ml or 5 litres
13. a saucepan
 200 ml or 2 litres

B

Copy and complete.

1. 1300 ml = ☐ litres
2. 750 ml = ☐ litres
3. 0·8 litres = ☐ ml
4. 1·25 litres = ☐ ml
5. 4750 ml = ☐ litres
6. 3600 ml = ☐ litres
7. 0·25 litres = ☐ ml
8. 0·4 litres = ☐ ml

Give the capacity shown by each arrow.

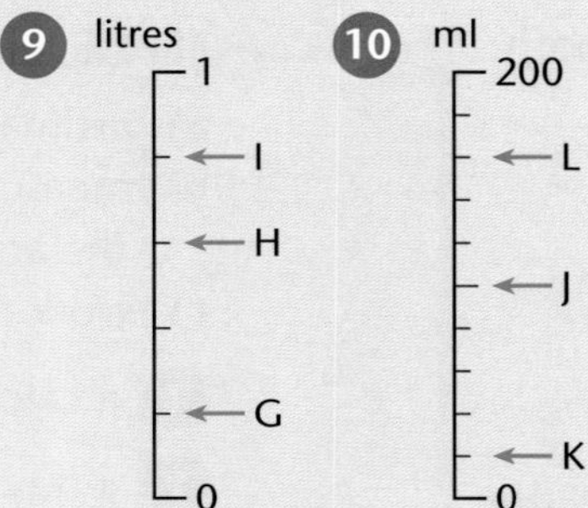

Suggest a suitable metric unit to measure these capacities.

11. a lake
12. a water pistol
13. a mug
14. a kitchen sink
15. a bottle of medicine

C

Copy and complete.

1. 1·95 litres = ☐ ml
2. 0·47 litres = ☐ ml
3. 3080 ml = ☐ litres
4. 60 ml = ☐ litres
5. 3·29 litres = ☐ ml
6. 10·4 litres = ☐ ml
7. 10 ml = ☐ litres
8. 2050 ml = ☐ litres

Give the capacity shown by each arrow.

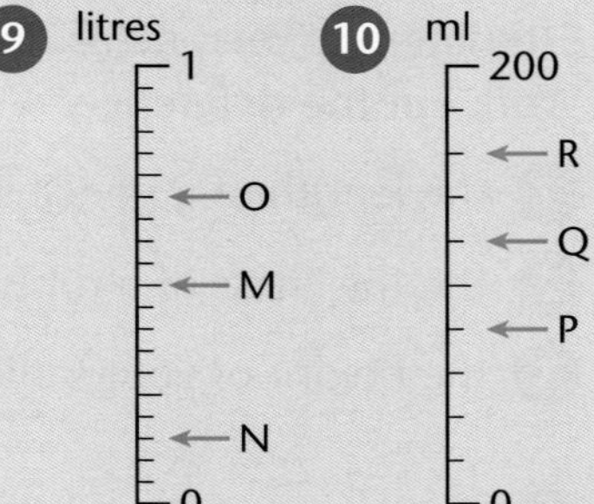

Write these capacities in order, smallest first.

11. 1·5 ℓ 1050 ml 115 ml
12. 0·23 ℓ 200 ml 2·3 ℓ
13. 47 ml 0·04 ℓ 0·07 ℓ
14. 6900 ml 6·69 ℓ 6·6 ℓ
15. 0·8 ℓ 508 ml 0·58 ℓ
16. 272 ml 0·27 ℓ 227 ml

D3 MEASURING LENGTHS

I can estimate and measure lengths in centimetres and millimetres.

Example

a) Estimate the length of the above line. Estimate = 9 cm
b) Measure the length. Length = 11·7 cm
c) Work out the difference between the estimate and the actual length. Difference = 11·7 cm–9 cm = 2·7 cm

Estimate the length of each line. Measure each length.
Work out the difference between your estimate and the actual length.

1
2
3
4
5
6

B

Estimate and then measure each length.
Work out the difference.

1 the length of a pencil in cm
2 the thickness of a rubber in mm
3 the height of your table in cm

4 the length of your little finger in mm
5 the length of your book in cm
6 the thickness of your book in mm

7 the width of your chair in cm
8 the width of your ruler in mm
9 the height of your chair in cm.

10 Find other lengths to measure in cm and mm.

C

For each item:
a) estimate the perimeter
b) measure length and width and work out the actual perimeter
c) work out the difference.

1 a calculator in cm
2 a tray in cm
3 your table in metres
4 a door in metres
5 your ruler in cm
6 your book in cm
7 the classroom in metres
8 the whiteboard in metres.

9 Find other perimeters to estimate and measure.

D3 TIME PROBLEMS

I can solve time problems by finding a time difference or by finding a start or end time.

Examples

A lesson starts at 9:40.

It lasts 50 minutes.

When does it finish?

20 mins 30 mins

9:40 10:00 ?

Answer 10:30

A lesson lasts 40 minutes.

It finishes at 11:15.

When does it start?

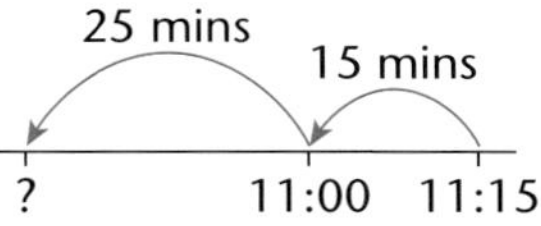

Answer 10:35

A

1. A television programme begins at 8:10 and finishes at 9:00. How long is the programme?
2. A netball match starts at 3:15 and finishes at 3:55. How long is the match?
3. Jose gets into the swimming pool at 1:40. He gets out at 2:30. How long is he in the pool?
4. A washing machine is switched on at 7:35. The wash finishes at 8:20. How long has it taken?
5. Nieve puts the chips in the oven at 4:45. They are ready at 5:15. How long have they taken?
6. Dance Club starts at 3:30. It finishes at 4:25. How long does it last?
7. Amir's watch is 20 minutes slow. It shows the time as 9:05. What is the real time?

B

1. Dean's bike ride takes 50 minutes. He arrives back at home at 12:15. When did he set off?
2. The music lesson lasts 40 minutes. It starts at 1:40. When does it finish?

3. Maria knows a clock is 15 minutes fast. The clock shows the time as 6:10. What is the real time?
4. A football match kicks off at 7:45. The first half takes 45 minutes. When is half-time?
5. Ryan notices the time is 5:30. He realises he has been playing the guitar for 55 minutes. When did he start playing?
6. Julie sees that the next bus is at 10:15. The time is 9:50. How long does she have to wait?

C

1. Davy hangs his washing on the line at 1:05. He takes it down at 2:55. How long has it been on the line?
2. Kitty finishes delivering newspapers at 11:25. Her round has taken 70 minutes. When did she start?
3. The ice show starts at 7:30. The first half lasts 80 minutes. When is the interval?
4. A ferry crossing takes 105 minutes. The ferry docks at 3:55. When did it sail?
5. Jack starts painting at 9:35. He finishes at 11:10. How long has he been painting?

6. A film lasts 95 minutes. It starts at 2:50. When does it finish?

I can find information in a timetable.

Every morning five buses run from the village to the nearest town.

	BUS 1	BUS 2	BUS 3	BUS 4	BUS 5
Village	6:30	7:45	8:55	10:15	11:25
Crossroads	6:35	7:50	9:00	10:20	11:30
Superstore	6:50	8:10	9:20	10:35	11:45
School	6:55	8:20	9:30	10:45	11:55
Train Station	7:05	8:45	9:45	10:55	12:05
Town Hall	7:15	9:05	10:05	11:15	12:20

Example

How long is the journey on Bus 1 from Crossroads to the Town Hall?

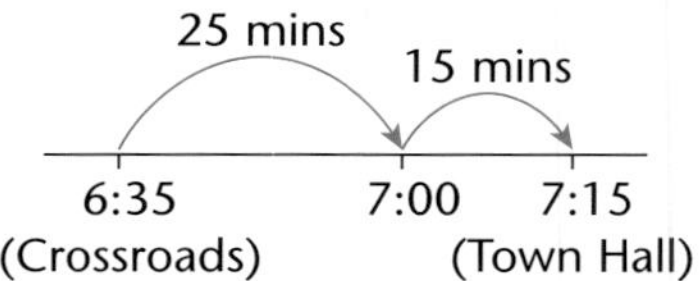

Answer *40 minutes*

A

1. At what time does Bus 1 leave the village?

At what time does Bus 1 stop at:

2. the superstore
3. the train station?

How long is the journey on Bus 1:

4. from the village to the superstore
5. from the train station to the Town Hall?

How long is the journey on Bus 3:

6. from Crossroads to the school
7. from the superstore to the train station?
8. Lee has to be on the 7:20 train. He takes Bus 1 from the village. How long will he have to wait at the station?

B

At what time would you reach:

1. the station on Bus 5
2. Crossroads on Bus 2
3. the superstore on Bus 4
4. the Town Hall on Bus 1
5. the school on Bus 5
6. the Town Hall on Bus 3?

How long is the journey:

7. on Bus 4 from the school to the Town Hall
8. on Bus 2 from the superstore to the school
9. on Bus 3 from Crossroads to the superstore
10. on Bus 5 from the village to the train station?
11. Which bus would you take from the village if you need to be at the train station:
    a) by 9:00
    b) by 12:00?

C

1. How long does each bus take to reach the Town Hall?

Which bus should someone take from the village if they need to be:

2. at school by 9:00
3. at a meeting at the Town Hall at 12:00
4. at work at the superstore by 10:00
5. on a train due to leave the station at 8:00?

At what time would you catch a bus at Crossroads to keep these appointments?

6. train station 12:00
7. superstore 12:00
8. Town Hall 9:00
9. school 9:00

D3 MEASUREMENT PROBLEMS

I can solve one and two-step problems involving measures.

Example

A cake weighs 2 kg.
It is cut into 10 slices.
Three slices are eaten.
How much cake is left?

2 kg ÷ 10 = 200 g
200 g × 3 = 600 g
2 kg or 2000 g − 600 g = 1400 g
Answer *1 kg 400 g of cake is left.*

A

1. A fence is 62 m long. 14 m is blown down. How much of the fence is left standing?
2. Ken saves 50p each day. How much does he save in one week?
3. A cake weighs 800 g. It is cut into four slices. How much does each slice weigh?
4. Eighty buckets of water fill a pond. Each bucket holds 2 litres. How much water does the pond hold?
5. Ten cherries weigh 60 g. What is the weight of one cherry?

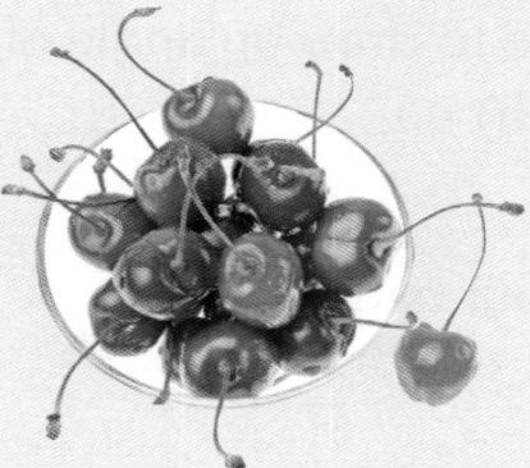

6. A string is 1 metre long. 10 cm is cut off. Another 20 cm is cut off. How long is the piece of string now?

B

1. A parcel weighs half a kilogram. Another weighs 300 g. What do they weigh together?
2. Ivy buys four cakes. She pays with a £5 note and receives £2·60 change. How much does each cake cost?
3. A piece of guttering is 4 m long. A plumber cuts off two 80 cm lengths. How much guttering is left?
4. Six 150 ml cups are filled from a jug holding one litre of water. How much water is left?
5. Joe has a set of 30 encyclopaedias. He needs 1·2 m of shelving to store them. How wide is each encyclopaedia?
6. One packet of biscuits costs 65p. Dick buys three packets for £1·50. How much has he saved?

C

1. Jack weighed four and a half kilograms at birth. Jessica weighed 750 g less. What was Jessica's weight?
2. A cyclist travels 300 m in one minute. How many kilometres does he travel in 20 minutes?
3. Hasina buys three 75p lollies and two 80p ice creams. She pays with a £10 note. How much change does she get?
4. A saucepan holds 2 litres of boiling water. One tenth of the water evaporates. How much water is left in the saucepan?
5. A plank is 3 m long. It is cut in half. 78 cm is cut from one of the two planks. How long is the shortest piece of wood?
6. Train tickets for two adults and two children cost £24 altogether. Children's tickets cost half price. How much is one adult's ticket?

I can compare the size of angles and use a set square to check.

Angles are measured in degrees (°).
A whole turn is 360°.
A half turn is 180°.
A quarter turn or right angle is 90°.

Examples

The minute hand of a clock turns:
360° in one hour
180° in 30 minutes
90° in 15 minutes.

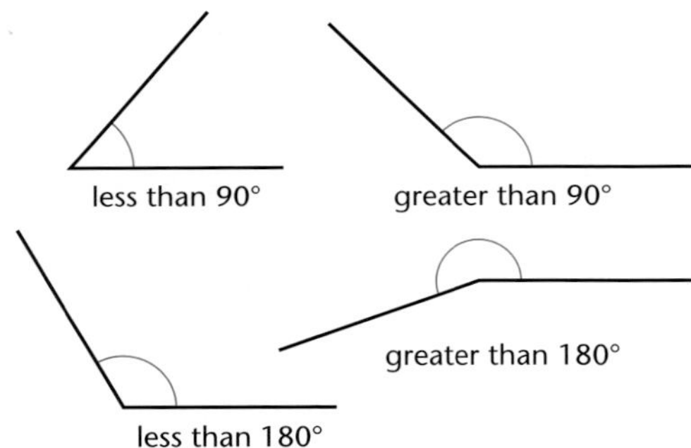

Set squares can be used to draw and measure some angles.

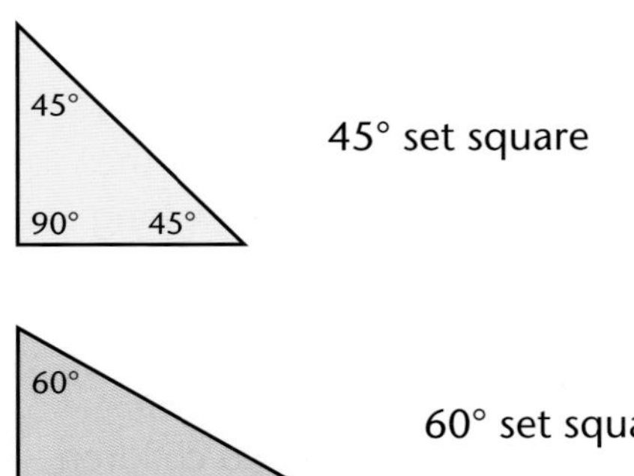

45° set square

60° set square

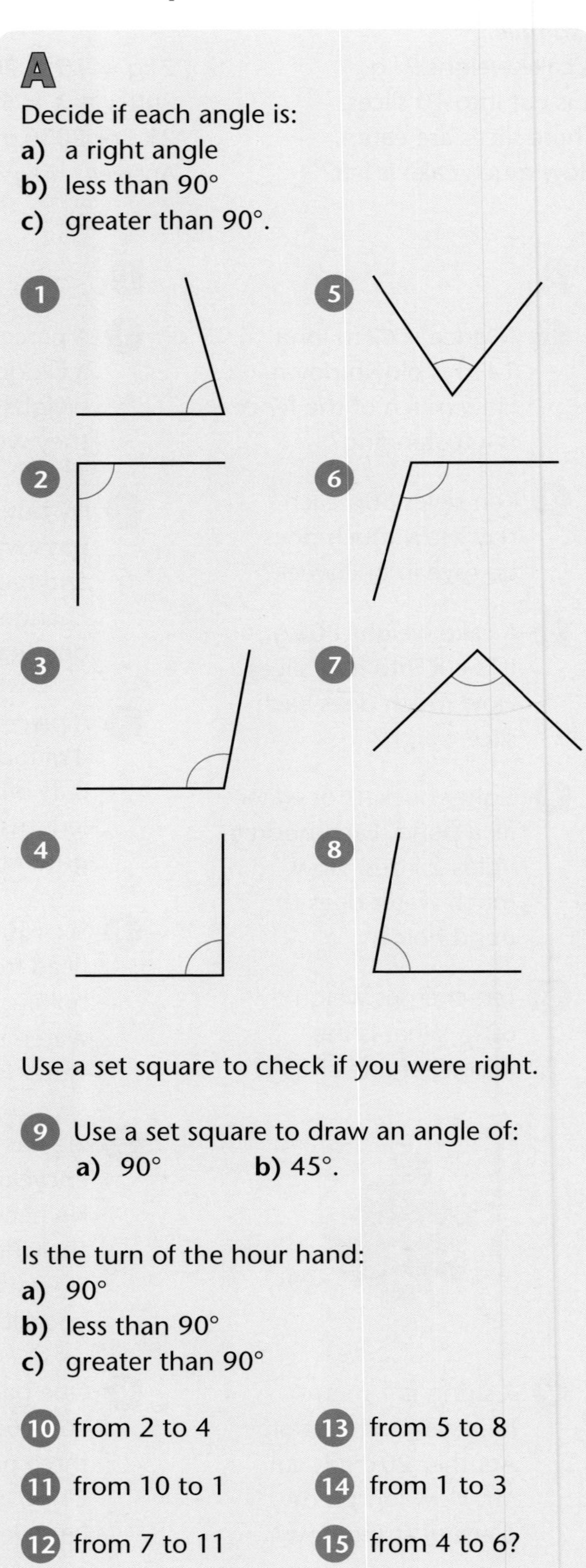

A

Decide if each angle is:
a) a right angle
b) less than 90°
c) greater than 90°.

1 **2** **3** **4** **5** **6** **7** **8**

Use a set square to check if you were right.

9 Use a set square to draw an angle of:
a) 90° **b)** 45°.

Is the turn of the hour hand:
a) 90°
b) less than 90°
c) greater than 90°

10 from 2 to 4
11 from 10 to 1
12 from 7 to 11
13 from 5 to 8
14 from 1 to 3
15 from 4 to 6?

Decide if each angle is:

a) less than 180°
b) greater than 180°.

1 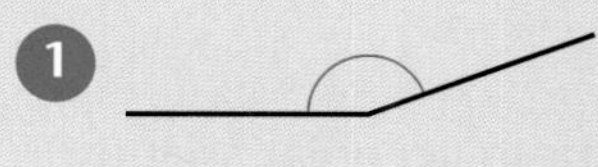

4

2 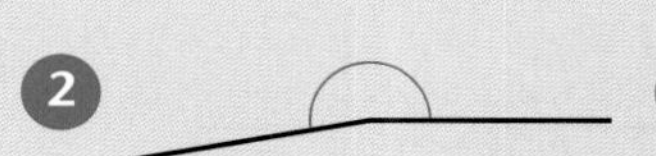

5 

3 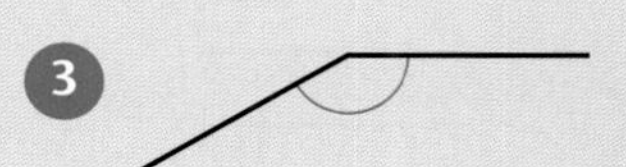

6 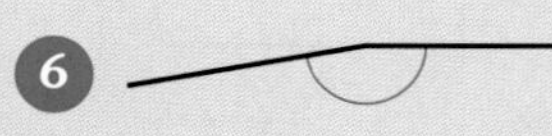

7 Use a set square to draw angles of:

a) 90° **c)** 45°
b) 60° **d)** 30°

Decide if each angle is:

a) less than 30°
b) 30°
c) between 30° and 60°
d) 60°
e) greater than 60°.

8 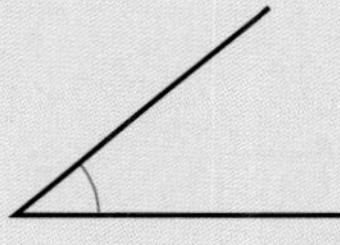

12 

9 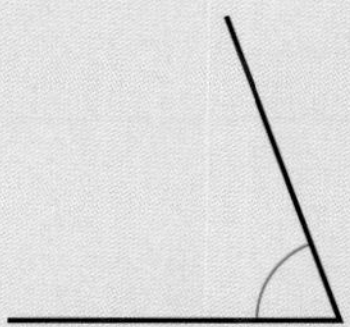

13 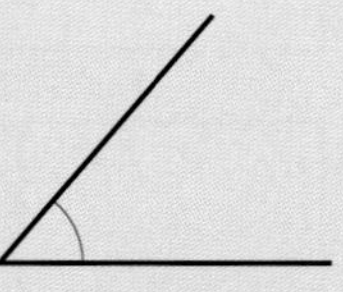

10 

14 

11 

15 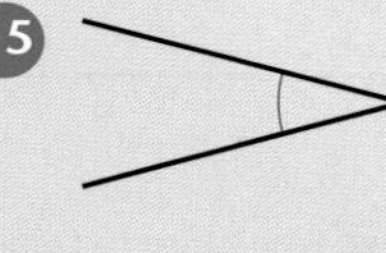

Use a set square to check.

C

What angle is made by turning in a clockwise direction from:

1 N to SE
2 SW to NW
3 S to E
4 NE to W
5 E to SE
6 SE to NW
7 W to NE
8 NW to W?

N
NW NE
W E
SW SE
S

9 Combine set squares to draw angles of:

a) 75° **c)** 120° **e)** 150°.
b) 105° **d)** 135°

10 Which one of these angles is:

a) 30° **b)** 60°?

Use a set square to check.

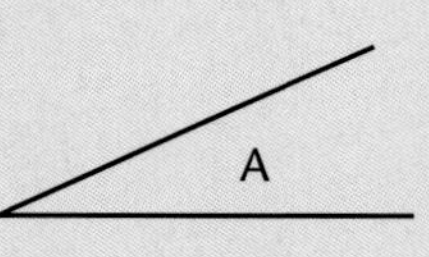

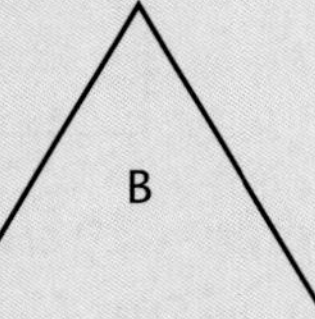

C

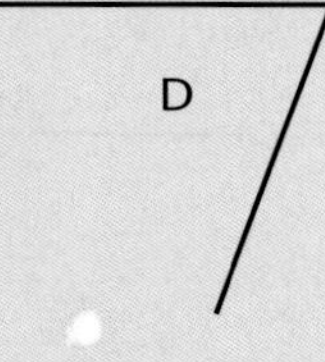

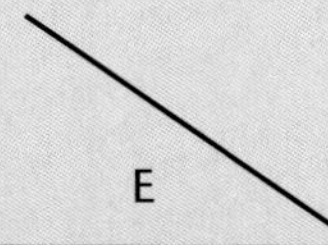

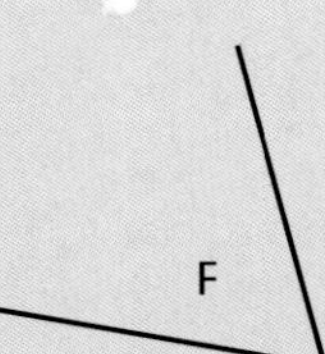

Write down the angle turned by the minute hand of a clock in:

11 15 minutes
12 30 minutes
13 5 minutes
14 25 minutes
15 40 minutes
16 55 minutes
17 10 minutes
18 35 minutes

I can find the area of irregular shapes by counting squares.

The area of a shape is the amount of surface it covers.

Area is measured in squares, usually square centimetres (cm^2) or square metres (m^2).

The perimeter of a shape is the distance around its edges.
The perimeter of a field is the length of the fence around it. The area is the field itself.

Examples

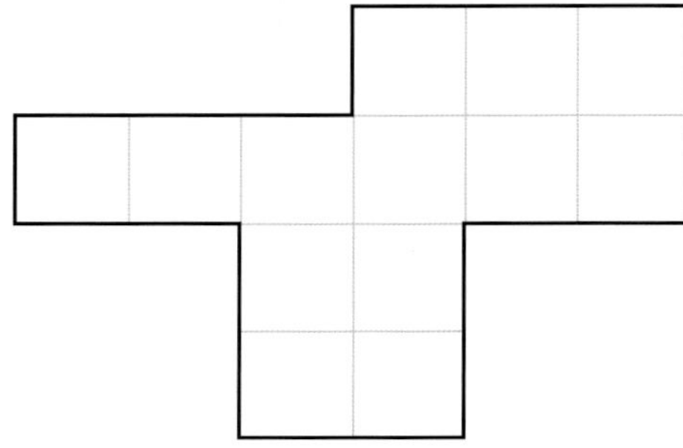

Perimeter = 20 cm
Area = 13 cm^2

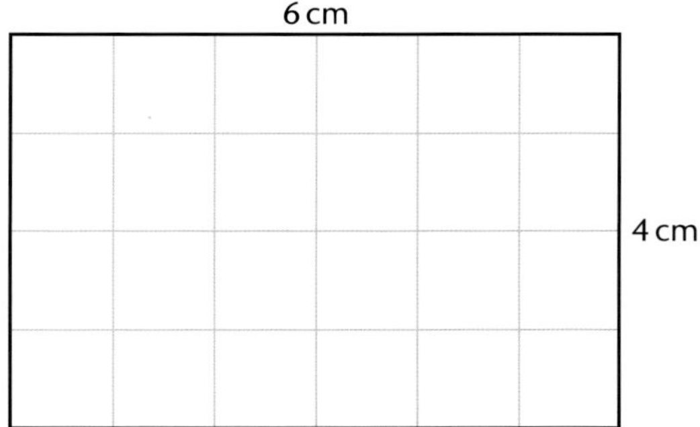

Area = length × width
= (6 × 4) cm^2
= 24 cm^2

Perimeter = (6 + 4 + 6 + 4) cm
= 20 cm

A

Find the area of each of these irregular shapes.

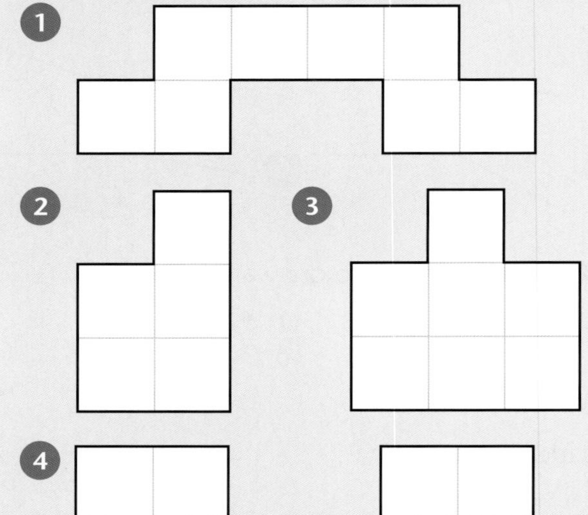

For each shape below work out:

a) the area
b) the perimeter.

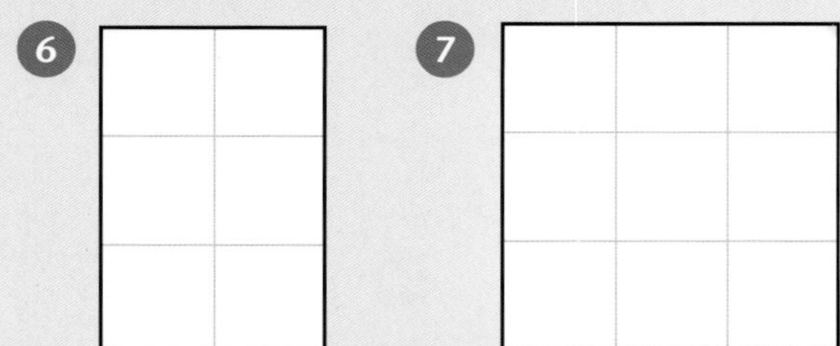

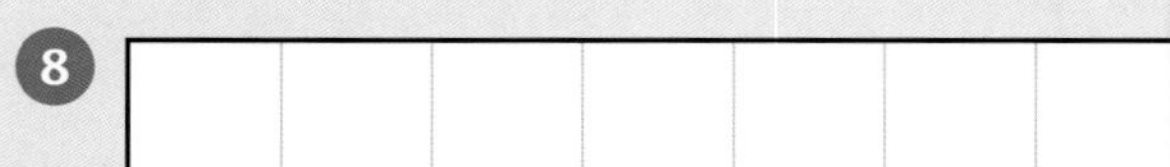

9 Use squared paper.
Draw three different irregular shapes with an area of 10 cm^2.

For each of these irregular shapes work out:

a) the area
b) the perimeter

1 2

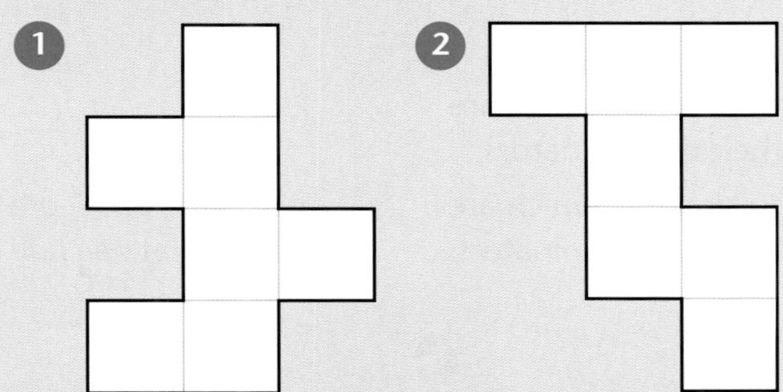

3

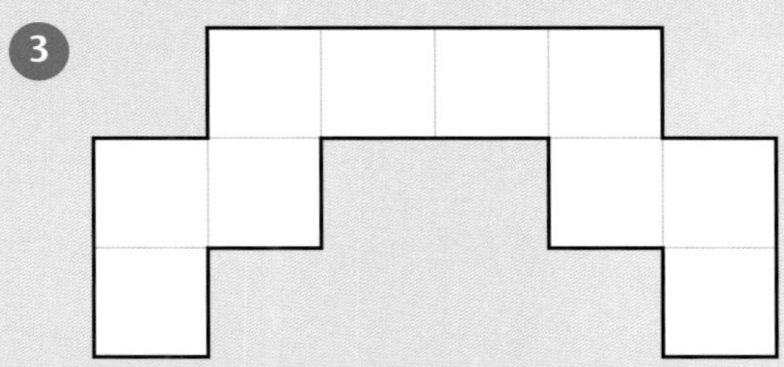

4 Draw three different rectangles with an area of 24 cm^2. Work out the perimeter of each.

5 Draw three different rectangles with a perimeter of 24 cm.
Work out the area of each.

6 Use 1 cm squared paper.
Draw three different irregular shapes with a perimeter of 20 cm.
Work out the area of each.

7 Work out the area of each letter by counting squares and half squares.

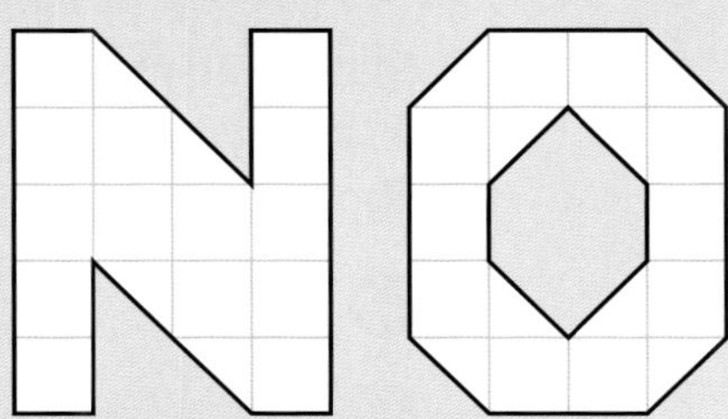

8 Make up your own drawings of letters using squared paper. You could draw your initials.
Work out the areas.

Measure these shapes and work out their perimeters.

1 3 2

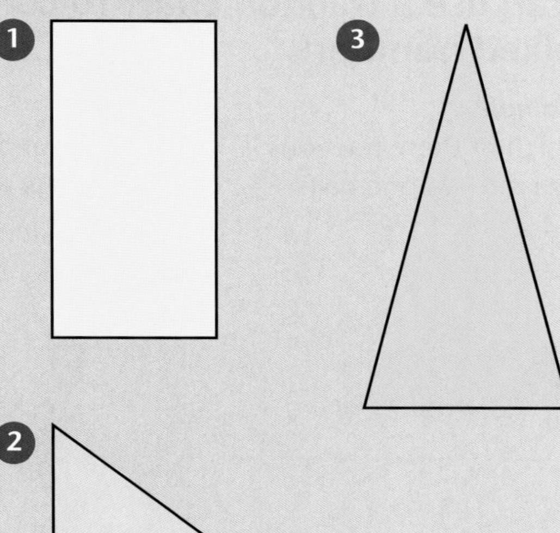

4 Copy and complete this table showing the measurement of rectangles.

Length	Width	Perim.	Area
7 cm	6 cm		
9 cm		24 cm	
	2 cm		40 cm^2
14 cm			70 cm^2
	7 cm	36 cm	
	4 cm		100 cm^2
		26 cm	40 cm^2
30 cm		62 cm	

5 How many square centimetres are there in a square metre?

6 A carpet costs £15 per square metre. A room is 4 metres long and 3 metres wide. How much will it cost to carpet the room?

7 A tin of paint covers 8 square metres of fence. A fence is 2 metres tall and 24 metres long. How many tins of paint will be needed?

E3 ORDERING FRACTIONS

I can use a fraction chart to compare fractions and I can order a set of mixed numbers.

Example

Which of these fractions is greater than one half?

$\frac{3}{8}$ $\frac{2}{3}$ $\frac{1}{5}$ $\frac{4}{7}$

$\frac{3}{8}$ and $\frac{1}{5}$ have numerators which are less than half their denominators.

$\frac{2}{3}$ and $\frac{4}{7}$ have numerators which are more than half their denominators.

Answer *$\frac{2}{3}$ and $\frac{4}{7}$ are greater than one half*

A

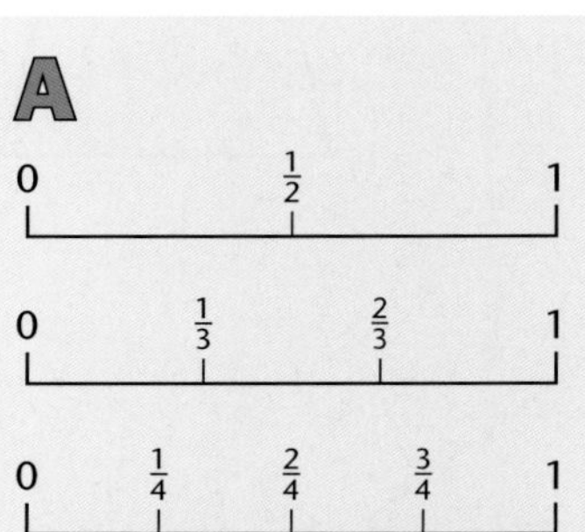

Look at the number lines. Write down if each fraction is:

greater than one half
or less than one half.

1. $\frac{2}{5}$
2. $\frac{2}{3}$
3. $\frac{4}{5}$
4. $\frac{1}{4}$
5. $\frac{3}{5}$
6. $\frac{3}{4}$
7. $\frac{1}{5}$
8. $\frac{1}{3}$

Write down if each fraction is:

equal to one half
or less than one half
or greater than one half.

9. $\frac{3}{6}$
10. $\frac{7}{10}$
11. $\frac{9}{100}$
12. $\frac{4}{8}$
13. $\frac{2}{4}$
14. $\frac{5}{12}$
15. $\frac{5}{10}$
16. $\frac{5}{8}$

B

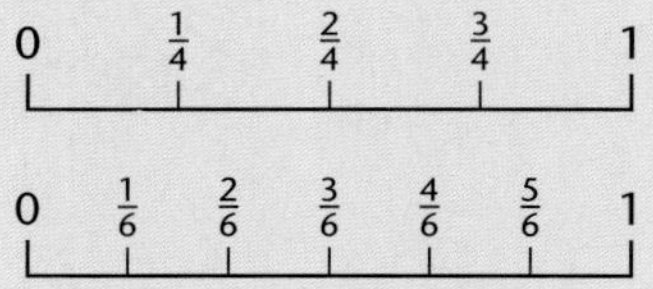

0 $\frac{1}{10}$ $\frac{2}{10}$ $\frac{3}{10}$ $\frac{4}{10}$ $\frac{5}{10}$ $\frac{6}{10}$ $\frac{7}{10}$ $\frac{8}{10}$ $\frac{9}{10}$ 1

0 $\frac{1}{12}$ $\frac{2}{12}$ $\frac{3}{12}$ $\frac{4}{12}$ $\frac{5}{12}$ $\frac{6}{12}$ $\frac{7}{12}$ $\frac{8}{12}$ $\frac{9}{12}$ $\frac{10}{12}$ $\frac{11}{12}$ 1

Look at the number lines. Write down the larger of each pair of fractions.

1. $\frac{3}{4}$ $\frac{8}{10}$
2. $\frac{2}{10}$ $\frac{1}{6}$
3. $\frac{2}{12}$ $\frac{1}{4}$
4. $\frac{5}{6}$ $\frac{9}{12}$
5. $\frac{3}{10}$ $\frac{4}{12}$
6. $\frac{1}{4}$ $\frac{2}{6}$
7. $\frac{5}{6}$ $\frac{8}{10}$
8. $\frac{10}{12}$ $\frac{9}{10}$

Write the next five numbers in each sequence.

9. $\frac{1}{2}$, 1, $1\frac{1}{2}$, 2
10. $\frac{1}{4}$, $\frac{1}{2}$, $\frac{3}{4}$, 1
11. $5\frac{7}{10}$, $5\frac{6}{10}$, $5\frac{5}{10}$, $5\frac{4}{10}$
12. 3, $2\frac{2}{3}$, $2\frac{1}{3}$, 2

Write in order, smallest first.

13. $2\frac{1}{5}$, $1\frac{3}{4}$, $3\frac{1}{10}$, $1\frac{1}{2}$
14. $4\frac{1}{3}$, $2\frac{2}{5}$, $2\frac{2}{10}$, $3\frac{1}{8}$
15. $2\frac{1}{2}$, $1\frac{2}{3}$, $2\frac{3}{7}$, $1\frac{1}{2}$
16. $4\frac{3}{10}$, $5\frac{1}{2}$, $5\frac{5}{8}$, $4\frac{1}{2}$

C

Write in order, smallest first.

1. $\frac{1}{2}$, $\frac{2}{3}$, $\frac{2}{6}$
2. $\frac{2}{5}$, $\frac{3}{10}$, $\frac{1}{2}$
3. $\frac{5}{8}$, $\frac{1}{2}$, $\frac{3}{4}$
4. $\frac{4}{9}$, $\frac{1}{3}$, $\frac{1}{2}$
5. $\frac{6}{10}$, $\frac{1}{2}$, $\frac{25}{100}$
6. $\frac{1}{2}$, $\frac{4}{7}$, $\frac{4}{9}$

Write the next three numbers in each sequence.

7. $\frac{1}{4}$, $\frac{3}{4}$, $1\frac{1}{4}$, $1\frac{3}{4}$
8. $\frac{2}{3}$, $1\frac{1}{3}$, 2, $2\frac{2}{3}$
9. $\frac{2}{9}$, $\frac{4}{9}$, $\frac{6}{9}$, $\frac{8}{9}$
10. $1\frac{1}{4}$, $2\frac{1}{2}$, $3\frac{3}{4}$, 5

0 A B C D E F G H 1

Match each fraction to a letter on the number line above.

11. $\frac{1}{6}$
12. $\frac{3}{4}$
13. $\frac{1}{3}$
14. $\frac{1}{12}$
15. $\frac{1}{2}$
16. $\frac{2}{3}$
17. $\frac{5}{6}$
18. $\frac{1}{4}$

E3 EQUIVALENT FRACTIONS

I can find other fractions that are equivalent to a given fraction.

Equivalent fractions are fractions that look different but are the same.

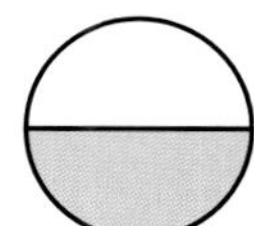 $\frac{1}{2} = \frac{2}{4}$ 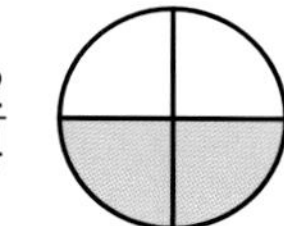

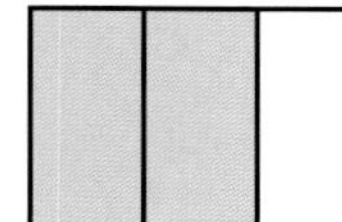 $\frac{2}{3} = \frac{4}{6}$ 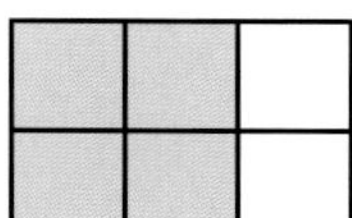

A

Write the equivalent fractions shown in each pair of diagrams.

1 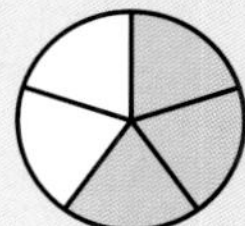 

2 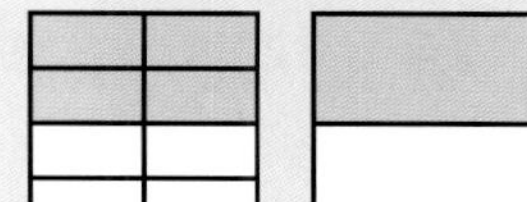

3 

4 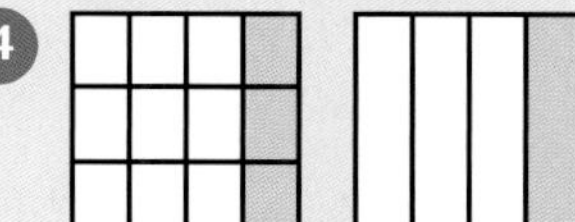

5 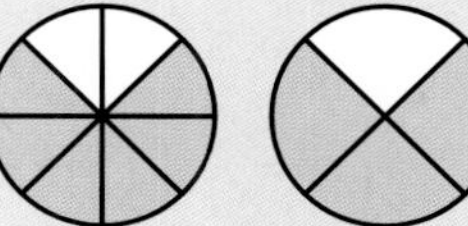

6 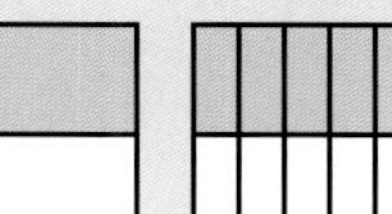

7 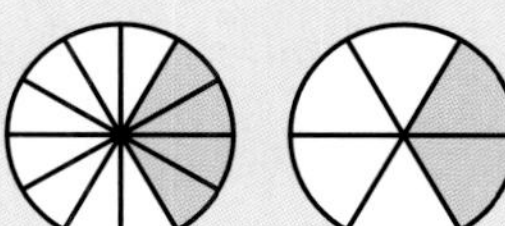

8 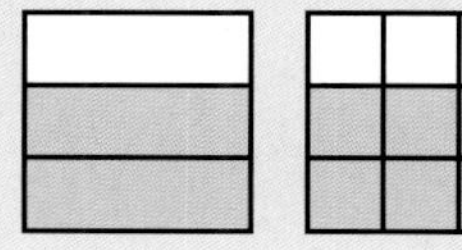

B

Write the equivalent fractions by the letters for each pair of number lines.

1 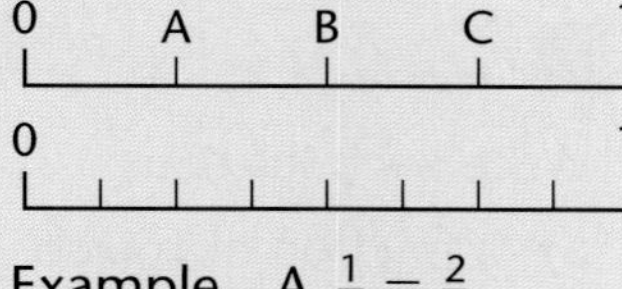

Example A $\frac{1}{4} = \frac{2}{8}$

2 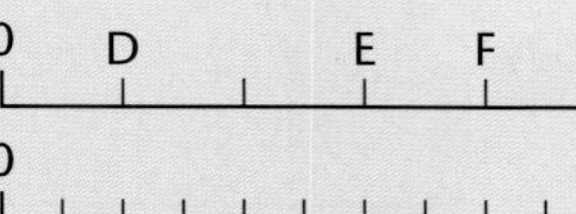

3 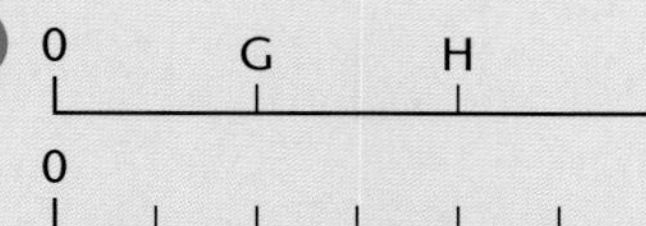

4 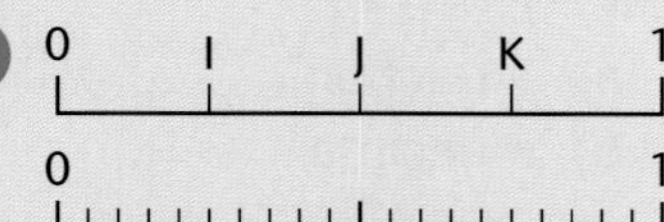

Use squared paper. Draw a pair of diagrams to show these equivalent fractions.

5 $\frac{1}{2} = \frac{6}{12}$

6 $\frac{1}{3} = \frac{4}{12}$

7 $\frac{2}{6} = \frac{6}{15}$

8 $\frac{3}{4} = \frac{12}{16}$

C

Copy and complete by writing $>$, $<$ or $=$ in the box.

1 $\frac{1}{2} \square \frac{3}{8}$

2 $\frac{1}{3} \square \frac{2}{6}$

3 $\frac{2}{5} \square \frac{5}{10}$

4 $\frac{3}{4} \square \frac{5}{10}$

5 $\frac{5}{6} \square \frac{10}{12}$

6 $\frac{3}{5} \square \frac{11}{20}$

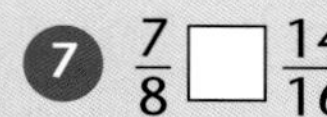

7 $\frac{7}{8} \square \frac{14}{16}$

8 $\frac{2}{3} \square \frac{9}{12}$

9 $\frac{1}{2} \square \frac{9}{20}$

10 $\frac{3}{4} \square \frac{12}{16}$

11 $\frac{1}{3} \square \frac{6}{12}$

12 $\frac{7}{10} \square \frac{13}{20}$

Which is/are the odd one(s) out in each set of fractions?

13 $\frac{7}{14}$ $\frac{8}{16}$ $\frac{4}{12}$ $\frac{9}{18}$ $\frac{3}{6}$

14 $\frac{6}{15}$ $\frac{14}{35}$ $\frac{4}{10}$ $\frac{10}{30}$ $\frac{8}{20}$

15 $\frac{8}{12}$ $\frac{27}{36}$ $\frac{18}{24}$ $\frac{6}{8}$ $\frac{21}{28}$

16 $\frac{30}{100}$ $\frac{20}{50}$ $\frac{6}{20}$ $\frac{21}{70}$ $\frac{12}{20}$

17 Write the next five terms in this sequence.

$\frac{5}{6} = \frac{10}{12} = \frac{15}{18}$

I can recognise equivalent fractions and decimals.

Examples

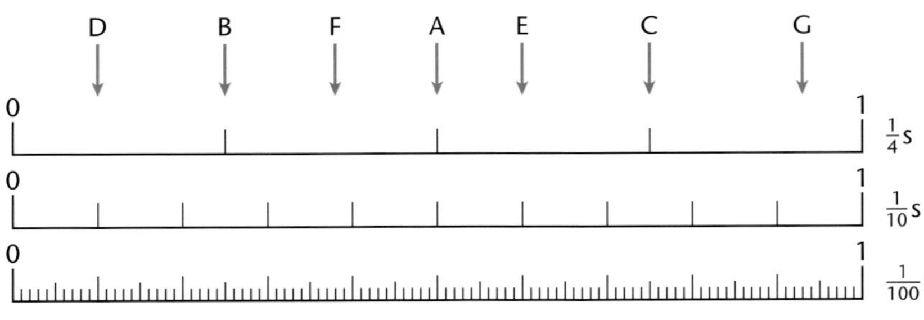

$A = \frac{1}{2} = \frac{5}{10} = 0{\cdot}5$

$B = \frac{1}{4} = \frac{25}{100} = 0{\cdot}25$

$C = \frac{3}{4} = \frac{75}{100} = 0{\cdot}75$

$D = \frac{1}{10} = \frac{10}{100} = 0{\cdot}1$

$E = \frac{6}{10} = \frac{60}{100} = 0{\cdot}6$

$F = \frac{38}{100} = 0{\cdot}38$

$G = \frac{93}{100} = 0{\cdot}93$

A

Write each letter as:

a) a fraction
b) a decimal.

1
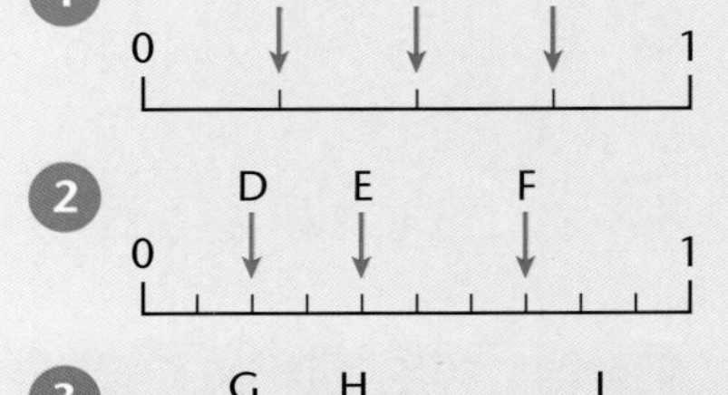

2

3
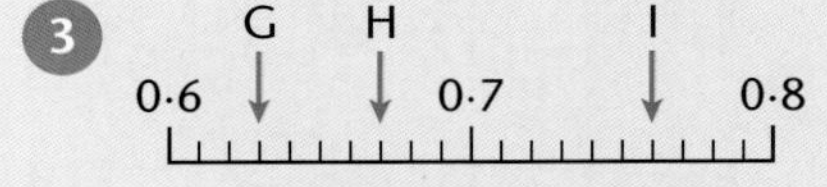

Write the shaded part of each shape as:

a) a fraction
b) a decimal.

4

7

5

8

6
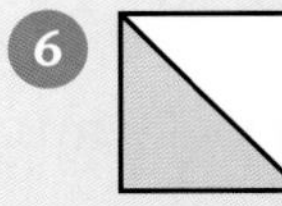

9

B

Write each letter as:

a) a fraction or mixed number
b) a decimal.

1
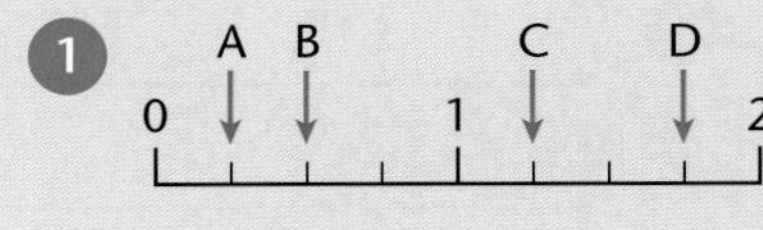

2
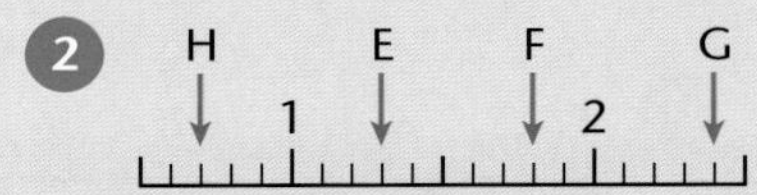

Write the shaded part of each shape as:

a) a fraction
b) a decimal.

3 6
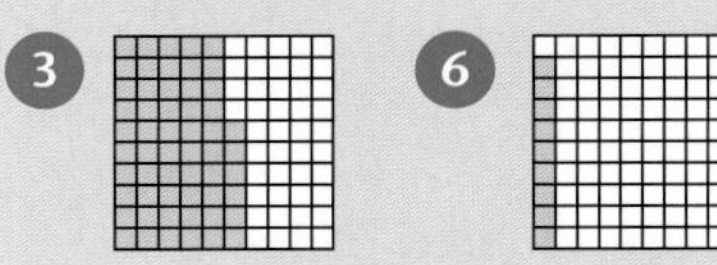

4 7
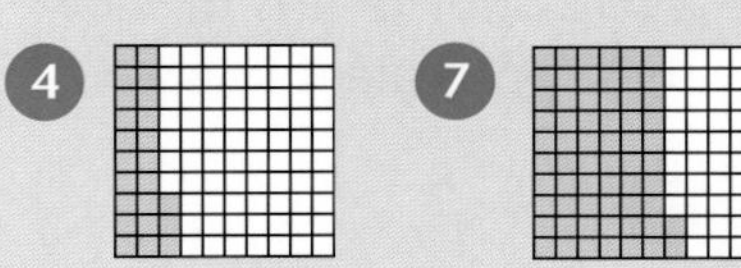

5 8
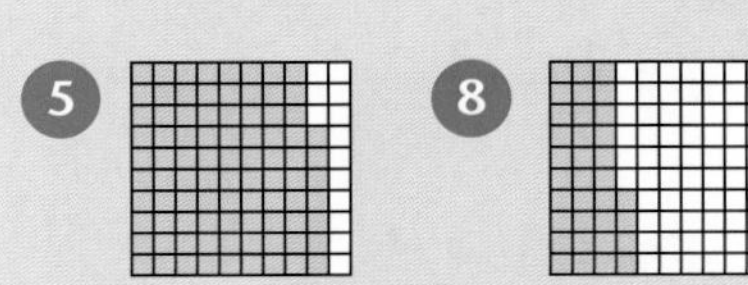

C

Write as mixed numbers.

1 2·82
2 9·07
3 5·61
4 4·25
5 1·3
6 7·08
7 4·5
8 3·94
9 2·01
10 6·42
11 8·75
12 5·19

Write as decimals.

13 $1\frac{6}{10}$
14 $3\frac{48}{100}$
15 $4\frac{1}{2}$
16 $6\frac{5}{100}$
17 $2\frac{67}{100}$
18 $9\frac{3}{4}$
19 $4\frac{2}{100}$
20 $1\frac{87}{100}$
21 $8\frac{4}{10}$
22 $5\frac{14}{100}$
23 $4\frac{1}{4}$
24 $7\frac{3}{100}$

Give the answer as a decimal.

25 $0{\cdot}9 - \frac{1}{4}$
26 $2{\cdot}4 - \frac{1}{2}$
27 $1\frac{7}{10} + 0{\cdot}61$
28 $2\frac{3}{4} + 0{\cdot}45$

I can find fractions of numbers and quantities.

Examples

$\frac{1}{5}$ of 30 = 30 ÷ 5
= 6

$\frac{3}{5}$ of 30 = (30 ÷ 5) × 3
= 6 × 3
= 18

What fraction of £1 is 5p?
Twenty 5ps make £1.
5p is $\frac{1}{20}$ of £1.

A

Find one half of:

1. 12
2. 24
3. 18
4. 100
5. 16p
6. 60p
7. 28 cm
8. 50 cm

Find one tenth of:

9. 30
10. 40
11. 90
12. 50
13. 80p
14. 20p
15. 100 cm
16. 60 cm

Find one fifth of:

17. 20
18. 100
19. 30
20. 25
21. 50p
22. 35p
23. 10 cm
24. 45 cm

25. Thirty paper planes are tested. One fifth fly more than 10 metres. One half fly less than 5 metres. How many planes fly between 5 and 10 metres?

B

Work out

1. $\frac{1}{10}$ of 80
2. $\frac{2}{10}$ of 80
3. $\frac{1}{4}$ of 24
4. $\frac{3}{4}$ of 24
5. $\frac{1}{3}$ of 15
6. $\frac{2}{3}$ of 15
7. $\frac{1}{6}$ of 42
8. $\frac{5}{6}$ of 42

Find

9. $\frac{4}{5}$ of 30
10. $\frac{3}{4}$ of 28
11. $\frac{5}{8}$ of 40
12. $\frac{2}{3}$ of 27
13. $\frac{9}{10}$ of 20
14. $\frac{2}{9}$ of 63
15. $\frac{4}{7}$ of 35
16. $\frac{7}{10}$ of 80

What fraction of £1 is:

17. 10p
18. 50p
19. 20p
20. 25p?

What fraction of 1 metre is:

21. 1 cm
22. 25 cm
23. 10 cm
24. 50 cm?

25. There are 24 eggs in a tray. Two thirds are broken. How many eggs are:
a) broken **b)** unbroken?

26. Sixty ice creams are sold. One third are vanilla. One quarter are mint. How many of the ice creams are:
a) vanilla
b) mint
c) other flavours?

C

Find

1. $\frac{2}{3}$ of £1·80
2. $\frac{3}{5}$ of £2·00
3. $\frac{3}{4}$ of £3·00
4. $\frac{7}{8}$ of £10·00
5. $\frac{9}{10}$ of 1 metre
6. $\frac{32}{100}$ of 1 metre
7. $\frac{6}{10}$ of 5 metres
8. $\frac{51}{100}$ of 2 metres

What fraction of £2 is:

9. 10p
10. 50p
11. 20p
12. 25p?

What fraction of 4 metres is:

13. 1 metre
14. 40 cm
15. 50 cm
16. 80 cm?

17. There are 28 children in a class. Five sevenths of the children use a pen. How many children do not use a pen?

18. One quarter of the children in a class chose blue as their favourite colour. Eighteen children chose other colours. How many children are there in the class?

E3 WRITTEN METHOD FOR MULTIPLICATION

I can multiply two-digit numbers by one-digit numbers.

Example 27×6

Approximate first

27 rounds to 30

$30 \times 6 = 180$

27×6 is less than 180

×	6
20	120
7	42
	162

	20 + 7
×	6
	120
	42
	162

	20 + 7	
×	6	
	120	20×6
	42	7×6
	162	

A

Work out

1. 15×2
2. 46×5
3. 28×3
4. 17×4
5. 59×3
6. 28×5
7. 39×4
8. 61×2
9. There were 42 cars going south and three times as many going north. How many cars were going north?
10. A phone call costs 4p for every minute. How much does a 26 minute call cost?
11. There are five oranges in each pack. How many oranges are there in 37 packs?

B

Work out

1. 45×6
2. 89×9
3. 62×7
4. 75×8
5. 63×9
6. 86×8
7. 18×6
8. 95×7
9. 94×8
10. 82×6
11. 73×7
12. 47×9
13. 53×8
14. 84×7
15. 52×9
16. 36×6
17. Mura earns 25p every time he does the washing up. How much does he earn if he does the washing up every day for a week?
18. There are 8 rolls in a packet and 72 packets in a box. How many rolls are in the box?
19. One can of dog food costs 49p. How much do six cans cost?
20. Each tray holds nine flowers. How many flowers are there in 37 trays?

C

Work out

1. 173×5
2. 369×6
3. 108×8
4. 287×7
5. 149×9
6. 450×4
7. 175×6
8. 249×8
9. 307×7
10. 267×9
11. 198×3
12. 280×6
13. 376×8
14. 525×4
15. 469×7
16. 138×9
17. A ferry carries 136 cars every crossing. It makes six crossings in a day. How many cars are carried in the day?
18. One dictionary weighs 325 g. How much do eight dictionaries weigh?
19. Tickets for a film cost £9. There are 537 people in the audience. How much is taken at the box office?
20. The losing candidate gained 156 votes. The winner gained seven times as many. How many people voted for the winner?

I can divide a two-digit number by a one-digit number.

Examples

$86 \div 5$

Estimate

$5 \times 10 = 50$

$5 \times 20 = 100$

$10 < 86 \div 5 < 20$

$$\begin{aligned} 86 \div 5 &= (50 + 36) \div 5 \\ &= 10 + 7\text{R}1 \\ &= 17\text{r}1 \end{aligned}$$

$$\begin{array}{rl} 86 & \\ -50 & (5 \times 10) \\ \hline 36 & \\ -35 & (5 \times 7) \\ \hline 1 & \end{array}$$

Answer 17r1

$186 \div 5$

$$\begin{array}{rl} 186 & \\ -150 & (5 \times 30) \\ \hline 36 & \\ -35 & (5 \times 7) \\ \hline 1 & \end{array}$$

Answer 37r1

A

Work out

1. $52 \div 4$
2. $39 \div 3$
3. $24 \div 2$
4. $75 \div 5$
5. $68 \div 4$
6. $45 \div 3$
7. $90 \div 5$
8. $32 \div 2$
9. $51 \div 3$
10. $28 \div 2$
11. $85 \div 5$
12. $60 \div 4$
13. $36 \div 2$
14. $65 \div 5$
15. $44 \div 4$
16. $39 \div 3$
17. $80 \div 5$
18. $54 \div 3$
19. $76 \div 4$
20. $30 \div 2$

B

Work out

1. $72 \div 4$
2. $84 \div 7$
3. $96 \div 6$
4. $126 \div 9$
5. $97 \div 5$
6. $104 \div 8$
7. $93 \div 7$
8. $84 \div 6$
9. $123 \div 9$
10. $57 \div 3$
11. $130 \div 7$
12. $128 \div 8$
13. $100 \div 6$
14. $187 \div 5$
15. $150 \div 8$
16. $138 \div 9$
17. Archy buys six pencils for 90p. How much does each pencil cost?
18. There are 112 guests at a wedding reception. They sit at tables of eight. How many tables are needed?
19. One ninth of the apples in a shop are green. There are 162 apples altogether. How many are green?

C

Work out

1. $111 \div 6$
2. $194 \div 9$
3. $146 \div 4$
4. $133 \div 7$
5. $216 \div 8$
6. $194 \div 5$
7. $306 \div 9$
8. $140 \div 6$
9. $169 \div 7$
10. $114 \div 3$
11. $150 \div 8$
12. $240 \div 9$
13. $222 \div 6$
14. $192 \div 4$
15. $218 \div 8$
16. $256 \div 7$
17. Nine biscuits weigh 216 g altogether. How much does one biscuit weigh?
18. Sharina's book has 195 pages. She has read one fifth of the book. How many pages has she read?
19. One eighth of the 184 customers in a shop spent more than £50. How many customers spent less than £50?
20. Joyce drives the same journey every day for a week. At the end of the week she has driven 266 miles. How long is the journey?

I can solve simple ratios and proportion problems.

Examples

1 

1 square in every 4 is green.
There is 1 green square to every 3 yellow squares.
There is 1 green square for every 3 yellow squares.

2 There are 2 girls to every 3 boys at a party.
There are 15 boys. How many girls are there?

Girls	2	4	6	8	10	
Boys	3	6	9	12	15	Answer *10*

3 There are 2 girls in every 3 children at a party.
There are 15 children at the party.
How many are boys?

Girls	2	4	6	8	10	
Boys	1	2	3	4	5	
Children	3	6	9	12	15	Answer *5*

4 There are 2 girls for every 3 boys at a party
There are 15 children.
How many are girls?
How many are boys?

Girls	2	4	6	Answers
Boys	3	6	9	*Girls 6*
Children	5	10	15	*Boys 9*

A

1 In a Lucky Dip 1 ticket in every 5 wins a prize.
Copy and complete the table.

Number of tickets	5									
Number of prizes	1	2	3	4	5	6	7	8	9	10

2 Make a similar table for a Lucky Dip in which 1 ticket in every 4 wins a prize.

3 Look at your table for 2.
a) How many prizes would there be if there are 36 tickets?
b) How many tickets would there be if there are 7 prizes?

4 There are 60 beads in a necklace. Two beads in every five are red. Copy and complete the table.

Number of red beads	2	4										
Number of beads	5											

5 Make a similar table for a necklace of 30 beads in which one bead in every three is blue.

6 Look at your table for 5.
a) How many blue beads are there if there are 18 beads altogether?
b) How many beads are there altogether if there are 8 blue beads?
c) How many beads are there altogether if there are 12 blue beads?

B

Copy and complete the sentences for each pattern.

1
a) 1 in every ☐ squares is red.
b) There are ☐ yellow squares to every red square.

2
a) There are ☐ blue circles for every orange circle.
b) 1 in every ☐ circles is orange.

3
a) There are ☐ red stars to every 3 blue stars.
b) There are 3 blue stars in every ☐ stars.

Use squared paper.
Draw a tile pattern as in Question 1 in which:

4 there is 1 red square to every 5 blue squares.

5 1 in every 2 squares is red.

6 there are 4 blue squares for every red square.

Look at this pattern of beads.

7 What fraction of the beads are:
a) yellow
b) blue?

8 If there are 10 yellow beads, how many blue beads would there be?

9 Look at the pattern in Question 1.
a) What fraction of the squares are red?
b) What fraction of the squares are yellow?

10 Look at the pattern in Question 3.
a) What fraction of the stars are red?
b) What fraction of the stars are blue?

C

A necklace has this pattern of beads.

1 What fraction of the beads are red?

2 What fraction are yellow?

3 What fraction are blue?

4 If there are 10 blue beads, how many red beads would there be?

5 If there are 30 red beads, how many would be yellow?

6 If there are 14 yellow beads, how many would be blue?

7 Ibrahim has 2 stickers for every 1 Gus has. Ibrahim has 12 stickers. How many does Gus have?

8 Ellie reads 3 pages to every 2 that Grace reads. Ellie reads 15 pages. How many does Grace read?

9 There are seven adults in every ten people on a bus. There are 70 people on the bus. How many are adults? How many are children?

10 A tennis player won four matches to every one she lost. She played 30 matches. How many did she lose? How many did she win?

11 Three in every seven ice creams sold are vanilla. Twelve vanilla ice creams are sold. How many ice creams are sold altogether?

12 At the Chess Club there are two girls for every five boys. There are six girls at the club. How many boys are there?

13 There are 36 cows in a field. Four in every nine are brown. How many cows are not brown?

14 One third of the pencils needed sharpening. 28 pencils did not need sharpening. How many pencils were there?

I can recall all multiplication and division facts and work out related facts.

A

What is

1. 7×4
2. 2×6
3. 8×7
4. 3×9
5. 6×10
6. 4×8
7. 9×3
8. 3×7
9. 8×8
10. 7×6
11. 10×2
12. 9×9
13. $30 \div 6$
14. $28 \div 7$
15. $36 \div 4$
16. $48 \div 8$
17. $35 \div 5$
18. $45 \div 9$
19. $21 \div 3$
20. $54 \div 6$
21. $72 \div 9$
22. $24 \div 8$
23. $20 \div 4$
24. $42 \div 7$

B

Copy and complete.

1. $\square \times 5 = 40$
2. $\square \times 6 = 18$
3. $\square \times 3 = 18$
4. $\square \times 8 = 56$
5. $\square \times 7 = 63$
6. $\square \times 9 = 90$
7. $\square \div 10 = 100$
8. $\square \div 8 = 40$
9. $\square \div 4 = 24$
10. $\square \div 7 = 14$
11. $\square \div 6 = 48$
12. $\square \div 9 = 54$

Write the answer only.

13. 8×30
14. 7×70
15. 4×60
16. 9×80
17. 8×20
18. 7×90
19. 60×6
20. 90×5
21. 40×8
22. 50×7
23. 80×4
24. 40×9
25. $300 \div 5$
26. $900 \div 9$
27. $640 \div 8$
28. $300 \div 10$
29. $210 \div 7$
30. $120 \div 6$
31. $280 \div 4$
32. $320 \div 8$
33. $300 \div 3$
34. $81 \div 9$
35. $420 \div 6$
36. $700 \div 7$

C

Copy and complete.

1. $\square \div 6 = 40$
2. $\square \div 4 = 90$
3. $\square \div 9 = 30$
4. $\square \div 20 = 7$
5. $\square \div 70 = 8$
6. $\square \div 80 = 6$
7. $\square \times 5 = 250$
8. $\square \times 9 = 630$
9. $\square \times 3 = 270$
10. $\square \times 60 = 480$
11. $\square \times 80 = 400$
12. $\square \times 70 = 630$

Write the answer only.

13. 6×400
14. 9×800
15. 3×600
16. 800×2
17. 400×7
18. 500×9
19. 7×500
20. 3×800
21. 8×1000
22. 400×6
23. 600×9
24. 200×7
25. $2100 \div 3$
26. $3600 \div 9$
27. $3500 \div 7$
28. $3200 \div 4$
29. $5400 \div 6$
30. $5600 \div 8$
31. $5000 \div 10$
32. $7200 \div 9$
33. $3600 \div 6$
34. $4500 \div 5$
35. $4900 \div 7$
36. $1600 \div 8$

Copy the crossnumber puzzles onto 1 cm squared paper.
Use the clues to solve the puzzles.

1	2		3	4
5			6	
	7	8		
9				10
11			12	

Clues across

1. 34 + 35
3. 36 − 9
5. 75 − 40
6. 6 × 5
7. 85 + 85
11. 32 − 15
12. 19 × 2

Clues down

1. 44 + 19
2. 1000 − 49
3. 23 × 10
4. 700 ÷ 10
8. 96 − 21
9. 54 + 7
10. 36 ÷ 2

B

Clues across

1. 28 ÷ 2
3. 49 + 19
5. 7 × 4
6. 100 − 81
7. 8·5 × 10
8. 7 × 3
10. 30 ÷ 2
11. 47 + 47

Clues down

1. 96 + 30
2. 12 × 4
3. 665 − 50
4. 101 − 12
7. 45 + 36
8. 50 ÷ 2
9. 6 × 4

1	2		3	4
5			6	
		7		
	8			9
10			11	

C

1	2			3
4			5	
		6		
7	8		9	10
11				

Clues across

1. 436 + 57
4. 101 − 14
5. 360 ÷ 4
6. 9 × 8
7. 113 − 44
9. 6 × 9
11. 40 × 8

Clues down

1. 8 × 6
2. 132 − 35
3. 0·6 × 100
5. 37 × 25
7. 9 × 7
8. 460 ÷ 5
10. 0·49 × 100

REVIEW PAGE - COUNTING AND NUMBER

Write in words.

1. 308
2. 1297
3. 4362
4. 1500
5. 2605
6. 3089
7. 5240
8. 8060

What is the value of the underlined digit?

9. 2<u>6</u>13
10. 15<u>7</u>0
11. 324<u>8</u>
12. <u>5</u>861
13. 33<u>8</u>6
14. <u>6</u>052
15. 793<u>4</u>
16. 9<u>5</u>29

Count on in 10s:

17. 50 from 237
18. 40 from 380
19. 70 from 536
20. 60 from 475.

Count on in 100s:

21. 400 from 1831
22. 800 from 2569
23. 300 from 4924
24. 700 from 3792.

Count back in 1000s:

25. 6000 from 8235
26. 3000 from 7810
27. 5000 from 6497
28. 4000 from 9063.

Multiply by 10.

29. 148
30. 53
31. 217
32. 570
33. 25
34. 781
35. 690
36. 436

Divide by 10.

37. 2000
38. 3240
39. 390
40. 4700
41. 8610
42. 5000
43. 1800
44. 6520

Write these numbers in order. Start with the smallest.

45. 7981 7198 8197 8719
46. 1782 2178 2187 1827
47. 3649 3469 3694 3496
48. 1573 1375 1735 1537

Estimate the numbers shown by the arrows.

49. 0 — 10
50. 0 — 20
51. 0 — 50
52. 0 — 100

Round to the nearest

(10) (100)

53. 73
54. 146
55. 325
56. 291
57. 620
58. 970
59. 340
60. 750

61. What number is shown by each arrow?

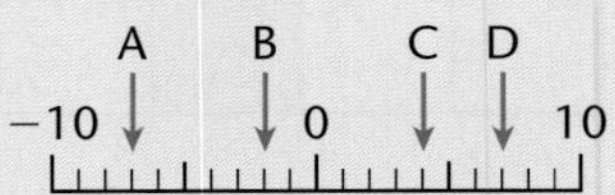

62. Which of these numbers are:
a) odd **b)** even?

47	316	23	38
270	5	54	91

Write the first six multiples of:

63. 10
64. 6
65. 4
66. 9

Write down the numbers in the box which are multiples of:

67. 2
68. 3
69. 5
70. 7

14	15	18	20
21	35	49	60

REVIEW PAGE – FRACTIONS AND DECIMALS

What fraction of each shape is shaded?

 1 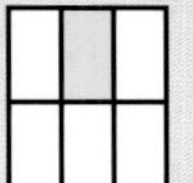

 5 

2 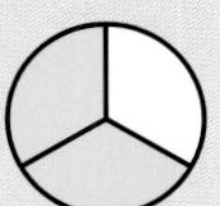

 6 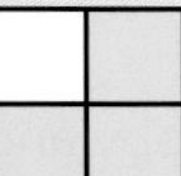

3 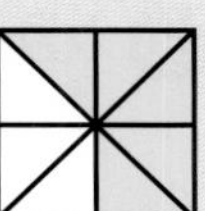

 7 

4 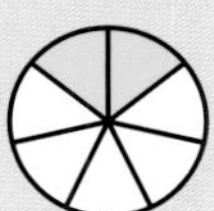

8 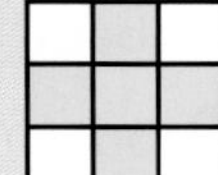

Write the equivalent fractions shown by each pair.

 9 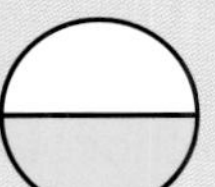 = 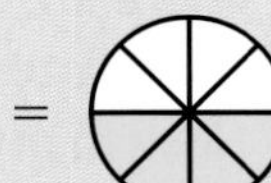

10 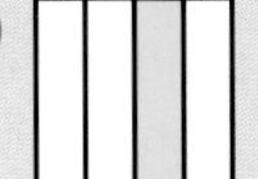 = 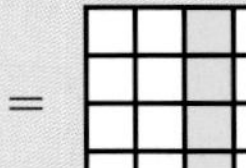

11 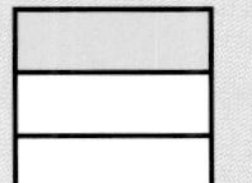 = 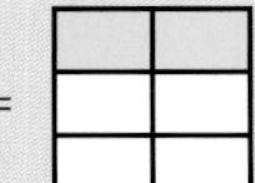

12  = 

Copy and complete the equivalent fractions. (You can use the fraction charts on page 42.)

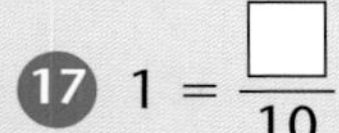

13 $\frac{1}{4} = \frac{\square}{8}$ 17 $1 = \frac{\square}{10}$

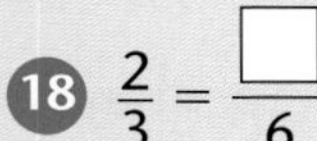

14 $\frac{1}{2} = \frac{\square}{6}$ 18 $\frac{2}{3} = \frac{\square}{6}$

15 $1 = \frac{\square}{3}$ 19 $\frac{2}{5} = \frac{\square}{10}$

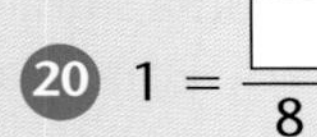

16 $\frac{1}{2} = \frac{\square}{10}$ 20 $1 = \frac{\square}{8}$

Find

21 $\frac{1}{2}$ of 30 25 $\frac{1}{4}$ of 32p

22 $\frac{1}{3}$ of 18 26 $\frac{1}{10}$ of 60 m

23 $\frac{1}{5}$ of 40 27 $\frac{1}{3}$ of £12

24 $\frac{1}{10}$ of 50 28 $\frac{1}{2}$ of 1 kg

What fraction of:

29 £1 is 50p

30 £1 is 20p

31 1 m is 1 cm

32 1 m is 25 cm?

Give the value of the underlined figure.

33 3·$\underline{2}$ 37 2·6$\underline{5}$

34 6·0$\underline{4}$ 38 $\underline{1}$8·3

35 0·$\underline{5}$3 39 7·$\underline{4}$1

36 1$\underline{9}$·7 40 0·8$\underline{9}$

Write as fractions.

41 0·1 45 0·5

42 0·25 46 0·82

43 0·67 47 0·05

44 0·03 48 0·75

Write as decimals.

49 $\frac{1}{2}$ 53 $\frac{3}{4}$

50 $\frac{2}{10}$ 54 $\frac{9}{100}$

51 1 55 $\frac{7}{10}$

52 $\frac{43}{100}$ 56 $\frac{1}{4}$

57 Write the numbers shown by the arrows as decimal fractions.

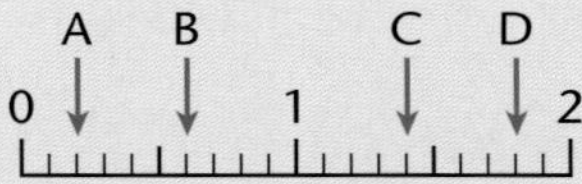

Work out

58 0·4 + 0·3 62 0·8 − 0·5

59 0·2 + 0·7 63 0·7 − 0·2

60 1·3 + 0·5 64 1·5 − 0·4

61 1·1 + 0·6 65 1·9 − 0·3

Arrange in order. Start with the smallest.

66 1·5 5·1 2·4 4·2

67 3·8 8·8 8·3 3·3

68 54 5·4 4·5 45

69 $3\frac{2}{3}$ $2\frac{1}{4}$ $3\frac{2}{5}$ $2\frac{1}{2}$

70 $2\frac{1}{2}$ $1\frac{1}{2}$ $2\frac{3}{5}$ $1\frac{3}{8}$

Copy and complete.

1. 135 + 39 = □
2. 48 + 27 = □
3. 600 + □ = 1300
4. 156 + □ = 200
5. □ + 40 = 151
6. □ + 76 = 119
7. 82 − 38 = □
8. 500 − 64 = □
9. 204 − □ = 197
10. 1000 − □ = 250
11. □ − 90 = 168
12. □ − 32 = 145

Work out

13. 138 + 91
14. 257 + 36
15. 592 + 57
16. 326 + 48
17. 217 − 81
18. 390 − 54
19. 626 − 64
20. 583 − 78

Set out correctly and find the totals.

21. 4 + 37 + 246 + 25
22. 54 + 123 + 9 + 16
23. £3·73 + 65p + 48p
24. £1·26 + 57p + £2·43

Set out correctly and find the differences.

25. 137 − 66
26. 392 − 58
27. £4·18 − £1·45
28. £3·60 − £1·32
29. Sam buys a coat for £79 and a pair of shoes for £26. How much does she spend?
30. Emma's grandmother is 91. Emma is 35. What is the difference in their ages?

Copy and complete.

31. 23 × 4 = □
32. 12 × 11 = □
33. 8 × □ = 32
34. 6 × □ = 0
35. □ × 2 = 58
36. □ × 7 = 35
37. 48 ÷ 6 = □
38. 4000 ÷ 100 = □
39. 16 ÷ □ = 16
40. 27 ÷ □ = 3
41. □ ÷ 10 = 600
42. □ ÷ 2 = 960

Copy and complete.

43. 25 × 6
44. 63 × 8
45. 34 × 9
46. 52 × 7

Copy and complete.

47. 5)85
48. 6)90
49. 4)72
50. 7)98

Work out and give the remainder as a whole number.

51. 36 ÷ 5
52. 165 ÷ 10
53. 26 ÷ 3
54. 27 ÷ 4

Work out

55. £43 ÷ 2
56. £67 ÷ 10
57. £33 ÷ 4
58. £11 ÷ 5
59. There are 24 chocolates in each box. How many chocolates are there in five boxes?
60. The 92 children in Year 4 are divided into four equal teams. How many children are there in each team?
61. What is the product of 23 and 7?
62. Eight friends share the cost of a meal equally. The bill is for £132. How much should each person pay?

REVIEW PAGE - MEASURES

Copy and complete.

1. 100 cm = ☐ m
2. $\frac{1}{2}$ m = ☐ cm
3. $\frac{1}{10}$ m = ☐ cm
4. 25 cm = ☐ m
5. 1 km = ☐ m
6. $\frac{1}{10}$ km = ☐ m
7. 500 m = ☐ km
8. $\frac{1}{10}$ cm = ☐ mm
9. 10 mm = ☐ cm
10. 50 mm = ☐ cm
11. 1 kg = ☐ g
12. 2000 g = ☐ kg
13. 100 g = ☐ kg
14. $\frac{1}{2}$ kg = ☐ g
15. 500 ml = ☐ litre
16. 4 litres = ☐ ml
17. 1000 ml = ☐ litre
18. $\frac{1}{10}$ litre = ☐ ml

Work out the measurement shown by each arrow.

19.

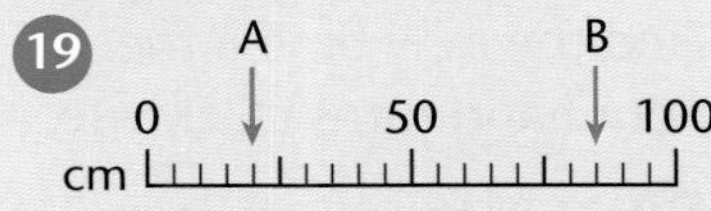

20.

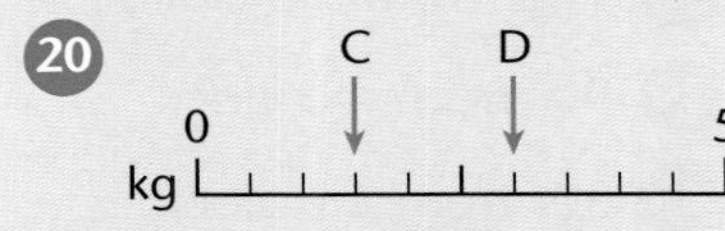

21. 22.

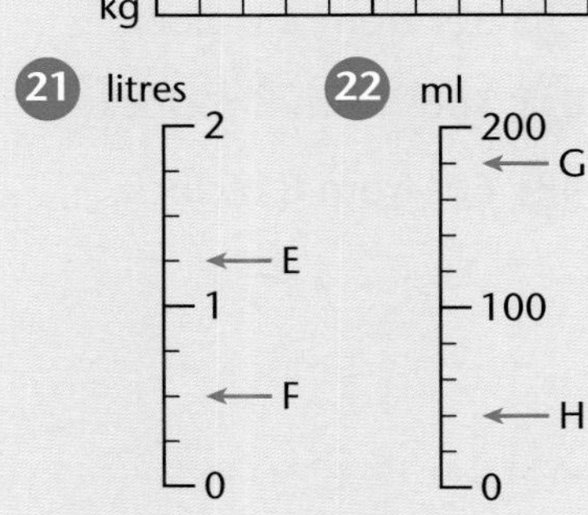

23. A plank of wood is 2 metres long. 65 cm is sawn off. How long is the plank which is left?
24. There are ten coins in a pile. Each coin is 3 mm thick. How high is the pile in centimetres?
25. Four cans of peaches weigh 2 kilograms. What does each can weigh?
26. Anna makes one and a half litres of orange juice. She pours 700 ml into a bottle. How much is left?
27. What is the area of the rectangle?
28. What is the perimeter of the rectangle?
29. Use squared paper. Draw rectangles with areas of:
    a) 12 cm^2
    b) 15 cm^2.
30. Work out the perimeters of the rectangles you have drawn.

Copy and complete.

31. 5 weeks = ☐ days
32. 180 seconds = ☐ minutes
33. 30 months = ☐ years
34. 4 hours = ☐ minutes
35. 2 days = ☐ hours
36. 8 decades = ☐ years
37. 3 years = ☐ weeks
38. 90 minutes = ☐ hours

How many days are there in these months?

39. September
40. October
41. November
42. December

Write each time shown:
a) in words
b) in figures, using am and pm.

43.

afternoon

44.

night

45. 8:51 morning
46. 6:14 evening

47. The first lesson after playtime ends at 11:35. The lesson lasts for 50 minutes. At what time does playtime end?
48. The next lesson lasts 40 minutes. When does lunchtime begin?

Write the name of each of these 2-D shapes.

 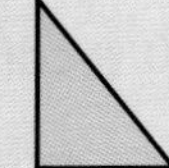

 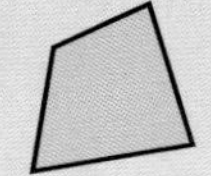

 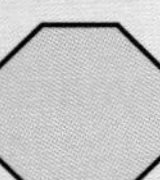

 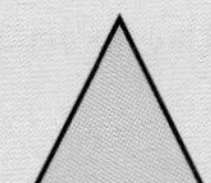

11 Which of the above shapes are regular?

12 How many lines of symmetry does each of the above shapes have?

13 Draw an irregular hexagon.

14 Draw a concave quadrilatral.

15 What is the maximum number of right angles possible in:

a) a quadrilateral which is not a square or a rectangle

b) an irregular pentagon?

Draw diagrams to illustrate your answer.

Write the name of each of these 3-D shapes.

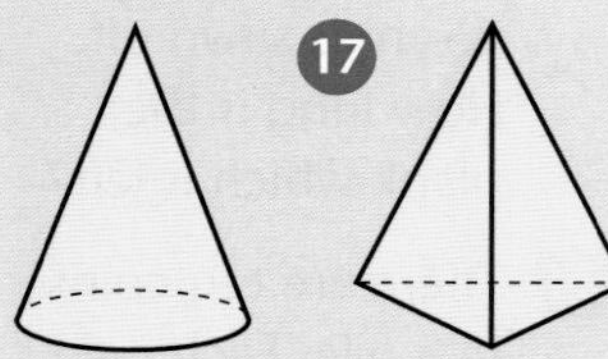

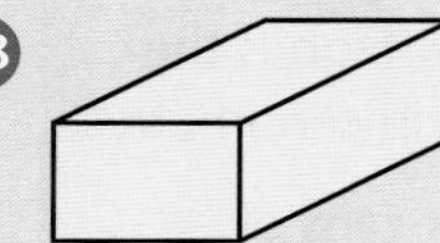

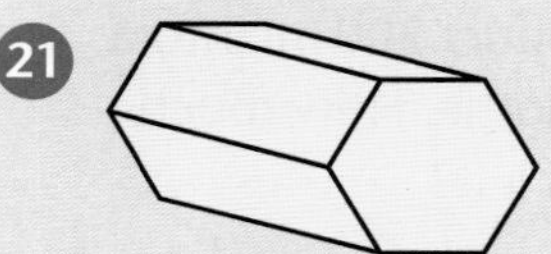

How many cubes are needed to build each of these shapes?

24 Draw a shape made from 10 cubes.

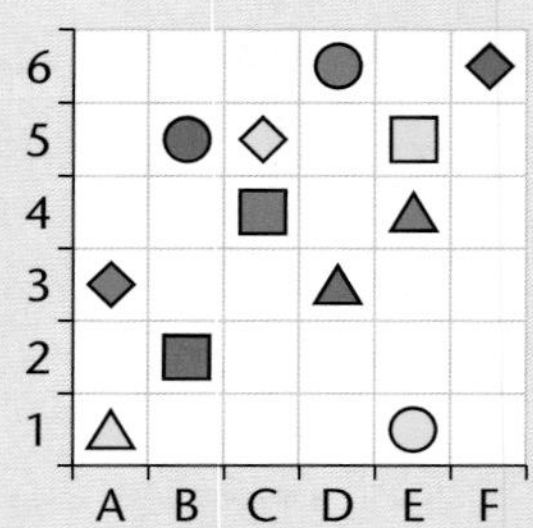

Draw the shape at

25 A1

26 C4

27 F6

28 B5

Give the position of these shapes.

29 ▲

30 ◇

31 ■

32 ●

How many degrees is the clockwise turn:

33 N to S

34 SE to SW

35 NE to E

36 SW to NE

37 W to NW?

Find the new time if the hour hand turns clockwise:

38 180° from 9 o'clock

39 90° from 4 o'clock

40 30° from 4 o'clock

41 360° from 8 o'clock

42 60° from 8 o'clock.

REVIEW PAGE – HANDLING DATA

1 Copy the Carroll diagram and use it to sort these numbers.

92	7	150	81
126	74	15	219
63	4	58	300

	even	not even
2-digits		
not 2-digits		

2 Copy the Venn diagram and write the letters in the correct places.

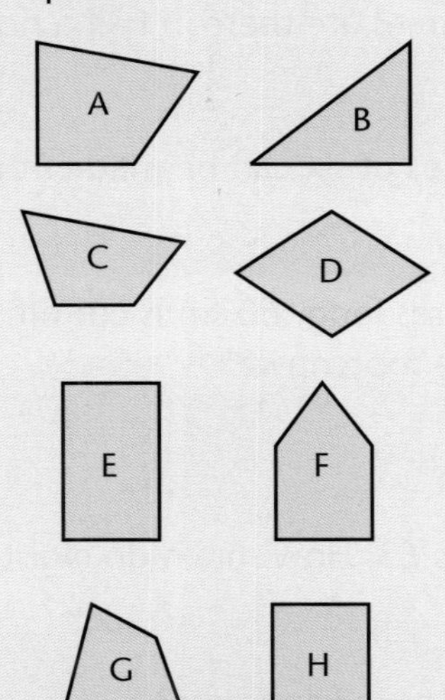

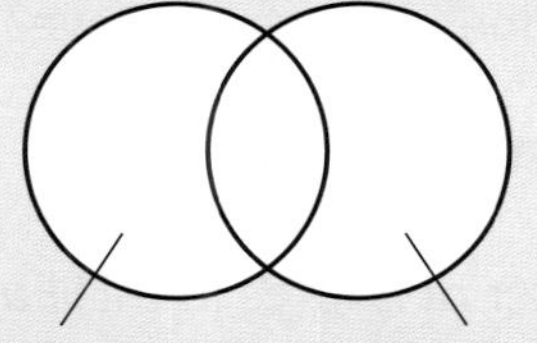

3 The children in Class 4 were asked whether they walked to school, or came by bus, by car or by train.
These are the results:

W B C W W T
C W B W C W
B W T C W B
W C W B C W
B W W C W C

Make a tally chart and then draw a pictogram to show the results.

4 This pictogram shows the number of children learning musical instruments at a school.

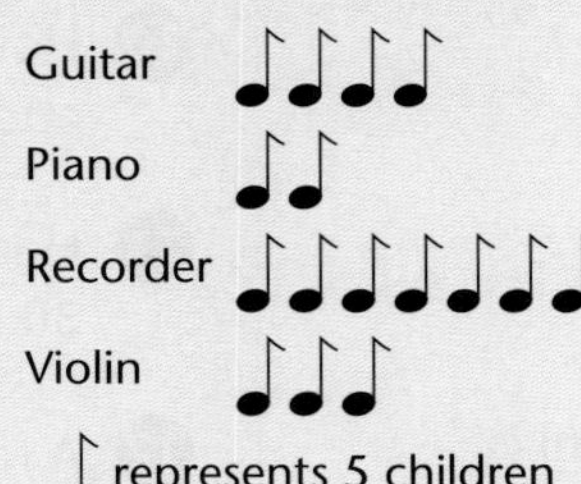

a) How many children were learning piano?

b) Which instrument was being learnt by 15 children?

c) Which instrument was being learnt by most children?

d) How many more children were learning guitar than violin?

e) How many children altogether were learning an instrument?

5 The diners at a canteen had a choice of eggs, fish, meat or salad. These are the meals chosen one lunchtime.

M S F F M M
S F M S M F
E F F M M S
F F S M M M
F E M S M S
E F M S M E

Make a tally chart and then draw a bar chart to show the results.

6 This bar chart shows the favourite colours of some children.

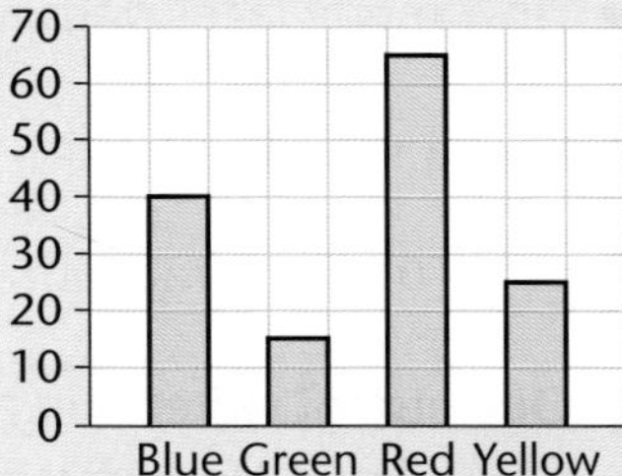

a) What was the most popular colour?

b) Which colour was chosen by 15 children?

c) What was the least popular colour?

d) How many children chose yellow?

e) How many more children chose blue than chose green?

f) How many children were asked to choose their favourite colour?

TEST 1

1. Write one thousand two hundred and thirty-eight in figures.
2. Round 452 to the nearest 100.
3. Add together 135 and 40.
4. How many quarters make one half?
5. What is the difference between 84 and 39?
6. How many centimetres are there in 2 metres?
7. What is the product of 7 and 4?
8. How many minutes are there in 3 hours?
9. Meena has one pound. She spends 42p. How much does she have left?
10. How many faces does a cube have?
11. Count on 6 from −2.
12. Write 0·3 as a fraction.
13. One litre of water is in a jug. 400 ml is poured out. How much water is left?
14. Write five to four in the afternoon in figures, using am or pm.
15. One book costs £6. What is the total cost of three books?
16. How many 5p coins make 40p?
17. Add 1·3 to 0·4.
18. One can weighs 400 g. What is the weight of five cans in kilograms?
19. How many degrees are there in two right-angles?
20. Write the first five multiples of 8.

TEST 2

1. What is the sum of 34 and 26?
2. How many fifths make one whole one?
3. The temperature is 3°C. It falls by 5°C. What is the new temperature?
4. Subtract 0·3 from 0·8.
5. How many days are there in 4 weeks?
6. What is the third multiple of 9?
7. Write two thousand and seventy-six in figures.
8. Divide 3160 by 10.
9. A dress costs £65. Zoe has £37. How much more does she need?
10. How many degrees are there in half a right-angle?
11. How many boxes of six can be made from 30 eggs?
12. A rope is 3 metres long. 60 cm is cut off. How long is the rope now?
13. From 97 take 41.
14. One ticket costs £3. How much do eight tickets cost?
15. Write 2000 grams in kilograms?
16. How many sides does a hexagon have?
17. What is double 280?
18. What is one quarter of 2 litres in millilitres?
19. A lesson starts at 10:55. It lasts 40 minutes. When does it finish?
20. What is one third of 60?

TEST 3

1. What is the difference between 100 and 72?
2. Write eight tenths as a decimal.
3. How many seconds are there in two minutes?
4. Four pencils cost £1. How much does one cost?
5. Write the fifth multiple of 6.
6. How many metres is one and a quarter kilometres?
7. Add 1000 to 3756.
8. How many degrees is the turn from north to south?
9. Victor is 48. His son is one sixth of his age. How old is his son?
10. Write one thousand three hundred and nine in figures.
11. Subtract 64 from 85.
12. One tin costs 40p. What is the cost of five tins?
13. Half a litre of cola is shared equally between two glasses. How much is in each glass in millilitres?
14. What is the perimeter of a rectangle 6 cm by 4 cm?
15. Round 763 to the nearest 100.
16. What is the sum of 1·6 and 0·3?
17. Each cake weighs 200 g. What is the weight of ten cakes?
18. How many thirds make one whole one?
19. What number is halfway between 150 and 200?
20. Subtract the number of days in June from the number of days in this year.

TEST 4

1. What is the product of 9 and 5?
2. The temperature is −1°C. It rises 4°C. What is the new temperature?
3. Add together 57 and 38.
4. Four tennis balls cost £3. How much does one ball cost?
5. Write two and a half litres as millilitres.
6. Subtract three tenths from one whole one.
7. How many sides does a quadrilateral have?
8. What is one fifth of £20?
9. How many 7s make 28?
10. A plank is 2 metres long. 60 cm is sawn off. How much is left?
11. Multiply 8 by 4.
12. Dilip buys a paper for 35p. How much change should he have if he pays with a £2 coin?
13. Write five thousand and seven in figures.
14. A TV programme starts at 6:45 and finishes at 7:20. How long does the programme last?
15. What is the total of 400 and 273?
16. Find the new time if the hour hand turns 90° from 7 o'clock.
17. Take 6 away from 2000.
18. One parcel weighs 800 g. Another weighs half a kilogram. What is their combined weight?
19. Write one quarter as a decimal.
20. Fifty-six children are divided into 8 teams. How many children are there in each team?

TIMES TABLES

How to learn a times table.

BY YOURSELF

1. Read the table over and over.
2. Cover the table and say it out loud or in your mind.
3. Say it more and more quickly
4. Try to say the table backwards.

WITH A FRIEND

Ask each other questions like:

What is 6 times 4?

Multiply 4 by 7.

How many fours make 32?

Divide 36 by 4.

1 × 1 = 1	1 × 2 = 2	1 × 3 = 3	1 × 4 = 4	1 × 5 = 5
2 × 1 = 2	2 × 2 = 4	2 × 3 = 6	2 × 4 = 8	2 × 5 = 10
3 × 1 = 3	3 × 2 = 6	3 × 3 = 9	3 × 4 = 12	3 × 5 = 15
4 × 1 = 4	4 × 2 = 8	4 × 3 = 12	4 × 4 = 16	4 × 5 = 20
5 × 1 = 5	5 × 2 = 10	5 × 3 = 15	5 × 4 = 20	5 × 5 = 25
6 × 1 = 6	6 × 2 = 12	6 × 3 = 18	6 × 4 = 24	6 × 5 = 30
7 × 1 = 7	7 × 2 = 14	7 × 3 = 21	7 × 4 = 28	7 × 5 = 35
8 × 1 = 8	8 × 2 = 16	8 × 3 = 24	8 × 4 = 32	8 × 5 = 40
9 × 1 = 9	9 × 2 = 18	9 × 3 = 27	9 × 4 = 36	9 × 5 = 45
10 × 1 = 10	10 × 2 = 20	10 × 3 = 30	10 × 4 = 40	10 × 5 = 50

1 × 6 = 6	1 × 7 = 7	1 × 8 = 8	1 × 9 = 9	1 × 10 = 10
2 × 6 = 12	2 × 7 = 14	2 × 8 = 16	2 × 9 = 18	2 × 10 = 20
3 × 6 = 18	3 × 7 = 21	3 × 8 = 24	3 × 9 = 27	3 × 10 = 30
4 × 6 = 24	4 × 7 = 28	4 × 8 = 32	4 × 9 = 36	4 × 10 = 40
5 × 6 = 30	5 × 7 = 35	5 × 8 = 40	5 × 9 = 45	5 × 10 = 50
6 × 6 = 36	6 × 7 = 42	6 × 8 = 48	6 × 9 = 54	6 × 10 = 60
7 × 6 = 42	7 × 7 = 49	7 × 8 = 56	7 × 9 = 63	7 × 10 = 70
8 × 6 = 48	8 × 7 = 56	8 × 8 = 64	8 × 9 = 72	8 × 10 = 80
9 × 6 = 54	9 × 7 = 63	9 × 8 = 72	9 × 9 = 81	9 × 10 = 90
10 × 6 = 60	10 × 7 = 70	10 × 8 = 80	10 × 9 = 90	10 × 10 = 100